NOVEL HOUSES

NOVEL HOUSES
Twenty Famous Fictional Dwellings

CHRISTINA HARDYMENT

Bodleian Library
UNIVERSITY OF OXFORD

First published in 2020 by the Bodleian Library
Broad Street, Oxford OX1 3BG
www.bodleianshop.co.uk

ISBN 978 1 85124 480 5

Text © Christina Hardyment, 2019

All images, unless specified on pp. 246–7,
© Bodleian Library, University of Oxford, 2019

Cover design by Dot Little at the Bodleian Library
Designed and typeset in 11 on 15 Garamond by illuminati, Grosmont
Printed and bound in Wales by Gomer Press Limited
on 115 gsm Munken Print paper

British Library Catalogue in Publishing Data
A CIP record of this publication is available from the British Library

CONTENTS

INTRODUCTION

The House as Hero

> [F]aced with the bestial hostility of the storm and the
> hurricane, the house's virtues of protection and resistance are
> transposed into human virtues. The house acquires the physical
> and moral energy of a human body. It braces itself to receive
> the downpour, it girds its loins... Such a house as this invites
> mankind to heroism of cosmic proportions. It is an instrument
> with which to confront the cosmos.
>
> Gaston Bachelard, *The Poetics of Space*, 1958[1]

Houses fascinate me. Not the little boxes squashed into sites too
small for them by modern developers, but well-established ones,
which have developed character over the decades or centuries.
When most women my age were throwing off the domestic shackles
of centuries, I was having babies, collecting sewing machines and
embarking on a book about the history of household technology.
I've set up home in earnest three times, and now I am settled for
good in a home that some may think is too densely lined with the
chattels of earlier homes, and especially with books. Although I
don't really believe that my Edwardian villa in an unfashionable
part of Oxford has 'the physical and moral energy of a human
body', it is, I like to think after a glass or two as I wander out into
the dark garden and gaze up at a quilt of stars, 'an instrument with

which to confront the cosmos'. Importantly, because I inherited a powerful streak of Norse wanderlust from my father, it is also a warm embrace to come back to; a safe, familiar haven. Well-found houses become second skins, defences against the world, nests.

Naturally, I have always been drawn to novels in which houses have character. As a child, I loved such fictional homes as Mole End in *The Wind in the Willows*, Moonacre Manor in Elizabeth Goudge's *The Little White Horse*, Laura Ingalls Wilder's *Little House on the Prairie*, L.M. Montgomery's Green Gables, Lucy Boston's Green Knowe, Villa Villekulla in *Pippi Longstocking*, and, stretching the meaning of home, Wild Cat Island in Arthur Ransome's *Swallows and Amazons*. The first time I was admitted to the adult part of Twickenham's magnificent Carnegie Library was to pursue the sequels to J.R.R. Tolkien's *The Hobbit*, and I was delighted to find that Bag End, to me one of the most enchanting homes in fiction, also featured largely in the *Lord of the Rings* trilogy. Once old enough to enter the mahogany portals of the main library as of right, I discovered that a great many adult novelists were as fascinated by place as I was, and I began a lifetime immersion in such fictions.

Over the last three decades I have written numerous books and articles about writers' fascination with place. I can make no claim to be a literary critic, however. My model is the informative and enthusiastic approach of Virginia Woolf's *The Common Reader*: a collection of essays intended for book-lovers who 'read for their own pleasure, rather than to impart knowledge or correct the opinions of others'. Offered the chance of creating a book for this audience out of twenty in-depth portraits of novels in which a dwelling plays a pivotal part, I jumped at it. Choosing just twenty was difficult – world literature offers innumerable candidates, and it gave me a pang to omit such personal favourites as Rumer Godden's *China Court* and Elizabeth Goudge's *The Herb of Grace*. But limiting the portraits to exceptionally famous English or American novels written in the last two hundred years provided chronological and literary coherence. Everyone will have read some of them, a few will have read all of them: *Novel Houses* is designed to be both an introduction to and a reminder of my featured fictions.

The books in which these remarkable dwellings appear are strikingly different from each other, in part because of the different eras in which they were written, in part because of the varied purposes of their authors. Some were written for fun, others for political punch. Some preach, some warn, some thrill, some are romantic, some satirical. All they have in common is the enduring fame of the imaginary place in which they are set. It is, admittedly, something of an exaggeration to call this introduction *The House as Hero*, but the phrase stuck fast in my mind: it sums up so succinctly what I feel about fictional places that act as guardians and springboards, inspirations and anchorages. Home is a recurring theme: childhood homes, homes under threat, homes lost and homes regained.

Looking at the novels through the single prism of place means that my portraits are inevitably one-sided. But I believe this approach illuminates their authors' motives in writing them. The buildings that dominate the books often have subtle secondary purpose. Behind the labyrinthine castle of Gormenghast is an affectionate evocation of Sark. Jane Austen was giving her own brothers advice in *Mansfield Park* as well as awarding her heroine a desirable residence. When I first read *Brideshead Revisited* I had no idea that it is at heart 'about God', as Waugh declared in a letter to Nancy Mitford. Nor had I realized that Walpole intended *The Castle of Otranto* as a critique of Tory absolutism, or how cleverly Harriet Beecher Stowe calculated that 'the Women of America, in whose hands rest the real destinies of the Republic' would make *Uncle Tom's Cabin* a potent spur to action against slavery because they were so horrified at its portrayal of the destruction of Tom's humble family circle. So expect the unexpected when you re-encounter these famous titles.

The chosen books are all literary landmarks, comets which trail behind them endless critical dust. Each has been discussed and dissected in countless ways, some illuminating, some hard to take seriously. Virginia Woolf remarks wryly in *Orlando* that

Every secret of a writer's soul, every experience of his life, every quality of his mind is written large in his works, yet we require critics to explain the one and biographers to expound the other. That time hangs heavy on people's hands is the only explanation of the monstrous growth.[2]

Taking this to heart, I rely more on quotations from novels and their author's letters than from the critics, but the page-referenced endnotes point the interested towards much scholarly erudition. To prompt memories and tempt new readers, I sketch plots, always emphasizing settings. I also explore the lives of the authors in order to establish why they were inspired to create such dwellings.

Many of the twenty fictional dwellings were directly inspired by real ones. Horace Walpole plucked the 'very sonorous' name Otranto from a map of Italy, but the groaning and ghost-haunted castle that inspired horror novels galore was a celebration of Strawberry Hill, the pretty little 'bauble' beside the Thames at Twickenham that he built as an antiquary's tribute to all things medieval. Jane Austen's brother inherited a house very similar indeed to Mansfield Park. Nathaniel Hawthorne wandered around the attics of his aunt's seven-gabled Salem house. John Galsworthy remembered his childhood high on Kingston Hill when he made it the site of Robin Hill, the house at the heart of *The Man of Property*. E.M. Forster's *Howards End* is a love-song to his childhood home Rooks Nest, and Virginia Woolf's *Orlando* celebrates Knole, the ancestral home of Vita Sackville-West. Dodie Smith came across Wingfield Castle when she was exploring Suffolk in 1934, and used it fifteen years later as Godsend, home of the indigent Mortmain family in *I Capture the Castle*. J.R.R. Tolkien never forgot the rural bliss of Sarehole.

But, though literary geography is great fun (and the Gazetteer at the end of the book lists a host of visitable locations), this is not primarily a book about matching fictions to places. It is an enquiry into what it was that made my twenty authors interest themselves in 'literary architecture', creating from a combination of experience and their own imaginations dwellings that expressed what they wanted to say. Themes emerge: the books could be grouped in innumerable different ways – those tinged with horror, ideal homes, childhood nests, trophy houses, traps, carefully constructed symbols, vast 'labyrinths of grandeur' and, most charismatic of all, heartlands. In the end, I decided to present them chronologically, not least because I enjoy the links between my authors.

Jane Austen satirized the multitude of 'horrid' novels inspired by Walpole's *The Castle of Otranto*, and Walter Scott praised her, remarking that 'it is no fool that can describe fools well'. Emily Brontë hero-worshipped Scott. Dickens admired Hawthorne's 'dark romance', and echoed it in *Bleak House*. Oddly, Henry James, a masterly creator of expressive houses, cuttingly dismissed Dickens as 'the greatest of superficial novelists' and described *Bleak House* as 'forced'. But Mervyn Peake saluted the fog-drenched opening of *Bleak House* in his description of darkness descending over Gormenghast. Stella Gibbons quotes Austen in the epigraphs of several novels, and wittily references her in *Cold Comfort Farm*. Daphne du Maurier made a pilgrimage to the Brontës' Haworth home and wrote a perceptive introduction to a 1955 edition of *Wuthering Heights*. Finally, J.K. Rowling salutes Jane Austen admiringly, naming Argus Filch's cat Mrs Norris and citing *Emma* as guiding light.

Limiting the book to famous English and American novels ruled out Victor Hugo's *Notre Dame*, Alain-Fournier's *The Lost Domain*, Thomas Mann's *Buddenbrooks*, Franz Kafka's *The Castle*, Umberto Eco's *The Name of the Rose*, Isabel Allende's *House of the Spirits* and a host of others. Even so, there are notable omissions. What about 'The Fall of the House of Usher'? Although probably the best fictional example extant of a sentient dwelling, I decided it was altogether too crude, too relentlessly focused to a single effect. Besides, it is a short story, rather than a novel with meat on its bones. I considered *Little Women*, but decided that the March family were more characterful than their house, and *Gone with the Wind*, but concluded that Rhett and Scarlett steal the stage from Tara.

In recent decades, property has been seen as the easiest way to obtain capital, and houses have become more associated with the accumulation of wealth than the establishment of a place to call home. Obsession with earning estate agents' superlatives is leading to a sad decline in characterful eccentricities. In the 2000s there was a flurry of interest by such authors as Kazuo Ishiguro (*The Remains of the Day*) and Ian McEwan (*Atonement*) in using the great country house as a symbol of civilized living, implicitly lamenting its decline, but such places have less literary charm now that they have become lookalike museums coddled by the National Trust or the gated retreats of the super-rich. More often, recent fictional homes are horrific. Writers have waxed satirical on dystopic apartment blocks and suburban dreariness in such novels as J.G. Ballard's *High-Rise*, Anthony Burgess's *A Clockwork Orange*, Julian Barnes's *Metroland* and John Lanchester's *Capital*. J.P. Delaney's *The Girl Before* stars an ultra-modern Chelsea des res that uses technology to manipulate the physical and mental wellbeing of its increasingly terrified tenant.

Rather than ending my catalogue of memorable dwellings among the gloomy predictions of such novels, I decided to look to a much more popular modern literary trend, one which, moreover, I personally prefer. In her introduction to *The Book of Fantasy*, edited by Jorge Luís Borges, Ursula Le Guin wrote that it was possible to believe that:

> our narrative fiction has for years been going, slowly and vaguely and massively, not in the wash and slap of fad and fashion but as a deep current, in one direction – towards rejoining the 'ocean of story', fantasy.[3]

For my final portraits, therefore, I offer three unforgettable fantasy dwellings: Gormenghast, Bag End and Hogwarts School.

A TRIUMPHANT ILLUSION

The Castle of Otranto and Horace Walpole

I waked one morning in the beginning of last June from a
dream, of which all I could recover was, that I had thought
myself in an ancient castle (a very natural dream for a head
like mine, filled with Gothic story), and that on the uppermost
banister of a great staircase I saw a gigantic hand in armour.

Horace Walpole, letter to Richard Cole, 9 March 1765

More than a dark stage set for the villain's persecution of the
maiden, the biologized castle has a body and a mind of its own.
It responds to Manfred's erotic villainy ... with all the vigor of
a revitalized corpse.

Frederick S. Frank, 2003[1]

Horace Walpole's innovative and original romance *The Castle of
Otranto* was written during the summer of 1764, and published on
Christmas Eve. It delighted literary London and can fairly claim
to have been the first (and funniest) of the 'horrid' supernatural
fantasies that would eventually be briskly parodied by Jane Austen's
Northanger Abbey. Full of calculated melodrama, it was a Yuletide
jeu d'esprit, a festive gift that paid secret tribute to the 'little Gothic
castle' of Strawberry Hill, which Horace had created on the banks
of the Thames near Twickenham. But it had a serious underlying
purpose. Walpole came from a political family, and although

Otranto is on one level a light-hearted taradiddle, it is also an attack on tyranny, symbolized by a grim and ghastly castle which has an extraordinarily active part to play in the plot.

The pace is hectic. On the morning of the wedding of the wealthy and beautiful Isabella to Conran, heir of Otranto, a giant plumed helmet crashes down into the castle's courtyard and crushes Conran to death. Desperate for a new heir, his ruthless father Count Manfred decides he will divorce his now infertile wife Hippolyta and marry Isabella himself. Isabella flees through intricate and gloomy cloisters, a creaky trapdoor with rusty hinges and a subterranean passage to sanctuary in the church of St Nicholas (patron saint of Christmas and oppressed women and children). She is helped on her way by Theodore, a young peasant who bears an uncanny resemblance to the portrait in the Long Gallery of Otranto's former ruler, Count Alfonso; he narrowly escapes being 'poignarded' by Manfred. After much confused to-ing and fro-ing between cloister, castle and caves, weeping by virtuous damsels, and the villainous Manfred's accidental murder of his own daughter, supernatural forces take over:

> A clap of thunder at that instant shook the castle to its foundations; the earth rocked, and the clank of more than mortal armour was heard behind. … the form of Alfonso, dilated to an immense magnitude, appeared in the centre of the ruins.
> 'Behold in Theodore the true heir of Alfonso! said the vision: And having pronounced those words, accompanied by a clap of thunder, it ascended solemnly towards heaven, where the clouds parting asunder, the form of St. Nicholas was seen, and receiving Alfonso's shade, they were soon wrapt from mortal eyes in a blaze of glory.[2]

Modern scholars have had a field day with *Otranto*. 'The castle possessed [Walpole] like a spirit', claims Angela Wright. Fiona Robertson sees its labyrinthine secret passages as analogous to the human brain. Elizabeth McAndrew feels that it 'becomes a lasting

The Knight of the Gigantic Sabre arrives at the Castle of Otranto to confront the usurper Manfred 'in complete armour, his lance in the rest, his face entirely concealed by his vizor, which was surmounted by a large plume of scarlet and black feathers'.

representation of the torments of the subconscious making a prison of the self'.[3] This is, I think, going too far. Although the castle is indeed made scarily sentient, Walpole intended the supernatural events to produce as much hilarity as horror, not least because many of the most active objects were familiar to his guests. The giant gauntlet came from a suit of armour in Walpole's collection, and it crashed down a staircase which had the same heraldic trimmings as Strawberry's stairwell. Alfonso's spectral figure steps out of a painting by Marcus Geeraerts of Henry Cary, Lord Falkland, dressed all in white, which then hung at Strawberry Hill.[4] Many other magical twists and turns of fortune hinge on the house's geography and furnishings.

How did Horace come to create Strawberry Hill? He was the youngest son of Sir Robert Walpole, first Earl of Orford, who dominated British politics between 1721 and 1742. He thoroughly disliked Houghton Hall, the huge neoclassical pile erected in the 1730s by Sir Robert, and destined to be a debt-ridden millstone around the necks of his two older brothers. Instead, he acquired a 'little plaything house' in 5 acres of grounds on the banks of the Thames near Twickenham. 'It is the prettiest bauble you have ever seen, set in enamelled meadows and filigree hedges.'[5] He decided to transform it into a miniature country seat, a reflection of his love of all things medieval, and succeeded in creating 'a triumphant illusion of barbarism and gloom'.[6] It was lined with fine works of art and redolent with cultural and personal reference. Walpole was influenced by Joseph Addison's 1712 'Essay on the Imagination', which recommends reading histories and fables, engaging with nature, and contemplating illustrious objects as ways of soothing the mind and eliciting pleasure. He approved of Addison's dictum that

> greatness of Manner in Architecture … has such force upon the Imagination, that a small Building, where it appears, shall give the Mind nobler ideas than one of twenty times the Bulk, where the Manner is ordinary or little.[7]

This was the age of the antiquary and the topographer, when cultured men and women roamed Britain with pens, crayons, paper and watercolour paints in their satchels, seeking out picturesque landscapes and armorial pedigrees. For several summers Walpole and the friends who made up his 'Committee of Taste' toured the country on what they called 'Gothic Pilgrimages', looking for medieval objects to buy, and seeking sources of inspiration for the design of Strawberry Hill from the chantry chapels and tombs of cathedrals and churches, and the interiors of crumbling medieval castles and fifteenth-century country houses. Horace was especially interested in anything connected with his own ancestors. It was

Horace Walpole celebrated his pretty mock-Gothic home Strawberry Hill by featuring elements of it in his spoof horror story *The Castle of Otranto* (1767). It boasted battlements and pinnacles, cloisters and an oratory, a miniature version of Windsor Castle's crenellated round tower, and an armoury stuffed with weapons and armour.

in the course of these travels that he coined the word 'serendipity' to describe the experience of coming across treasures he hadn't known existed but instantly recognized as relevant to his project. It derived, he explained in a January 1754 letter to Horace Mann, from a Persian fairy tale entitled 'The Three Princes of Serendip', who, as they travelled, 'were always making discoveries, by accident and sagacity, of things which they were not in quest of'.

Soon Strawberry Hill boasted battlements and pinnacles, cloisters and an oratory, a miniature version of Windsor Castle's crenellated round tower and an armoury stuffed with weapons and armour. Its panelling, chimney breasts, windows and bookcases were modelled on real medieval tombs and fan vaults. In 1762 Walpole invited

Thomas Warton (1728–1790), Oxford's Professor of Poetry, down to admire it:

> You would find some attempts at Gothic, some miniatures
> of scenes which I am pleased to find you love – cloisters,
> screens, round towers, and a printing house, all indeed of
> baby dimensions, would put you a little in mind of the age of
> Caxton and Wynken. You might play at fancying yourself in a
> castle described by Spenser.[8]

Visitors were guided through the house by way of a series of theatri-cally arranged spaces, densely lined with objects that contrasted dramatically in size and type and stimulated the imagination, es-pecially Walpole's own. As Marion Harney perceptively writes, Strawberry Hill is 'essentially an autobiographical site'.[9] All it lacked was a romance of its own. Walpole decided to write *Otranto* to celebrate it. Its form was influenced by the melodramatic Italian pantomimes then playing in London theatres. He further justified the novel's theatricality by claiming in its preface 'that great master of nature, Shakespeare' as his model. He likened his own 'yokels' to the gravedigger in *Hamlet*, and pointed out that England's national bard also enjoyed employing the supernatural in the form of ghosts, sprites and witches.

To conceal his authorship, Walpole arranged for *Otranto* to be printed by a London printer rather than in his own printing house at Strawberry Hill. Its preface announced that it was an English transla-tion of a story of crusading times written in Italian by one 'Onuphrio Muralto' (a cryptogram of his own name), printed in Naples 'in the black letter'[10] in 1529, and only recently unearthed in the library of 'an ancient Catholic family in the north of England'. Tongue firmly in cheek, Walpole praised 'the beauty of the diction' and 'the zeal' and 'singular judgment' of the author. 'Terror, the author's principal engine, prevents the story from ever languishing; and it is so often contrasted by pity, that the mind is kept up in a constant vicissitude of interesting passions.' Finally, perhaps chuckling a little as he glanced around his cod-medieval library, he declared that

Though the machinery is invention, and the names of the actors imaginary, I cannot but believe that the groundwork of the story is founded on truth. The scene is undoubtedly laid in some real castle. The author seems frequently, without design, to describe particular parts. 'The chamber,' says he, 'on the right hand;' 'the door on the left hand;' 'the distance from the chapel to Conrad's apartment': these and other passages are strong presumptions that the author had some certain building in his eye.[11]

Which of course he did, as he revealed in a letter to his crony Richard Cole in March 1765:

Your partiality to me and Strawberry have I hope inclined you to excuse the wildness of the story. You will even have found some traits to put you in mind of this place. When you read of the picture quitting its panel, did not you recollect the portrait of Lord Falkland, all in white, in my gallery?[12]

The letter proves how symbiotically linked Strawberry Hill and *Otranto* were. A telling sentence in it runs: 'The work grew on my hands and I grew fond of it – add that I was very glad to think of any thing rather than politics.' It points to a neglected aspect of *Otranto*: the political twist in the tale. Horace had good cause to seek distraction. His political inclinations were, like his father's, Whiggish – anti-absolutist and pro-constitution, but the Whigs were now out of favour: the Jacobite rebellion of 1745 inclined the government to extreme conservatism. Walpole's much-admired cousin General Henry Seymour Conway, whose interests he had promoted whenever he could, was sacked from his regiment in April 1764 and given short shrift from the rigidly Tory Court party that was gathering around the inexperienced new king George III. Both Conway and Walpole expressed their disapproval of the government's use of the dubiously legal 'general warrant' to arrest the radical journalist John Wilkes, then a popular hero whose name had become synonymous with Liberty.

Disillusioned and weary, Walpole abandoned politics, retreated to Strawberry Hill and began work on *Otranto*, which is at heart about defeating tyranny: Manfred imprisons people arbitrarily, threatens to summarily execute Theodore, and murders his own daughter. This serious subtext is emphasized in the subtitle *A Gothic Story* that Walpole gave to the second edition of the novel, this time published under his own imprimatur: the Officina Arbuteana at Strawberry Hill. The word 'Gothic' did not have the meaning that it would later acquire. Walpole liked to call himself a Goth, but he certainly didn't dress in black and sleep with vampires. He meant that he was a defender of the ancient liberties enshrined in Magna Carta. Walpole's love of all things medieval was inseparably associated with his belief in the ancient laws of England, which the legendary jurist William Blackstone (1723–1780) would describe a few years later in his *Commentaries on the Laws of England* as 'an old Gothic castle, erected in the days of chivalry, but fitted up for a modern inhabitant'.[13] When Walpole set pen to paper, one of his motives was to warn against the debilitating absolutism then being imposed by Louis XV on the French. The wrecking of Otranto Castle symbolizes the defeat of despotism. In 1781 this anti-absolutist message was pointed up in a version for the London stage by Robert Jephson, who set it in France and called it *The Count of Narbonne*.

Why did Walpole initially conceal his identity? He might well have been nervous at acknowledging authorship. If critics slammed *Otranto* it would deal a blow to a reputation that was already reeling under cruel political strokes of fate. In the event, he need not have worried. The reading public loved the book because, for all its absurdities, it is a romp of a read. A second edition was required within three months. This time, Walpole came clean, and even supplied an ingenious literary justification for the book in a new preface. Personal diffidence and 'the novelty of the attempt' had, he claimed, prevented him from revealing that he had written it himself, in 'an attempt to blend the two kinds of romance, the ancient and the modern'. By 'modern' he meant such contemporary moralizing novels as Samuel Richardson's *Pamela; or, Virtue Rewarded*

(1740), Eliza Haywood's *The History of Miss Betsy Thoughtless* (1751) and Frances Sheridan's *Memoirs of Miss Sidney Biddulph* (1761).

> In the former, all was imagination and improbability: in the latter, nature is always intended to be, and sometimes has been, copied with success. Invention has not been wanting; but the great resources of fancy have been dammed up, by a strict adherence to common life.[14]

Walpole enjoyed making fun of both ancient and modern traditions. His was the age of satire, of Daniel Defoe and Alexander Pope, and of Laurence Sterne and Henry Fielding, who both wrote parodies of the long and tedious 'sentimental' novels of the time. What he didn't foresee was that countless bored women, tired of the interminable improving offerings from the circulating libraries, would welcome *Otranto*'s wild action, haunted castle, dank cloisters, determined young heroines and handsome young hero, and that a good many would set out to write their own 'shudder novels'. The trickle of 'Gothic' romances in atmospheric settings that *Otranto* inspired, notably J. Clara Reeve's *The Old English Baron* (1777)[15] and Sophia Lee's *The Recess* (1785), increased to a flood with Ann Radcliffe's *The Mysteries of Udolpho* (1794), Matthew Lewis's *The Monk* (1796) and Eleanor Sleath's *The Orphan of the Rhine* (1798).

History has not dealt kindly with Horace Walpole. The wealthy youngest son of a prime minister in an age when allotting lucrative sinecures, seats in rotten boroughs and posts in government to one's friends and relations was assumed to be one of the benefits of high office, he has long been written off as a fey dilettante who indulged himself to the point of absurdity. But he was in truth a knowledgeable connoisseur of literature, painting and all aspects of the arts. Strawberry Hill was not just 'a small capricious house … built to please my own taste, and in some degree to realize my own visions'. It was intended as an architectural pattern book, which he hoped would inspire others to admire the wonders of medieval invention and the patriotic symbolism of Gothic architecture, and re-create them. In 1774 he published a detailed and densely illustrated *Description of the Villa of Mr. Horace Walpole, younger son of the Earl of Orford, at Strawberry-Hill near Twickenham, Middlesex. With an Inventory of the Furniture, Pictures, Curiosities, etc.* It points out the many symbolic connections of the four thousand and more works of art and ancient and exotic curiosities he had brought together there.

Walpole's voluminous correspondence (now collected in the magnificent 48-volume Yale edition) was not just a way of passing the time. It was a deliberate construct, a set of memoirs in the style of Madame de Sévigné that were intended to offer future historians a unique contemporary source from a man who described his times with elegance and perception. His *Historic Doubts on the Life and Reign of King Richard the Third* (1768) was one of the earliest attempts to defend the much-vilified monarch. He also wrote a wittily opinionated *Catalogue of the Royal and Noble Authors of England* (1758), *The History of the Modern Taste in Gardening* (1771) and the four-volume *Anecdotes of Painting in England* (1762–71). The only other fictions Walpole wrote were notably unsuccessful: a notorious tragedy about mother–son incest entitled *The Mysterious Mother* (1768), which Byron would later admire, and the weirdly surreal *Hieroglyphic Tales* (1766–72), written 'when I was out of my mind', and not published in his lifetime.

What of the real Otranto? Although Walpole toured Italy early in the 1750s, he never got as far as Otranto, although he must have come across many dramatic little fortified medieval castles in the Val d'Aosta and the Apennines. He claimed that he picked the 'very sonorous name' off a map, and was delighted when, twenty years after the novel's publication, a friend sent him a drawing of the actual castle, which was, he crowed, 'just as I imagined it'. At one point he likened the great court of his fiction to that of Trinity College, in his alma mater Cambridge, and it is tempting to imagine Otranto's 'great staircase' as that of his friend John Chute's at his Hampshire house, The Vyne.[16] But his imagined *Otranto* was above all a tribute to his carefully constructed heartland of

Strawberry Hill: the quaintly exquisite retreat he had designed with deliberate care to be a luxuriously comfortable home of his own, full of antique and heraldic objects whose significance he carefully spelt out in his *Description* of Strawberry Hill.

Most touching of all, perhaps, is the presence in the house's chapel-like 'Cabinet' of a facsimile of the statue to his mother that Horace had installed in the Henry VII Chapel in Westminster Abbey; the Chapel's fan vaulting was replicated in Strawberry Hill's Long Gallery. Sir Robert was a notorious womanizer; for the last ten years of his marriage he had lived openly with his glamorous and wealthy mistress Maria Skerrett at Houghton and Richmond Park in 'a confusion of wine and bawdy and hunting and tobacco'.[17] Horace's mother Lady Catherine, who lived in Chelsea, was certainly no angel (rumour had it that Horace's real father was Lord Hervey) but Horace adored her, and was devastated by her death in 1737, when he was barely 20. Walpole's biographer Robert Ketton-Cremer believed that love for his mother 'was the most powerful emotion of his entire life'.[18] Sir Robert Walpole married his mistress with indecent haste in 1738. A prominent theme of *The Castle of Otranto* is the selfish perfidy of husbands and the self-abnegating nature of wives. Manfred's eventual reconciliation with his hard-done-by wife Hippolyta was wistful wish-fulfilment on Horace's part. Strawberry Hill had the same quality – a womb of fantasies spun around an imagined past, created to comfort a brilliant, puzzled man-child.

THE BEWILDERED HOUSE
Mansfield Park and Jane Austen

They admire *Mansfield Park* exceedingly. Mr Cooke says 'it is the most sensible novel he ever read', and the manner in which I treat the clergy delights them very much.

Jane Austen, letter to Cassandra, 13 June 1814[1]

Keep the young generations in hail,
And bequeath them no tumbled house!

George Meredith, 'The Empty Purse', 1892[2]

To turn from *Otranto* to *Mansfield Park* (1814) is to move from playful, though freighted, artifice to subtle and purposeful art. Jane Austen (1775–1817) was deeply interested in place, and she would certainly have read *Otranto*; she lampooned the cod-medieval settings of the Gothic romances that it inspired in *Northanger Abbey*, the first novel she finished.[3] Houses are given distinct personality in her novels, and always reflect the character of their occupants. In *Pride and Prejudice*, touring Pemberley, 'a large, handsome stone building, standing well on rising ground', whose master is, the housekeeper assures her, 'the best landlord, and the best master … that ever lived', changes Elizabeth Bennet's mind about the merits of Mr Darcy. In *Emma*, Donwell Abbey 'was just what it ought to be, and it looked what it was', and confirms the merits of Mr Knightley for Emma Woodhouse.

In *Mansfield Park* (1814) Austen goes much further. It is a consciously original book about the restoration of order to a house that is divided against itself because of Sir Thomas and Lady Bertram's failures as parents. The moral preservation of the Bertram children is at stake. The 'airy and well-situated' Northamptonshire house that gives the book its title takes centre stage, both architecturally and as a symbol of the family who occupy it. Set in 'a real park, five miles round', it is

> a spacious modern-built house, so well placed and well screened as to deserve to be in any collection of engravings of gentlemen's seats in the kingdom.[4]

However, instead of portraying a great house faithful to its traditions like Pemberley or Donwell Abbey, Austen presents one that is only superficially impressive. The profligacy of Sir Thomas's eldest son Tom has impaired its finances, so his brother Edmund's inheritance stands to be reduced. Moreover, Sir Bertram has interests in slave plantations in the Caribbean, a source of wealth which in the eyes of many, including Austen, was morally tainted.[5]

We are introduced to the Bertrams through the medium of a highly unusual heroine. Daringly, instead of offering the charming sisters of *Pride and Prejudice* and *Sense and Sensibility*, Austen offers Fanny Price, a shrinking violet, whose name she borrowed from a 'lovely' and 'chaste' heroine pursued by a rake in George Crabbe's 1807 poem *The Parish Register* (Fanny has Crabbe's *Tales* on her bookshelf). In an even more original twist, Fanny's eventual reward is not Mansfield Park, but Mansfield Parsonage. Nor is this intended as a second best. Austen herself preferred cosy parsonages to grand mansions, and the duties of the country clergy are a significant theme in the novel.[6] Running in parallel to her barbed reflections on the Bertrams' parenting is criticism of clergymen who neglected their flocks, or who held more than one living, and were therefore distant from many of their parishioners. Discussion of the responsibilities of the clergy recurs. Sir Thomas explains to

Henry Crawford, who wants to rent Thornton Lacey Parsonage to be near Fanny, that he can't because Edmund will be resident there.

> 'a parish has wants and claims which can be known only by a clergyman constantly resident... Edmund ... might ... be the clergyman of Thornton Lacey every seventh day, for three or four hours, if that would content him. But it will not. He knows that human nature needs more lessons than a weekly sermon can convey; and that if he does not live among his parishioners, and prove himself by constant attention their well-wisher and friend, he does very little either for their good or his own.'[7]

The novel opens when 10-year-old Fanny Price is removed from a large and indigent family to be a useful companion to her mother's sisters.[8] She is to live with her aunt Lady Bertram and her formidable husband Sir Thomas in a mansion dauntingly different from her turbulent Portsmouth home.

> The grandeur of the house astonished, but could not console her. The rooms were too large for her to move in with ease: whatever she touched she expected to injure, and she crept about in constant terror of something or other; often retreating towards her own chamber to cry.[9]

She is mocked by her cousins Maria and Julia, who pronounce her 'prodigiously stupid'; the boys remark on her small size and shyness. Her mother's other sister Aunt Norris, married to Mansfield's parson, busies herself with interfering at the Park, indulging Maria and Julia and putting Fanny down. 'Remember,' she tells her, 'wherever you are, you must be the lowest and last'. The Bertrams are distracted parents. Lady Bertram pays 'not the smallest attention' to the education of her daughters.

> She had not time for such cares. She was a woman who spent her days in sitting nicely dressed on a sofa, doing some long piece of needlework, of little use and no beauty, thinking more of her pug than her children, but very indulgent to the latter, when it did not put herself to inconvenience.[10]

Sir Thomas, preoccupied with making money, leaves far too much of their charge to Mrs Norris.

Fanny does find comfort in her cousin Edmund, Tom's serious-minded younger brother. He finds her weeping on the stairs to her chilly attic bedroom one day, and from then on takes an interest in her. He imbues her with his own high principles and fights her corner when thoughtless neglect of her becomes positively unkind. By the time she is 18, Fanny worships the ground Edmund walks on, but his mind is on his forthcoming ordination, and his heart tempted by the fascinating Mary Crawford, a wealthy London heiress who comes to stay with her sister Mrs Grant at Mansfield Parsonage, as does her equally wealthy and charming brother Henry. Serpents have entered Eden. The extent to which Mary's nature has been corrupted is established early on, when in a careless aside about the admiral uncle under whose roof they have been living, she makes an exceptionally vulgar naval pun: 'of *Rears*, and *Vices*, I saw enough'.[11] Mansfield Park's defences are down. Sir Thomas Bertram has gone to Antigua to see to his sugar plantations. Lady Bertram snores on the sofa, and Mrs Norris is engineering what she sees as a highly desirable match between Maria and the rich and stupid James Rushworth. The rot setting in at Mansfield Park is signalled by three set pieces, in all of which a home is a significant element, and in the course of which shy little Fanny will emerge as an infallible moral compass.

The first points up the decay of traditional values. The Crawfords, the Bertram children and Fanny go to visit Sotherton Court, which Maria's fiancé has inherited, along with several thousand acres and ancient manorial rights. Edmund admires it: 'The house was built in Elizabeth's time, and is a large, regular, brick building – heavy, but respectable looking, and has many good rooms', but Rushworth derides it as 'a dismal old prison', and plans to hire Humphrey Repton to 'improve' its grounds, and to open up its 'prospect' by cutting down its long oak avenue. Fanny expresses regret to Edmund in an undertone, quoting from William Cowper's then popular didactic poem *The Task*: 'Ye fallen avenues, once more I mourn your fate unmerited'. *The Task* praises rural simplicities: its most famous line is 'God made the country, and man made the town'. It also pillories slavery.[12] Later, when they are shown the plain oblong chapel, and are told that the Rushworths no longer hold family prayers, Mary quips cynically that 'every generation has its improvements'. Fanny, quoting that arch traditionalist Sir Walter Scott, regrets both the ending of the tradition and the absence of ancient heraldry in the chapel.

> This is not my idea of a chapel. There is nothing awful here,
> nothing melancholy, nothing grand. Here are no aisles, no
> arches, no inscriptions, no banners. No banners, cousin, to be
> 'blown by the night wind of heaven.' No signs that a 'Scottish
> monarch sleeps below'.[13]

Henry Crawford flirts first with Julia and then, despite her engagement, with Maria, encouraging her to escape Rushworth by showing her a way around the iron fence and the ha-ha that symbolically imprisons her inside Sotherton's formal garden; they disappear into the freedom of the park's informal 'wilderness', pursued by a rightly suspicious Rushworth. Edmund wanders off into the woods with Mary, leaving Fanny forlorn on a bench. There is an unreal air akin to *A Midsummer Night's Dream* about the whole episode: 'We were all … bewildered', Henry will say apologetically later on. The word 'bewildered' recurs no less than six times as matters at Mansfield go from bad to worse.

In the second set piece, the disordering of Mansfield's actual fabric by the putting on of a risqué play parallels the growing moral disorder. Tom Bertram and his theatre-mad friend Mr Yates insist, despite Edmund and Fanny's protests, on performing Elizabeth Inchbald's *Lovers' Vows*, a tale of aristocratic bad behaviour, adultery and bastardy. Austen assigns the parts aptly. The dastardly baron is played by Mr Yates, and the woman he seduced long ago by Maria, who can thus enjoy much fond embracing with Henry Crawford, who is cast as their son. The baron's impudently forward

Fanny Price watches nervously as Maria Bertram climbs around a locked gate and pursues the dashing Henry Crawford across the park: Joan Hassall's exquisite wood engravings for the Folio Society's 1959 edition of *Mansfield Park* captured its most significant scenes perfectly.

daughter is Mary Crawford, who declares her love for her tutor (Edmund), rather than the foppish cavalier (James Rushworth) who is her father's choice for her. Fanny strong-mindedly refuses to join in, but has to suffer the agony of seeing the man she loves rehearsing love scenes with a woman she feels is unworthy of him. The moral world is topsy-turvy: when Sir Thomas unexpectedly returns from Antigua during a rehearsal, his family find his homecoming not a joy but 'a moment of absolute horror!' Sir Thomas discovers that the bookcase in his much-loved study has been moved, and the billiards room transformed to a theatre in which a 'ranting young man ... appeared likely to knock him down backwards'. He finds himself 'bewildered in his own house'.

Sir Thomas restores order at Mansfield, but only superficially. Despite her feelings for Henry, Maria marries Mr Rushworth, and disappears with Julia to queen it first in Brighton and then among Wimpole Street's notoriously fast and fashionable set. Tom goes to Newmarket to join his rackety friends. The Crawfords remain, however, unexpectedly becoming converts to the Mansfield ethos as it was intended to be. Although Mary sneers at Edmund because he is going to be a clergyman, she is very drawn to him. Edmund, Mary and Henry talk of the clergy, each in the process revealing their true characters. Edmund emphasizes the 'spirit of improvement' in preaching, Henry confesses that 'nineteen times out of twenty I am thinking how such a prayer ought to be read, and longing to have it to read myself', Mary is all for absentee vicars.

Henry also decides to amuse himself by seducing Fanny (now grown 'absolutely pretty'), but has no success; instead he falls deeply in love with her and, after the coming-out ball Sir Thomas gives for her, proposes marriage. Now it is Fanny's turn to be assailed. Sir Thomas, Edmund and Henry himself put pressure on her to accept him. Each in turn invades the private sanctum she has established in the East room. Austen describes the contents of this 'nest of comforts' in unusual detail, something she rarely does in her novels, but she wants to make a distinction between the moral vacuity of the formal interiors of Sotherton and Mansfield and the emotional reassurance Fanny gets from being among her beloved possessions.

> She could go there after anything unpleasant below, and find immediate consolation ... Her plants, her books ... her writing-desk, and her works of charity and ingenuity, ... she could scarcely see an object in that room which had not an interesting remembrance connected with it. Every thing was a friend, or bore her thoughts to a friend...[14]

As Sir Thomas, Henry and Edmund all try to persuade her, she too grows 'bewildered', wondering if her scruples are misguided. But she stands fast, only to be expelled from her beloved nest when Sir Thomas decides that a long visit to her family in Portsmouth might make her better appreciate what she was rejecting.

The third set piece sees Fanny in 'bewildered, broken, sorrowful contemplation' of the noisy chaos that is life in the Prices' cramped little Portsmouth home.

> The smallness of the house, and thinness of the walls, brought every thing so close to her, that, added to the fatigue of her journey, and all her recent agitation, she hardly knew how to bear it.[15]

She is affectionately welcomed, but has lost her position there. She longs for Mansfield, recalling its spacious, civilized elegance, and even looks more kindly on Henry, the only person to visit her in Portsmouth:

> She was willing to allow he might have more good qualities than she had been wont to suppose. She began to feel the possibility of his turning out well at last...[16]

But the Mansfield she dreams of is on the point of collapse. Tom falls ill, and is soon near enough to death to make Mary Crawford advance again on Edmund, because he now seems likely to inherit Mansfield. Maria leaves Rushworth to live in sin with Henry Crawford, who has been flirting with her while deprived of Fanny, and Julia elopes to Scotland with Mr Yates. 'There is no end to the evil let loose upon us', writes Edmund, summoning Fanny back to Mansfield on behalf of his father and mother.

She returns with her sister Susan, and soon emerges as the family's prop and mainstay. When Mary is revealed to be as perfidious as her brother, Edmund abandons hope of her, making Fanny the confidante of his broken heart. All's not quite well, but it is going to end as best it may, announces Austen, marching on stage as the omniscient narrator.

> Let other pens dwell on guilt and misery. I quit such odious subjects as soon as I can, impatient to restore every body, not greatly in fault themselves, to tolerable comfort, and to have done with all the rest.[17]

Tolerable comfort is achieved in the space of one hectic last chapter. In time, we hear, Edmund 'did cease to care about Miss Crawford, and became as anxious to marry Fanny as Fanny herself could desire'. Sir Thomas is delighted, realizing that in Fanny he has the perfect daughter-in-law. Julia marries Mr Yates, who turns out to be happy to take advice from a father-in-law 'now conscious of errors in his own conduct as a parent'. Maria, the book's unforgiven pariah, is banished to a 'remote' part of the country with the ghastly Mrs Norris. The Crawfords retreat, sadder, perhaps a little wiser. Tom Bertram, chastened by his illness and shocked at the outcome of his theatricals, 'became what he ought to be, useful to his father, steady and quiet'. Mansfield's moral foundations strengthened, the house becomes altogether pleasanter as Sir Thomas mellows, Lady Bertram finds another Fanny in her sister Susan, and Fanny and Edmund settle nearby.

Improvement (another word that recurs) is general, both moral and architectural. Fanny's final home is Mansfield Parsonage, which has evolved just as she has. Run down with parsimony by Aunt Norris, it was luxuriously improved by Mr and Mrs Grant, who laid out fine gardens and a shrubbery for contemplating nature. After Fanny and Edmund move in, it 'soon grew as dear to her heart, and as thoroughly perfect in her eyes, as everything else within the view and patronage of Mansfield Park had long been'.

Mansfield Parsonage was not in Austen's opinion a consolation prize. Parsonages were her preferred dwellings in both fact and fiction. Attractive examples recur in her novels: Hunsford Parsonage in *Pride and Prejudice*, Delaford Parsonage in *Sense and Sensibility* and Woodston Parsonage in *Northanger Abbey*, about which Catherine Morland ('she, who had so longed to be in an abbey!') reflects: 'There was nothing so charming to her imagination as the unpretending comfort of a well-connected parsonage.' Jane grew up in just such a house, and always regretted her expulsion from Steventon Rectory, which she had to quit when her brother James succeeded her father as rector in 1801. The family moved first to Bath, full of the hustle and bustle of a watering place, and then, after the death of Jane's father, to Southampton. These domestic circumstances led to Jane's writing going on hold until 1809 when she settled with her mother, her sister Cassandra and a childhood friend Martha Lloyd in a house in the village of Chawton, in Hampshire, the second of the great estates inherited by her brother Edward. It was, recorded her niece Caroline, quite as good as the generality of Parsonage houses then – and much in the same old style – the ceilings low and roughly finished – *some* bedrooms very small – *none* very large but in number sufficient to accommodate the inmates and several guests.[18]

The move transformed Jane's life, providing her at last with a peaceful place in which to write.

Where did the inspiration for *Mansfield Park* come from? Fanny has something of the upright saintliness of the eponymous hero of Richardson's *Sir Charles Grandison*, one of Jane Austen's favourite books. Its heroine, Harriet Byron, comes from Northamptonshire, which is where Mansfield Park is said to be, and one of Sir Charles's good deeds is to restore the family fortunes of Sir Thomas and Lady Mansfield and their family; they have a daughter called Fanny and live in Mansfield House. But paying homage to a favourite book by borrowing names from it is not the same as being inspired by it. I believe that a succession of formative events in the fortunes of the Austen family lay behind *Mansfield Park*. In 1780 Jane's brother Edward was adopted at the age of 12 by their mother's wealthy but childless cousins, Thomas and Constance Knight, with a view to making him their heir. Two years after Thomas Knight's death in 1798 Mrs Knight decided to retire to Winchester and hand over the estates to Edward. His principal residence became Godmersham, near Ashford in Kent. A substantial Palladian mansion built in 1732, it closely resembles Mansfield Park in appearance. Discussion of the right management of estates recurs in *Mansfield Park*: Henry Crawford takes a more active interest in his hitherto neglected estate with an eye to impressing Fanny.

Another theme in *Mansfield Park* is the right upbringing of children. In 1808 Edward's wife Elizabeth died. Edward was left with eleven children on his hands, ranging in age from 15 to a newborn. He did not marry again, relying instead on help from his own family, especially Jane and Cassandra. A year after Elizabeth's death, he provided his mother and sisters with their cherished

Chawton home. Chawton House itself is an Elizabethan manor house like Mr Rushworth's Sotherton, and its grounds still include a wilderness and a ha-ha.[19] Edward spent five summer months there in 1813 there, 'improving' it. He added a billiards room and landscaping in the style of Humphrey Repton. That year, his oldest child Fanny, a favourite of Jane's, was close to coming of age; that and the upbringing of Fanny's rumbustious brothers[20] must have been in her aunt's thoughts as she strolled the short distance between her village home and Chawton House, mentally constructing *Mansfield Park*. Jane expressed misgivings about her nephews' 'sporting Mania' and 'habit of Luxury' in a letter written later that autumn (12 October 1813). It was to be expected, sighed Cassandra, 'with so indulgent a father and so liberal a stile [*sic*] of living'.[21] Jane makes Edmund declare in *Mansfield Park*, 'It is the habits of wealth that I fear.'

Chawton also has a rectory, of which Jane's brother Henry was curate for four years. Handsome, clever and a notable actor, Henry had all his fictional namesake Henry Crawford's charm, and was Jane's favourite brother. He originally considered the Church as a career, but in 1797 he married his widowed cousin, the glamorous Eliza de Feuillide, spirited, witty, vain and musical, and as averse to a clerical husband as was Mary Crawford. Henry entered the militia instead of the Church; he subsequently became a banker. Though far from approving of Eliza's outrageous ways, Jane was very fond of her. She was with her when she died of cancer in April 1813, just as *Mansfield Park* was being sketched out. I think that the subtle drawing of Mary Crawford's character reflects Jane's mixed feelings about Eliza. After her death, and the collapse of his business in 1815, Henry took orders, and served as curate of Chawton from 1816 to 1820, when he succeeded his brother James as rector of Steventon, which was in Edward's gift.

Austen's use of place to point up her purposes continued in her next novel, *Emma* (1815), in which George Knightley's good management of Donwell Abbey (another house that resembled Chawton House) is symbolic of his fine character, and in *Persuasion* (1818), in

Elements of the Great House at Chawton informed Jane Austen's *Mansfield Park* (1814). Her brother Edward inherited it in 1798, and added a ha-ha around its church and garden, and a wilderness. In 1809 he settled his mother, Jane and Cassandra in a pretty house in the village, a ten-minute walk away.

which the loss of Kellynch Hall makes manifest the threat that once stood over Mansfield Park. Jane herself could rest content with her parsonage-like Chawton home. These lines from her rhyming letter to her brother Frank soon after their move there perfectly expresses its importance to her:

Our Chawton home – how much we find
Already in it, to our mind,
And how convinced that when complete,
It will all other Houses beat
That ever have been made or mended,
With rooms concise, or rooms distended.[22]

BRIDGING TWO WORLDS
Tully-Veolan and Walter Scott

The minds of men are formed by their habitations.
> Walter Scott, *Tales of a Grandfather*, 1831[1]

The Scots baronial mansion, in imitation of Tully-Veolan …
with its angle turrets, crow-stepped gables, and battlements,
sprang up, seemingly overnight, in England and Ireland.
> Mavis Batey, 1983[2]

Sir Walter Scott (1771–1832) was the J.K. Rowling of his age, read by
old and young alike and adored for his ebullient humour, colourful
characters, carefully researched settings, thrilling historical incidents
and impeccable morality. He addressed his readers as old friends,
nudging them into fuller appreciation of his message with paren-
theses and footnotes, and rousing their hearts to high endeavours:

> One hour of life, crowded to the full with glorious action, and
> filled with noble risks, is worth whole years of those mean
> observances of paltry decorum, in which men steal through
> existence, like sluggish waters through a marsh, without either
> honour or observation.[3]

He dreamed of reawakening the medieval traditions of chivalry
in the breast of all red-blooded men and women. He devoted his

hugely productive writing years to presenting the history, actual and mythical, of Scotland and England in an immensely palatable fashion, and to a definite purpose: the reconciliation of Highlanders and Lowlanders, Jacobites and Hanoverians, the English landed gentry and the troubled working class. In *Waverley* he uses the fictional Tully-Veolan Castle, the eventual home of his English hero and Scottish heroine, as the symbol of such reconciliation. From the profits of his writing he converted a Tweed-side farmhouse into what he liked to call his 'Conundrum Castle'. Abbotsford was Tully-Veolan made actual: it combined the romance of Scottish baronial trimmings with the latest English domestic conveniences. Not only did it herald a nationwide architectural fashion – dwellings great and small were topped with castellations and a rash of turrets. It was also a magnificent architectural reinforcement of *Waverley*'s argument for national unity.

Scott's vision of Anglo-Scottish reconciliation was inspired by his own background. His grandfather was a confirmed Jacobite, known as Beardie because he had sworn never to shave his beard unless a Stuart regained the throne. His father, a dry-as-dust Edinburgh lawyer, was as confirmed a Hanoverian; his hobby was Calvinist church history. The smog-filled city was no place to bring up a child, especially one lamed by polio, and Walter spent much of his early childhood and later his school holidays with his grandparents on the banks of the Tweed, revelling in the open-air life and drinking in their stirring tales of the old days in the borders. His withered leg ruled out the military career he had hoped for, but he grew up into a striking figure of a man, described by an admiring American visitor in 1820 as 'tall, well formed, … neither fat nor thin, with forehead very high, nose short, upper lip long and face rather fleshy, complexion fresh and clear, eyes very blue, shrewd and penetrating'.[4] Scott recalls that after he arrived at Edinburgh University at the age of 12, he 'fastened … like a tiger upon every collection of old songs or romances which chance threw my way, or which my scrutiny was able to discover on the dusty shelves of

James Sibbald's circulating library in the Parliament Square'. He read Classics, then qualified as a lawyer, touring the Highlands for his father and drinking in tales of the Jacobite rebellions from the survivors of the most recent, that of 1745. He collected stories and ballads galore, and published a three-volume collection entitled *Minstrelsy of the Border* in 1802–3.

Scott began work on long narrative poems set in a glamorized medieval past, in which young Lochinvar galloped out of the west, and Thomas the Rhymer encountered the Queen of Elfland in the Eildon hills. *The Lay of the Last Minstrel* (1805) brought him national fame. It bounces along in memorable couplets. 'O'er ptarmigan and venison / The priest had spoke his benison' is my own favourite, but the best known is undoubtedly

> Breathes there the man, with soul so dead,
> Who never to himself hath said,
> This is my own, my native land!

Scott explained in the *Lay*'s preface that it was 'intended to illustrate the customs and manners which anciently prevailed on the Borders of England and Scotland'. More long poems followed, notably *Marmion, a Tale of Flodden* (1808) and *The Lady of the Lake* (1810). These became deeply lodged in the nation's literary imagination, and even today we quote, usually unknowingly, from them: 'O, what a tangled web we weave / When first we practise to deceive!' is from *Marmion* and 'Hail to the Chief' from *The Lady of the Lake*.

But in 1812 a new literary star entered the firmament. The first cantos of Lord Byron's *Childe Harold's Pilgrimage* electrified the reading public, and after his subversive and shocking satiric epic *Don Juan* appeared Byron was the most sought-after literary lion in London. 'He beat me out of the field in description of the stronger passions and in deep-seated knowledge of the human heart', Scott admitted to his son-in-law John Lockhart.[5] Scott turned instead to preaching his message using a new form of fiction: the historical novel. He started writing *Waverley* in 1805, inspired by the ambitious desire of composing a tale of chivalry, which was to be in the style of the *Castle of Otranto*, with plenty of Border characters, and supernatural incident.[6]

He put it aside and returned to poetry, but took it up again in the winter of 1813, and finished it in July 1814.

By now, Scott had new literary influences. One was Jane Austen. 'That young lady had a talent for describing the involvements and feelings and characters of ordinary life, which is to me the most wonderful I ever met with', he wrote.

> The Big Bow-wow strain I can do myself like any now going; but the exquisite touch, which renders ordinary commonplace things and characters interesting, from the truth of the description and the sentiment, is denied me.[7]

More relevant to *Waverley*, however, was Maria Edgeworth (1768–1849), who has been called the author of 'the first historical novel, the first regional novel in English, the first Anglo-Irish novel, the first Big House novel and the first saga novel'.[8] Scott admired her 'rich humour, pathetic tenderness and admirable tact', but was even more impressed by the effective way in which first *Castle Rackrent* (1800) and then *The Absentee* (1812) approached the vexed question of absentee Anglo-Irish landlords. In 1800 and 1801, Acts of Union between Great Britain and Ireland had been passed, but relations between the Irish and their rapacious English landlords remained at a low ebb. By addressing such evils head-on, Scott believed that Edgeworth 'may truly be said to have done more towards completing the Union than perhaps all the legislative enactments by which it has been followed up'.[9]

Scott hoped that *Waverley* would perform the same miracle for relations between disaffected Jacobites and English Whigs overly convinced of their own superiority. Set in 1745, the year of the second Jacobite rebellion, the novel's central character is Edward Waverley, an impressionable puppet pulled this way and that by his cautious Westminster Whig father Richard and his defiantly high-Tory pro-Stuart uncle, Everard Waverley of Waverley-Honour, 'an old English gentleman of an ancient descent and opulent fortune'. Edward grows up spending much of each year in his childless uncle's atmospheric old house, hung with scutcheons and battle trophies. In its library, 'a large Gothic room, with double arches and a gallery', he fills his head with chivalric romances, rather as Scott himself did as a boy, and roams its romantic grounds, enjoying their 'savage character'.

When sent to Scotland by his father as captain of a troop to defend the Hanoverian cause, he is easily diverted from his post in Dundee by an invitation to visit his uncle's Jacobite friend Baron Cosmo Bradwardine. The baron's ancestral seat Tully-Veolan Castle is the crux of the book. Scott gave it elements of such ancient Scottish houses and castles as Traquair House (notable for its bear gates, kept closed ever since 1745), Grandtully Castle, Murthly Castle, and the House of Dean and Old Ravelston (both now demolished) in Edinburgh.

On his approach to Tully-Veolan, Edward is shocked by the rundown state of its village, beggarly in comparison to 'the smiling neatness of English cottages'.

> The houses seemed miserable in the extreme. ... They stood, without any respect for regularity, on each side of a straggling kind of unpaved street, where children, almost in a primitive state of nakedness, lay sprawling, as if to be crushed by the hoofs of the first passing horse. ... [A]lmost every hut was fenced in front by a huge black stack of turf on one side of the door, while on the other the family dunghill ascended in noble emulation.[10]

But his heart begins to stir as he arrives at the walled park around the castle, rides up a double avenue of horse-chestnut trees, and through a battlemented gateway surmounted by 'two large weather-beaten mutilated masses of upright stone', which 'had once represented ... two rampant Bears'. There are pepper-pot turrets at each corner of the battlements, 'dungeon-looking stables' with

Edward Waverley admiring the carved bears on the battlemented gateway into Tully-Veolan Castle, from an 1885 edition of *Waverley*, illustrated by Louis Bombled. Scott made Tully-Veolan's destruction and reconstruction symbolize the reconciliation of Scotland and England.

granaries above them, a 'tun-bellied' pigeon house, and a fountain in the form of a huge stone bear, the family emblem. More bears, 'small and large, demi or in full proportion', are carved over the windows, and on gables, gutter spouts and turrets. The ancient family motto, 'Beware the Bear', is everywhere. One supports a sundial 'of large circumference inscribed with more diagrams than

Edward's mathematics enabled him to decipher', others act as balustrades around the terrace.

In this 'enchanted mansion' Edward meets Baron Cosmo, 'a tall, thin, athletic figure, old indeed and grey-haired, but with every muscle rendered as tough as whip-cord by constant exercise'. He expresses his delight in seeing his old friend's nephew, with tears in his eyes and a welter of Latin epigrams, and presents him to his daughter Rose, 'a very pretty girl of the Scotch cast of beauty, that is, with a profusion of hair of paley gold, and a skin like the snow of her own mountains in whiteness'. They dine in a 'great dining parlour, wainscoted with black oak, and hung round with the pictures of his ancestry'. Scott fills three chapters with picturesque details of the buildings, rooms, furnishings, gardens and servants of Tully-Veolan.

After enjoying lavish baronial hospitality, Edward is lured into wild Highland territory, first to the savagely primitive mountain cavern of the freebooter Donald Bean Lean, and then to stay in remote Glennaquoich, 'a high rude-looking square tower', with a young chieftain called Fergus Mac-Ivor. Fergus's sister Flora, aware of Edward's naivety, takes him to a 'sylvan ampitheatre' in a romantic glen and he falls in love with her. A tangled web of misunderstandings leads to a warrant for his arrest being issued, and he decides to throw in his lot with Fergus and Flora, who take him to meet Bonnie Prince Charlie, who is about to capture Edinburgh. Enraptured, Edward joins the Jacobite army on its march into England. It gets as far as Derby before being forced to turn back because of lack of support. Edward saves the life of a captured English soldier, Colonel Talbot, an act of mercy that will save his own life when the Stuart cause is irretrievably lost, and he finds himself in danger of trial for treason. Tully-Veolan Castle is sacked and burnt, its trees and bears brutally felled.

> The towers and pinnacles of the main building were scorched
> and blackened; the pavement of the court broken and
> shattered; the doors torn down entirely, or hanging by a single

hinge; the windows dashed in and demolished; and the court strewed with articles of furniture broken into fragments.[11]

But all is not lost. Thanks to Colonel Talbot, Edward is pardoned. Rose agrees to marry him, and Colonel Talbot and Sir Everard Waverley conspire to rebuild and even improve Tully-Veolan. New bears are carved, airy new stables erected, a glasshouse provided for the garden, and Baron Cosmo is restored to his ancestral home. With a final flourish, Talbot unveils

> a large and spirited painting, representing Fergus Mac-Ivor and Waverley in their Highland dress, the scene a wild, rocky, and mountainous pass, down which the clan were descending in the background ... the ardent, fiery, and impetuous character of the unfortunate Chief of Glennaquoich was finely contrasted with the contemplative, fanciful, and enthusiastic expression of his happier friend.[12]

It symbolically consigns the Jacobite cause and its romantic admirers to history. Edward has graduated from admiration of the romances in his uncle's library at Waverley-Honour and of the craggy wildness of Glennaquoich to appreciating the middle way represented by the improved Tully-Veolan. The rebuilt castle and its modern conveniences represent the victory of civilized compromise over the twin extremes of Hanoverian oppression and Jacobite romance. In time Edward and Rose will inherit, English and Scots blood mingling in mutually beneficial friendship between the two nations.

Like both Walpole and Austen, Scott published his first novel anonymously, wanting it to be regarded as an exciting new departure rather than trading on his established reputation as a poet. It was a huge success, real historical meat after the frothy Gothick syllabubs. Although a great many people quickly guessed who had written it, his anonymity was jovially maintained for the next thirteen years, and all his later novels were published as 'by the Author of Waverley'. Many of them would feature evocatively described ancestral seats, but the most significant building ever imagined by Walter Scott was the one that he made real, a 'romance in stone and lime' that he called Abbotsford: a family seat that was, like Walpole's Strawberry Hill, tailor-made to his own requirements.

Abbotsford began life as humble Clarty Hole Farm. The land it stood on and the ford beside it were once owned by Melrose Abbey, so Scott felt it apt to rename it Abbotsford; he also acquired any available relic of the by-then-ruined Melrose (already much-visited by literary pilgrims as it was the setting of *The Lay of the Last Minstrel*). Scott projected the final form of Abbotsford in his description of Jonathan Oldbuck's home Monkbarns in *The Antiquary* (1816), his own favourite among his novels.

> It was an irregular old-fashioned building, some part of which had belonged to a grange, or solitary farmhouse, inhabited by the bailiff, or steward, of the monastery, when the place was in possession of the monks.[13]

Both were approached through an ancient gateway, and surrounded by ornaments, terraces and yew hedges. Built in 1822, Scott's study closely resembled Oldbuck's *sanctum sanctorum*,

> a lofty room of middling size, obscurely lighted by high, narrow, latticed windows. One end was entirely occupied by book-shelves, greatly too limited in space for the number of volumes placed upon them, which were, therefore, drawn up in ranks of two or three files deep, while numberless others littered the floor and the tables, amid a chaos of maps, engravings, scraps of parchment, bundles of papers, pieces of old armour, swords, dirks, helmets, and Highland targets.[14]

Like Strawberry Hill, Abbotsford was a museum of significant objects, some symbolizing past splendours, some more personal mementoes. Scott had acquired Napoleon's blotting book and pen tray, locks of Nelson's and Wellington's hair, Bonny Prince Charlie's quaich (drinking cup) and a lock of his hair, Rob Roy's purse, Flora MacDonald's pocket book, and a tumbler once used by Robert

Sir Walter Scott wrote tirelessly in order to embellish the baronial estate of his 'Conundrum Castle' of Abbotsford. This posthumous portrait by William Allan pictures him dictating to his daughter Anne in its Armoury (1844).

Burns.[15] When Edinburgh's historic Tolbooth Prison was pulled down in 1817, Scott, who featured it in *The Heart of Midlothian* (1818), acquired its ancient gate, and used it as the entrance to his farm.

Washington Irving visited in 1817, and accurately caught both Scott's character and the atmosphere of Abbotsford when he described just such a house in his preface to *Bracebridge Hall* (1822), calling it 'the ancientest house, and the best for housekeeping in this county or the next; and though the master of it write but squire, I know no lord like him.' Scott prided himself on his 'housekeeping', by which both he and Irving meant the old tradition of keeping a generously hospitable house. By 1822 the 'Enchanter of the North' could proudly write 'Baronet' after his name, and the coats of arms on the ceiling of his entrance hall multiplied. 'Abbotsford has the appearance of a castle built of pastry something like those we see on a supper table' wrote the acid-tongued Frances, Lady Shelley (1787–1873) in her diary after a visit in 1818, 'but one must not quiz the castle or criticise the whims of such a genius.'

Adding to Abbotsford and its environs became an obsession. As Scott's novels took on grander themes – the mighty English castles of *Kenilworth* and *Ivanhoe*, rather than the modest strongholds of the Highlands and Borders – Abbotsford grew longer and higher and more turreted and crenellated. Although consciously antique, Abbotsford pioneered domestic technology. It had gas lighting (Scott was chairman of Edinburgh's first gas company), air-compression bells and patent stoves. Steam central heating was installed in 1823. Careful thought was given to guests' comfort.

> At Abbotsford … not only each table in the recesses of the library, but in every sleeping apartment, had its portefeuille with store of paper, pens, ink, and sealing-wax.[16]

More and more land was added, often acquired at ridiculous expense from sellers who knew their man. Scott's estate grew to 1,400 acres. As if he was single-handedly trying to compensate for the Highland Clearances, he planted thousands and thousands of trees, preferably using seeds and saplings from historic Scottish dwellings. Literary associations also mattered: birch saplings came from Loch Katrine, the setting for *The Lady of the Lake*; he named his Rhymer's Glen after the thirteenth-century Border poet and oracle Thomas the Rhymer.

By the mid-1820s Scott's debts had mounted impossibly high, not all of them due to profligate expenditure. He had invested heavily in his own publisher and printer James Ballantyne, hoping to improve sales of his books, without knowing Ballantyne's extreme ineptitude as a businessman. The London financial crash of 1825 added to his woes. When he was finally forced to declare himself bankrupt in 1826, he refused help and set to work doggedly to write himself out of debt, still cheerfully maintaining the laird-of-the-castle role that had become second nature. By 1829 he had restored his fortunes at the cost of broken health. Advised to try sunnier climes as a last resort, he took a cruise around the Mediterranean in September 1831. Typically, he began to map out a romance involving the Knights of Rhodes, and eyed up the picturesque fortified buildings with pepper-pot towers around Valletta's harbour, wondering if he could further embellish Abbotsford with 'a screen on the west side of the old Barn with a fanciful wall decorated with towers to enclose the Bleaching Green ornamented with watch towers such as these, of which I can get drawings while I am here'.[17] He barely made it home. Thousands flocked to his funeral, and followed his cortège to his grave in Dryburgh Abbey. Abbotsford, his domestic delight and his financial nemesis, has been a place of literary pilgrimage ever since.

Waverley transformed English perceptions of Highlanders from primitive traitors to romantic but loyal British subjects. Tartan became all the rage. When George IV visited Edinburgh in the royal yacht in 1822 in order to meet him, the portly king wore a tartan kilt and a huge sporran; cartoonists had a field day. When Scott turned to writing romances set in the Middle Ages, he made

England too look at its history with new eyes. Robin Hood's image as a champion of freedom and justice was created by *Ivanhoe*; written at the height of the post-Napoleonic Wars depression, it preached the message that the different classes of society could work together, just as the Saxons and Normans learn to in *Ivanhoe*.

Scott's forte was fictional architecture on a heroic scale. His enormously popular poems and novels created a domestic fashion for medievalism that ranged from vast mock castles such as Balmoral, the soaring skyline of Augustus Pugin's 1835 Palace of Westminster, and Jeffry Wyatville's enlarged and romanticized Windsor Castle to provincial town halls, gentlemen's mansions and suburban villas. He established the historical novel as an exceptionally healthy branch of popular fiction in which realism was as important as romance. His love of charismatic dwellings was echoed in Victor Hugo's *Notre-Dame de Paris* (1831) and William Harrison Ainsworth's *The Tower of London* (1840) and *Old Saint Paul's* (1841).

A PLAGUE ON BOTH YOUR HOUSES

Wuthering Heights and Emily Brontë

I've been greatly interested in Wuthering Heights, the first novel I've read for an age, and the best (as regards power and sound style) for two ages… But it is a fiend of a book – an incredible monster… The action is laid in hell, – only it seems places and people have English names there. Did you ever read it?

Dante Gabriel Rossetti to William Allingham,
19 September 1854[1]

Wuthering Heights is the name of Mr Heathcliff's dwelling. 'Wuthering' being a significant provincial adjective, descriptive of the atmospheric tumult to which its station is exposed in stormy weather.

Emily Brontë, *Wuthering Heights*, 1847[2]

Wuthering Heights, a brutally told tale of jealousy and cruelty, love and loss, is dominated by the house it is named for: the Earnshaws' ancient Yorkshire family seat, scene of the all-consuming passion that develops between Cathy Earnshaw, the daughter of the house, and the foundling Heathcliff. Home is at the heart of things throughout the story, more especially the lost home. Hunger for home permeates *Wuthering Heights*, as it permeated Emily's own heart and soul. 'What on earth is half so dear – / So longed for – as the hearth of home?' runs one of her poems.

To increase dramatic effect, Emily begins her story *in media res*, but the extent to which it is built around the idea of home is better appreciated when summarized chronologically. While on a business trip to Liverpool in 1771, Cathy's father Mr Earnshaw finds a 'houseless' five-year-old, 'dirty, ragged, black-haired … and as good as dumb'. He takes him into the Heights as one of the family, and names him Heathcliff after his dead first son. The partiality that Mr Earnshaw shows to the boy makes their loutish 14-year-old second son Hindley loathe him, but 6-year-old Cathy grows up to identify deeply with him. 'He's more myself than I am', she later wails. 'Whatever our souls are made of, his and mine are the same.'

After the death of his parents, Hindley reduces Heathcliff to a servant, treating him with a cruelty calculated 'to make a fiend out of a saint'. Cathy stays loyal, and they roam the moors together. One day they snoop through the lighted windows of Thrushcross Grange, home of the wealthy Linton family. Seeing them, the children call the servants, who let out a savage bulldog, which closes its jaws around Cathy's ankle. Heathcliff fearlessly attacks it with a rock until the servants arrive. Cathy, recognized as an Earnshaw, is brought in and made much of; Heathcliff is sent packing. She convalesces at the Grange, entranced by its crimson carpets, glittering chandeliers and leisured wealth, and the Lintons' son Edgar is entranced by her. Heathcliff is furiously jealous. He runs away, and Cathy marries Edgar Linton. But she soon realizes that her heart and her soul are still rooted in her childhood home high on the moor and Heathcliff.[3] The scene is set for a battle for dominance between two houses: Thrushcross Grange, luxuriating in the green and pleasant land of its enormous park, and Wuthering Heights, high on the windswept moors 4 miles away.

Heathcliff returns, now a man of means, and begins his revenge. Hindley borrows so much money from him to gamble with that after his death, in 1784, Wuthering Heights belongs to Heathcliff, rather than Hindley's son Hareton. He then elopes with Edgar Linton's sister Isabella. After the tragedy of Cathy's death in childbirth,

Emily Brontë's *Wuthering Heights* was modestly first published in 1847 as by 'Ellis Bell', together with *Agnes Grey*, by her sister Anne, writing as 'Acton Bell'. The literary world was instantly outraged. Dante Gabriel Rossetti called it 'a fiend of a book – an incredible monster'.

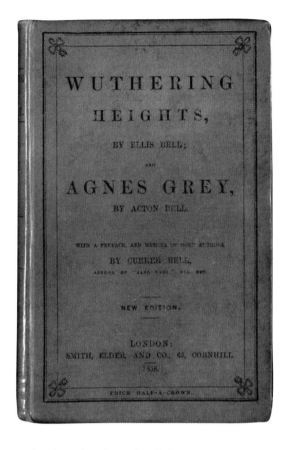

Heathcliff and Isabella's son Linton, rather than Cathy and Edgar's daughter Catherine, will inherit Thrushcross Grange, as it is entailed in the male line.[4] Abused and unloved ('the more the worms writhe, the more I yearn to crush out their entrails!' snarls Heathcliff), Isabella escapes by wriggling through the little garret window of Cathy's long-empty box bed, and puts the length of England between herself and her tormentor. After her death in 1797, Linton returns to Yorkshire. Heathcliff entices Catherine to Wuthering Heights, and forces her to marry Linton. After the deaths of both Edgar and Linton, he takes possession of the two houses, letting Thrushcross Grange out to a tenant and creating a strange parody of his childhood at Wuthering Heights, with Hareton in his own abused position and Cathy's daughter Catherine in Cathy's.

The novel itself opens in 1801, told by Thrushcross Grange's tenant Mr Lockwood, a jaded Londoner who heads north, finding the moors 'a perfect misanthropist's heaven'. He visits Heathcliff at the Heights, which has 'gaunt thorns all stretching their limbs one way, as if craving alms of the sun'. Its narrow windows are 'deeply set in the wall, and the corners defended with large jutting stones'. There is 'a quantity of grotesque carving lavished over the front, and especially about the principal door'. Above this, 'among a wilderness of crumbling griffins and shameless little boys', he sees 'the date "1500", and the name "Hareton Earnshaw"'. Inside he admires 'a vast oak dresser ... immense pewter dishes, interspersed with silver jugs and tankards', tower row on row to the roof. Under it is 'a huge, liver-coloured bitch pointer, surrounded by a swarm of squealing puppies'. When the pointer and a pack of other dogs attack Lockwood, the morose and surly Heathcliff merely laughs.

Lockwood later returns, and is grudgingly given tea in a 'huge, warm, cheerful apartment' which 'glowed delightfully in the radiance of an immense fire, compounded of coal, peat, and wood'. So much snow falls that he has to stay the night, and is given Cathy's garret box bed to sleep in. All night he is assailed by wild dreams caused, he decides, by a tree branch tapping at the nailed-up window. He breaks a pane and stretches out his arm to seize it.

> [I]nstead of which, my fingers closed on the fingers of a little, ice-cold hand! The intense horror of nightmare came over me: I tried to draw back my arm, but the hand clung to it, and a most melancholy voice sobbed, 'Let me in – let me in!' 'Who are you?' I asked, struggling, meanwhile, to disengage myself. 'Catherine Linton,' it replied, shiveringly ... 'I'm come home: I'd lost my way on the moor!' As it spoke, I discerned, obscurely, a child's face looking through the window. Terror made me cruel; and, finding it useless to attempt shaking the creature off, I pulled its wrist on to the broken pane, and rubbed it to and fro till the blood ran down and soaked the bedclothes: still it wailed, 'Let me in!' and maintained its tenacious gripe, almost maddening me with fear.

Lockwood's shrieking summons Heathcliff, whereupon he describes his dream. Heathcliff hurls himself on the bed, and wrenches open the lattice, bursting, as he pulled at it, into an uncontrollable passion of tears. 'Come in! come in!' he sobbed. 'Cathy, do come. Oh, do – *once* more! Oh! my heart's darling! hear me *this* time, Catherine, at last!'[5]

Lockwood staggers back to the Grange and takes to his bed, grateful for the ministrations of the Grange's housekeeper, Nelly Dean. Formerly a servant at the Heights, she explains his strange reception by recounting the events of the last forty years, from Heathcliff's arrival as a foundling to his present status, the dark lord of all he surveys, still mourning his lost love, for whom, she tells Lockwood, he had 'howled, not like a man, but like a savage beast being goaded to death with knives and spears'.

Heathcliff's end echoes Lockwood's dream. Decided on death, he stops eating, spending long days out on the moor and at night climbing into the box bed in the attic, and turning his face to its open lattice. Nelly finds him there one morning, lying on his back.

> His eyes met mine so keen and fierce, I started; and then he seemed to smile. I could not think him dead: but his face and throat were washed with rain; the bed-clothes dripped, and he was perfectly still. The lattice, flapping to and fro, had grazed one hand that rested on the sill; no blood trickled from the broken skin…
>
> I hasped the window; I combed his black long hair from his forehead; I tried to close his eyes: to extinguish, if possible, that frightful, life-like gaze of exultation before any one else beheld it. They would not shut: they seemed to sneer at my attempts: and his parted lips and sharp white teeth sneered too![6]

With this third appearance of a box bed, the architectural symmetry of the book becomes evident. It is a tale of three generations. Its framing wings are the three opening chapters, in which Lockwood describes his first experience of Heathcliff, and the three concluding ones, in which he returns after a year and discovers what has become of the warring spirits that he left. Firm chronological foundations underpin the plot, with a coherent but only obliquely revealed timeline that spans thirty years of its characters' lives.[7]

Emily's careful grounding of her hero and heroine in time and place makes them better able to soar. In this hurricane of a novel, Heathcliff and Cathy are elementals, rock and sky respectively, one tramping the moors in all weathers, with dogs at his heels, the other entranced by swaying in a tree on a windy day, watching birds wing and whirl around her. They are finally united in the earth that links their natures, in a specially contrived grave that will allow their coffins' sides to be removed so that Heathcliff's mortal remains can mingle with Cathy's. While they live, however, bricks and mortar rule. The outdoor scenes are largely accounts of journeys between the two houses around which the plot revolves.

The Heights changes character in the course of the story. Under Mr and Mrs Earnshaw, and Nelly Dean's care, it is well-kept, and Hindley plans 'a pretty parlour' for his wife Frances. At Christmas time, Nelly complacently recalls that she

> smelt the rich scent of the heating spices; and admired the shining kitchen utensils, the polished clock, decked in holly, the silver mugs ranged on a tray ready to be filled with mulled ale for supper; and above all, the speckless purity of my particular care – the scoured and well-swept floor.[8]

But when Frances dies, the Heights, like Hindley, deteriorates rapidly. Isabella finds the kitchen 'a dingy, untidy hole' when she and Heathcliff return from Gretna, the other rooms 'damp uninhabited chambers', and the 'house' little better:

> There was a great fire, and that was all the light in the huge apartment, whose floor had grown a uniform grey; and the once brilliant pewter dishes, which used to attract my gaze when I was a girl, partook of a similar obscurity, created by tarnish and dust.[9]

After Isabella flees, Heathcliff improves the house, but it declines again as he abandons hope. As he approaches his death, he observes to Nelly:

'It is a poor conclusion, is it not? ... an absurd termination to my violent exertions? I get levers and mattocks to demolish the two houses, and train myself to be capable of working like Hercules, and when everything is ready and in my power, I find the will to lift a slate off either roof has vanished!'[10]

Everything is transformed on Lockwood's last visit to Wuthering Heights, where he finds

a fragrance of stocks and wallflowers wafted on the air from amongst the homely fruit-trees. Both doors and lattices were open; and yet, as is usually the case in a coal district, a fine red fire illumined the chimney. ... [A]t the door sat my old friend Nelly Dean, sewing and singing a song...[11]

Catherine and Hareton, their heads bent over books together, are on the way to becoming lovers. Heathcliff's revenge on their respective houses has failed.

In the course of the story, a series of domestic invasions dictate the direction of the action. They are countered by locked gates, doors and windows; these in turn are violently shattered by the breaking of glass, the smashing of locks with stones, and vaultings over protective walls. Lockwood's initial invasion of the Heights is the first intrusion, Heathcliff's introduction into the family the second. Cathy and Heathcliff trespass on the Grange and have the dogs set on them. Edgar Linton nervously comes to Wuthering Heights in search of her. When Heathcliff returns after making his fortune he calls at the Grange, 'his fingers on the latch as if intending to open for himself'. When Cathy is ill, Heathcliff lurks in the park, and then walks into the house uninvited. Heathcliff's servant Joseph goes to Thrushcross Grange to take away Linton Heathcliff, and Cathy's daughter Catherine rides to Wuthering Heights in search of Linton. Hindley and Isabella lock out Heathcliff, but he batters his way in by smashing the mullion of a window. Finally Nelly invades the locked attic to find Heathcliff exultant in death.

Matching the invasions are imprisonments and escapes. Cathy's wounded ankle requires her to stay at Thrushcross Grange, though she longs for the Heights both then and when she has married Edgar and has to live at Thrushcross Grange. The Lintons are similarly held captive in Wuthering Heights: first Isabella, then Linton Heathcliff and finally Nelly Dean and Catherine Linton. Isabella succeeds in escaping, Nelly is released after Catherine is forcibly married, Catherine escapes to bid her dying father farewell.

When *Wuthering Heights* was published, under the pseudonym Ellis Bell, in December 1847, two months after the appearance of Charlotte Brontë's very successful *Jane Eyre*, the violence of its language appalled literary London. 'It is wild, confused, disjointed, and improbable; and the people who make up the drama … are savages ruder than those who lived before the days of Homer', thundered *The Examiner* (8 January 1848). American critics were even fiercer: 'How a man could have attempted such a book as the present without committing suicide before he had finished a dozen chapters, is a mystery. It is a compound of vulgar depravity and unnatural horrors', gasped *Graham's Lady's Magazine* (July 1848). No one dreamt that it had been written by the daughter of a country clergyman.

Patrick Brontë (1777–1861) was a self-taught Irishman of formidable intellectual talent and fierce temper, who won a place at Cambridge University. In 1807 he was ordained and married Maria Branwell of Penzance. After their sixth child was born in 1820 the family moved to Haworth, on the edge of the Yorkshire Moors. A year later Maria died of uterine cancer, and her rigidly Methodist sister Elizabeth came to housekeep. After his two oldest daughters died while away at their exceptionally harsh school, Patrick decided to bring up Branwell, Charlotte, Emily and Anne himself, giving them a generously broad education that included the Greek and Roman classics, Shakespeare's plays and Bunyan's *The Pilgrim's Progress*. He also gave them a box of 12-inch figures, known as the Young Men, who became the heroes of an imaginary world invented by the children. Each figure was named, and each child elected a 'chief'. Emily's was Sir Walter Scott, but the heroine of her invented world of Gondal was Augusta, named for the half-sister of Lord Byron, the heart-throb of every literary-minded female.

All four of the children showed precocious literary talent, which Charlotte called 'scribblemania'. 'We wove a web in childhood, / A web of sunny air' runs one of her poems. Emily was still writing Gondal poems while she worked on *Wuthering Heights*, and there is no doubt that Cathy and Heathcliff are close kin to the heroes of Gondal. Cathy could certainly have cried out, as a Gondal heroine does, that 'No coward soul' was hers, 'No trembler in the world's storm-troubled sphere', and Heathcliff could have mourned

> Cold in the earth – and fifteen wild Decembers,
> From those brown hills, have melted into spring:
> Faithful, indeed, is the spirit that remembers
> After such years of change and suffering.[12]

What else nourished Emily's imagination? She read and reread the poetry and novels of her childhood hero Sir Walter Scott, and there is no doubting his influence on her writing. Like Cathy, *Rob Roy*'s Diana Vernon 'has been left alone and deserted on the face of this wide earth, and left to ride, and run, and scamper at her own silly pleasure'. The violence of Heathcliff's fantasy of 'flinging Joseph off the highest gable, and painting the house-front with Hindley's blood!' pales in comparison with *Rob Roy*'s Helen Campbell telling Dougal to

> cut out their tongues and put them into each other's throats, to
> try which would there best knap Southron, or to tear out their
> hearts and put them into each other's breasts, to see which
> would there best plot treason against the MacGregor.[13]

The Scott novel that inspired Emily most was *The Black Dwarf* (1816). It, too, is told in retrospect, and its hero is a young man called Earnscliff, a curious elision of Earnshaw and Heathcliff. She borrowed elements of its plot, and the dwarfish Elshie's language is as violent as Heathcliff's: he curses the villain as 'a man who had annihilated my soul's dearest hope – who had torn my heart to mammocks, and seared my brain till it glowed like a volcano'.

Just as home is of central importance in her novel, so it was to Emily. After a few failed attempts at teaching, she spent all her life at Haworth Parsonage, writing endlessly, roaming her beloved moors, but also enjoying domestic pursuits. Haworth was a thriving mill town, only 3 miles from Keighley, to which the Brontës walked to borrow books from the Mechanics Institute and the circulating library.

Were there models for Wuthering Heights and Thrushcross Grange? The splendidly situated ruined farmhouse of Top Withens is frequently said to be Wuthering Heights, but it was never as substantial as the Earnshaws' ancient home. Lyndall Gordon has pointed to Ponden Hall, 3 miles away from Haworth, and to the fact that Emily may have had an inclination towards Robert Heaton of Royd: R. Heaton is, Gordon notes, an anagram of Hareton, and the sisters were notoriously fond of codes and puzzles.[14] As to Thrushcross Grange, in her annotated *Wuthering Heights*, Susan Gazali suggests that Shibden Hall, not far from Law Hill, where Emily had her ill-fated employment as a schoolteacher, has the right substantial country-house feel and elegantly landscaped park. Eight years before Emily might have known it, its resourceful and independent-minded owner Anne Lister (1791–1840) added a library in a Gothic tower, and the garden boasted cascades, a flower-filled terrace and rock gardens.

Emily died in December 1848, a year after the publication of *Wuthering Heights*. At first, the Victorian reading public preferred Charlotte's and Anne's novels, but Emily's masterpiece proved as irrepressible as Cathy Earnshaw's unquiet spirit. Interest in it smouldered into life in 1855, when Matthew Arnold visited Haworth and penned a poem which declared that Emily's soul 'Knew no fellow for might, / Passion, vehemence, grief, / Daring, since Byron died'.[15] Appreciation grew steadily, and the novel became an acclaimed

Top Withens, a remote and dramatically positioned farmhouse high above Haworth, the Yorkshire home of the Brontë family, has a setting similar to Wuthering Heights. Photograph by Fay Godwin.

literary classic.[16] Its popular glamour peaked in the 2000s, when it emerged that Bella Swan, the vampire heroine of Stephanie Meyer's *Twilight* series, has read and reread it, and identifies closely with Cathy; her vampire lover Edward is as jealous of her as Heathcliff is of Cathy. Today hundreds of thousands of pilgrims visit Haworth every year, and, as I write, Kate Bush's song 'Wuthering Heights' boasts over 37 million hits on YouTube.

DARK ROMANCE

The House of the Seven Gables and Nathaniel Hawthorne

[U]nder those seven gables ... through a portion of three
centuries, there has been perpetual remorse of conscience, a
constantly defeated hope, strife amongst kindred, various misery,
a strange form of death, dark suspicion, unspeakable disgrace...
> Nathaniel Hawthorne, *The House of the Seven Gables*, 1851[1]

[B]lack conceit pervades [Hawthorne] through and through.
You may be witched by his sunlight, – transported by the
bright gildings in the skies he builds over you; but there is the
blackness of darkness beyond; and even his bright gildings but
fringe and play upon the edges of thunder-clouds.
> Herman Melville, 'Hawthorne and his Mosses', 1850[2]

Few houses in fiction inhabit the tale spun around them more
physically than Nathaniel Hawthorne's *The House of the Seven
Gables*. Its first paragraph introduces 'the rusty wooden house'
with 'seven acutely peaked gables'; later it is described as 'breath-
ing through the spiracles of one great chimney'. Recollecting the
house in Salem that inspired his 'wild, chimney-corner legend',
Hawthorne wrote that

> The aspect of the venerable mansion has always affected me
> like a human countenance, bearing the traces not merely of
> outward storm and sunshine, but expressive, also, of the long

lapse of mortal life, and accompanying vicissitudes that have passed within.[3]

His first chapter sketches the house's ominous origins: it had replaced a humble thatched hut on a plot of land notable for a fine freshwater spring that belonged to one Matthew Maule. Colonel Pyncheon, an 'iron-hearted' Puritan who coveted the site, engineered a death sentence for Maule during the judicial massacres of the 1690s Salem witch-hunts. On the scaffold, Maule cursed him, saying 'God will give him blood to drink'. Undismayed, Pyncheon took possession of the plot and built a fine mansion for his family.

> it rose, a little withdrawn from the line of the street, but in pride, not modesty. Its whole visible exterior was ornamented with quaint figures, conceived in the grotesqueness of a Gothic fancy.[4]

But when the guests arrive for a great house-warming party at Pyncheon House, they find the colonel dead on a great oak chair in his study, with blood saturating his hoary beard and his snowy ruff. Was his death caused by his building his ostentatious palace on the unquiet grave of the wizard Maule, or by an apoplexy? And what has become of the 'Indian deed' by which the General Court gave the Pyncheons rights over 'a vast and as yet unexplored and unmeasured tract of Eastern lands'?

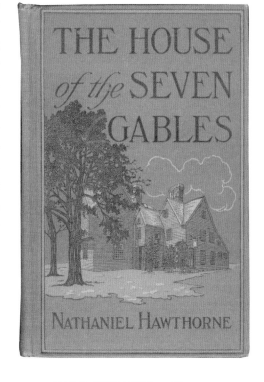

Nathaniel Hawthorne described *The House of the Seven Gables* as 'like a great human heart, with a life of its own, and full of rich and sombre reminiscences'. Cover of the 1913 Houghton Mifflin edition.

So begins what a youthful Arthur Ransome perceptively called a 'Moral Romance' in his *History of Story-Telling*.[5] Pyncheon House itself seems to protest at the family's refusal to admit that a wrong has been done. Hawthorne briefly sketches the fortunes and misfortunes of the ever more haunted house over the centuries.

> [S]o much had been suffered, and something, too, enjoyed … that the very timbers were oozy, as with the moisture of a heart. It was itself like a great human heart, with a life of its own, and full of rich and sombre reminiscences.[6]

Colonel Pyncheon's gloomy likeness in his study is 'so intimately connected with the fate of the house, and so magically built into its walls, that, if once it should be removed, that very instant the whole edifice would come thundering down in a heap of dusty ruin'. Soon there is another sudden bloody death of a Pyncheon in the same oak chair, and many fruitless attempts are made to find the Indian deed. When the house has benign owners, it smiles hopefully upon them. Under the colonel's son Gervayse

> [it] had that pleasant aspect of life which is like the cheery expression of comfortable activity in the human countenance. … it was a substantial, jolly-looking mansion, and seemed fit to be the residence of a patriarch, who might establish his own headquarters in the front gable and assign one of the remainder to each of his six children, while the great chimney in the centre should symbolize the old fellow's hospitable heart, which kept them all warm, and made a great whole of the seven smaller ones.[7]

But when a descendant of Matthew Maule comes to plead for restitution of his rights, Gervayse refuses. In revenge, Maule hypnotizes Gervayse's proud and beautiful daughter Alice into obsessive love for him, then summons her to wait upon him and his bride on their wedding night; she dies of exposure. Three decades before the narrative begins, there is a third death in the chair, this time of a Pyncheon who wanted to make restitution to the wronged Maules.

The crime is laid at the door of his heir, a nephew called Clifford, who was imprisoned for thirty years. In truth, the murderer was another nephew, Judge Jaffrey Pyncheon, who plans to claim the house for himself.

Seven Gables has seven significant characters, and numerous ghosts. Looming largest of the living is Judge Jaffrey, who has settled a little out of town in a brand-new mansion. He appears to be a pillar of the community, 'displaying every grace and virtue … befitting the Christian, the good citizen, the horticulturalist and the gentleman'. But, reversing his likening of the Pyncheon House to a person, Hawthorne likens the judge to a building: a 'tall and stately edifice', with 'splendid halls', gilded cornices and a 'lofty dome'. He then warns that

> in some low and obscure nook, – some narrow closet on the
> ground-floor, shut, locked and bolted, and the key flung away,
> – or beneath the marble pavement, in a stagnant water-puddle,
> with the richest pattern of mosaic-work above, – may lie a
> corpse, half decayed, and still decaying, and diffusing its death-
> scent all through the palace![8]

Contrasting with Jaffrey in every way is Clifford's sister Hepzibah, who has a life interest in the house, and lives there as a recluse: 'her very brain was impregnated with the dry-rot of its timbers'. Once attractive, she is now wrinkled and faded, and with a perpetual scowl, caused by her chronic shortsightedness.

> But her heart never frowned. It was naturally tender, sensitive,
> and full of little tremors and palpitations; all of which
> weaknesses it retained, while her visage was growing so
> perversely stern, and even fierce.[9]

She still loves her brother deeply. When she hears he is to be released, she humbles her pride by opening a little shop in the lowest of the house's gables so that she can earn enough to buy the little luxuries that she knows his 'sensitive, but ruined mind, critical and fastidious', requires. She has already taken in a lodger, a daguerrotypist called Holgrave, a radical idealist impatient of old-fashioned ways whose craft enables him to reveal character with brutal accuracy. But he tactfully stays in the background when Clifford returns, broken by three decades in prison and still terrified of Jaffrey. Clifford slumps limply on a cushioned chair, appalled by Hepzibah's ugliness and suspicious of Holgrave. Soon, however, all three find solace in the story's fifth main character Phoebe, a country cousin who justifies her sunny name by lighting up the life of everyone in the house. She is an archetypal homemaker, 'a little figure of the cheeriest household-life', and

> the battered visage of the House of the Seven Gables, black and heavy-browed as it still certainly looked, must have shown a kind of cheerfulness glimmering through its dusky windows as Phoebe passed to and fro in the interior.[10]

Describing Clifford watching her, Hawthorne again changes his house as living entity metaphor to human heart as house.

> [T]here would be a flickering taper-gleam in his eyeballs. It betokened that his spiritual part had returned, and was doing its best to kindle the heart's household fire, and light up intellectual lamps in the dark and ruinous mansion, where it was doomed to be a forlorn inhabitant.[11]

As this 'little circle of not unkindly souls' get to know each other better, they bond into a kind of family. Phoebe runs the shop in the gable efficiently, and the house cheers up. 'The gnawing tooth of the dry-rot was stayed among the old timbers of its skeleton frame', and its 'grime and sordidness' vanish away.

> Phoebe's presence made a home about her, – that very sphere which the outcast, the prisoner, the potentate, – the wretch beneath mankind, the wretch aside from it, or the wretch above it, – instinctively pines after, – a home![12]

Together, Holgrave and Phoebe check the rampant wilderness of the garden. Roses blossom, and squashes, cucumbers and tomatoes promise 'an early and abundant harvest'; even the attenuated and feeble Pyncheon poultry begin to thrive. But when Phoebe goes home for a visit, the household fires die down and the tendrils of happiness wither. A great storm arrives 'boisterously from the northwest', and

> taking hold of the aged framework of the Seven Gables,
> gives it a shake, like a wrestler that would try strength with
> his antagonist. Another and another sturdy tussle with the
> blast! The old house creaks again, and makes a vociferous but
> somewhat unintelligible bellowing in its sooty throat (the big
> flue, we mean, of its wide chimney), partly in complaint at
> the rude wind, but rather, as befits their century and a half of
> hostile intimacy, in tough defiance.[13]

A myriad ghosts throng the ancient house's mirrors and lurk in the tainted waters of Maule's well. Two are more persistent than the rest. Colonel Pyncheon glares down from his portrait, 'frowning, clenching [his] fist, and giving many … proofs of excessive discomposure', and the ghost of Alice Pyncheon strums on her coffin-shaped harpsichord and nourishes the clumps of flowers known as Alice's Posies that flourish in the gutters of the gables. History seems set on repeating itself when Phoebe comes close to being mesmerized like Alice, unaware that Holgrave is a descendant of the Maules. But Alice is a kindlier ghost than the colonel, and approves the mutual love that develops between Phoebe and Holgrave with a 'flaunting' full blooming of her roof posies and a trill on her harpsichord. A much worse fate awaits Judge Jaffrey, who arrives, intent on bullying Clifford into telling him where the Indian deed is hidden, and settles himself in the great oak chair. There, Hawthorne tells us in a long crescendo of sarcasm at his helplessness, he chokes on his own blood while the shades of past Pyncheons, first among them that of the colonel, troop past him.

Windows are animate throughout. Expressive under the gables, they are the eyes of the house, sometimes cheerful, sometimes frowning disapproval. Clifford's face has 'no more light in its expression than might have come through the iron grates of a prison-window'. The tiny panes of the shop, through which Hepzibah anxiously stares, frightening passers-by with her scowl, also entice customers with their display of her wares. The arched window from which Clifford spies on the busy street life outside his first-floor sanctuary, and listens to the merry tunes of a barrel organ, offers escape to the world outside the ghost-haunted house. Another favourite symbol is the hearth, something Hawthorne held very dear, deploring the modern preference for 'the cheerless and ungenial stove' in his essay 'Fire-Worship'.[14] Hepzibah, who has 'neither sunshine nor household-fire' in her heart, sits on a stiff, comfortless chair beside just such a stove in the Pyncheon House parlour, but Phoebe, 'as pleasant about the house as a gleam of sunshine falling on the floor through a shadow of twinkling leaves, or as a ray of firelight that dances on the wall while evening is drawing nigh', builds up a roaring blaze in the open kitchen fire and cooks delicious meals.

Despite Hawthorne's genius for Gothic forebodings, much admired by his contemporaries Edgar Allan Poe and Herman Melville (who dedicated *Moby Dick* to Hawthorne), the book ends hopefully. After Jaffrey's death, Clifford and Hepzibah manage a sortie into the outside world, taking a train ride out into the country. They discover how much else there is to life – though Hepzibah can't keep Pyncheon House out of her mind.

> [It] was everywhere! It transported its great, lumbering bulk with more than railroad speed, and set itself phlegmatically down on whatever spot she glanced at.[15]

They return to find that the judge's death is accepted as natural. Then word arrives that his heir has died in Europe, The aged siblings inherit his vast fortune, and remove with Holgrave and Phoebe to the judge's country house to start a new life together. 'I have a presentiment', announces the once radical Holgrave, 'that, hereafter, it will be my lot to set out trees, to make fences, – perhaps, even, in due time, to build a house for another generation'.

Such a settled existence was never Hawthorne's own lot. More than any of his other writings, *Seven Gables* expressed his haunted sense of domestic deprivation. His father, a Salem sea captain, had died of yellow fever in Surinam in 1808 when Nathaniel was 4 years old, and the family had lived with relatives until he was 12, when they moved into a house built for them by his maternal uncles. Nathaniel was packed off first to school, then to college, then to a sequence of lodgings before settling in 1839 in an 'owl's nest' of a Boston attic room (surely the inspiration for Holgrave's quarters in *Seven Gables*), where he worked in the Custom House. In 1842 he married Sophia Peabody, invalid sister of the formidable educator Elizabeth Peabody. They rented the Old Manse, in Concord, for the first three years of their married life, then moved in 1846 to Salem, as Hawthorne had been appointed Surveyor of Customs. Their three children were all born there, and Hawthorne's undemanding job provided the money and time he needed to establish himself as a writer of short stories and essays.

In his preface to *Seven Gables* Hawthorne explains that its inspiration was a house in Turner Street, Salem, owned by his wealthy cousin Susannah Ingersoll. He describes an 1840 visit to see 'the Duchess', as he liked to call her, to see how she, and the house, had weathered the great storm that had struck Salem a month earlier.

> I had a more than ordinary pleasant visit, and among other
> things, in speaking of the old house, she said it has had in
> the history of its changes and alterations Seven Gables. The
> expression was new and struck me very forcibly; I think I shall
> make something of it. I expressed a wish to go all over the
> house; she assented and I repaired to the Attic, and there was
> no corner or dark hole I did not peep into.[16]

Over tea, Susannah Ingersoll suggested that he wrote a story around the elaborately carved oak chair in her parlour. 'It is an old Puritan relict', she told him, 'and you can make a biographical

Hawthorne based *The House of the Seven Gables* (1851) on a 1668 colonial mansion in Salem's Turner Street belonging to his cousin Susannah Ingersoll. Pictured here suitably 'black and heavy-browed' in a 1931 postcard, it is now a much-visited memorial of his famous novel.

sketch of each old Puritan who became in succession the owner of the chair.' Hawthorne did just that, publishing *The Whole History of Grandfather's Chair*, a lively telling of New England history for children, in time for Christmas 1840. The chair soon becomes much more than a mere seat for a succession of historical figures; it talks back to the narrator and his grandchildren, concluding with oracular insistence that 'JUSTICE, TRUTH, and LOVE are the chief ingredients of every happy life'. Just such an oak chair is central to the plot in *Seven Gables*.

Hawthorne was influenced by the discursive, tale-in-tale methods of oriental storytellers, and fantasized about becoming 'an itinerant novelist, reciting my own extemporaneous fictions to such audiences as I could collect'. Perrault's famous tale of the Sleeping Beauty comes to mind in the fate of Alice Pyncheon and the rampant roses and vines encroaching on the 'rusty, crazy, creaky, dry-rotted, dingy, dark, and miserable old dungeon' of a house. Hawthorne was also fascinated by American history, 'not romance and chivalry, but the immediate past of vanished dignity and faded fashions'. He explains in his preface that *Seven Gables* was 'an attempt to connect a bygone time with the very present that is flitting away from us'. He was guiltily aware that his own Salem ancestor John Hathorne had been the only Salem judge not to repent of the 'passionate errors' and judicial murders during the mass hysteria of the witch-hunting years of the early 1690s, and added a *w* to his name to distance himself from Hathorne.

He dealt with the period in *Grandfather's Chair*, then addressed it more directly in his most famous book, *The Scarlet Letter*, which was published the year before *Seven Gables*. It was critically acclaimed, but its frank portrayal of the hypocrisy and self-serving of the pillars of Salem society ensured it a furious reception in his hometown, and he was sacked from his comfortable sinecure at the Salem Customs. In *Seven Gables*, he uses Holgrave as a mouthpiece for his opinions:

> 'Shall we never, never get rid of this Past? … It lies upon the
> Present like a giant's dead body! In fact, the case is just as
> if a young giant were compelled to waste all his strength in
> carrying about the corpse of the old giant, his grandfather, who
> died a long while ago, and only needs to be decently buried.'

Holgrave is given many similarities to Hawthorne – he too worked on a community farm, and wrote stories for *Godey's Lady's Book* and other women's magazines. Daguerrotypists are analogous to writers, revealing more of the truth than their subjects relish. Judge Pyncheon seems to have 'an exceedingly pleasant countenance, indicative of benevolence, openness of heart, sunny good humor, and other praiseworthy qualities of that cast', but in the daguerreotype Holgrave makes of him his face is 'sly, subtle, hard, imperious, and, withal, cold as ice'.

But Hawthorne was in other ways more like Clifford, a sensitive recluse longing for a permanent home. In 1852 the Hawthornes moved into The Hillside, once the home of Louisa May Alcott's family, renaming it The Wayside. It was the most settled home that Hawthorne ever had, although the family left it for Europe between 1853 and 1860. 'The experience of homelessness determined his sense of his relation to the world', writes Edgar A. Dryden, quoting Hawthorne's son Julian's remark that his father 'never found any permanent rest anywhere'.[17] More than any of his other writings, *Seven Gables* expressed Hawthorne's haunted sense of both paternal and domestic deprivation.

> The gloomy and desolate old house, deserted of life, and with awful Death sitting sternly in its solitude, was the emblem of many a human heart, which, nevertheless, is compelled to hear the thrill and echo of the world's gayety around it.

TOMB FOR THE LIVING

Bleak House and Charles Dickens

[T]here is no hurry there; there, in that ancient house, rooted
in that quiet park ... where the sun-dial on the terrace has
dumbly recorded for centuries that time which was as much
the property of every Dedlock – while he lasted – as the house
and lands.

Charles Dickens, *Bleak House*, 1853[1]

It is country cottages and middle-class villas that embody
traditional country house virtues in Dickens: the misleadingly
named Bleak House of Mr. Jarndyce, or Miss Betsey
Trotwood's abode in David Copperfield ... Dickens's great
houses are tombs for the living, like Sir Leicester Dedlock's
Chesney Wold in Bleak House...

Peter W. Graham, 2002[2]

Giving houses personalities as vivid as their occupants' came naturally to Charles Dickens. Though prone to amorous adventures,
he was a deeply domestic man, who valued the home highly. Its
importance had been drummed into him in the uncertain days of
his childhood, during which his Micawber-like father was sent to
a debtors' prison and he worked in a blacking factory. *Household
Words*, the densely informative 24-page weekly magazine which he
founded in the spring of 1850, addressed social issues, including

such domestic threats as slum dwellings and contagious diseases, as well as surveying parliamentary and international affairs, reviewing literature and art, and publishing fiction. Its purpose was, he wrote in the first issue, 'to show to all, that in all familiar things, even those which are repellant on the surface, there is Romance enough, if we will find it out.' This declaration is exactly echoed in the last line of his preface to *Bleak House*: 'I have purposely dwelt upon the romantic side of familiar things.' Despite this promise, the dominant note of Dickens's longest and most immediately successful novel is mournful. Disease and death dog its characters good and bad, and allusions to tombs recur. It is a state-of-the-nation story. With a potent mix of virulence and ridicule it attacks the political influence of the pretentious and time-locked aristocracy, the ancient and constipated legal system which benefits only the wealthy, the lawyers who prey like vultures on gullible clients, the cholera-ridden slums ruled by predatory moneylenders, the misery of workers in the booming brick industry and the inadequacies of welfare provision. The 'romantic side' it offers are the loving and benevolent human beings who manage against the odds to salvage human dignity and even happiness from the squalor of London. Both the abuses and the saving graces of the tale are pointed up by meticulously tailored architectural settings.

Dickens began thinking about *Bleak House* in the summer of 1851, quite possibly inspired by Hawthorne's *Seven Gables*, which he reviewed admiringly in *Household Words* in April 1851. He began writing in November 1851, and published it in *Household Words* in twenty monthly instalments, beginning in March 1852 and ending with a double instalment in September 1853. The alternative titles with which he toyed (*The Ruined House*, *The Solitary House That never knew happiness / That was always shut up*) show it to centre around a property with a story to tell. But which property?

The narrative opens in 1830s' London, in 'implacable November weather'. The streets around Holborn are mired in mud, soot flakes splash down with the rain, and gaslamps are lit before their time,

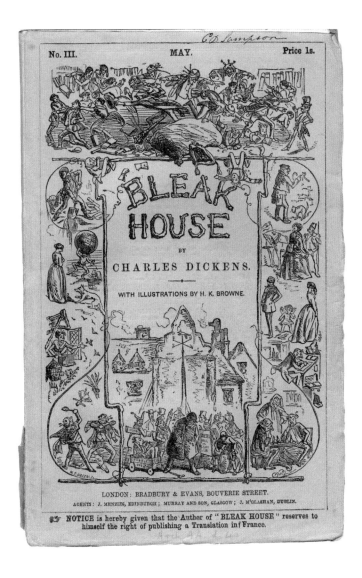

Charles Dickens's *Bleak House* was originally issued in 1852 in twenty monthly parts, each with the book's illustrator H.K. Browne's suitably chaotic rendering of its many dramatic scenes on its cover.

'as the gas seems to know, for it has a haggard and unwilling look'. There is fog everywhere, and at its heart, in Lincoln's Inn Hall, sits the Lord High Chancellor in his High Court of Chancery.

Never can there come fog too thick, never can there come mud and mire too deep, to assort with the groping and floundering condition which this High Court of Chancery, most pestilent of hoary sinners, holds this day in the sight of heaven and earth.[3]

Its appearance on the novel's first page raises the possibility that Chancery is itself the 'bleak house' of the book, a paralysing spectre arching over almost every character, 'which has its decaying houses and its blighted lands in every shire, which has its worn-out lunatic in every madhouse and its dead in every churchyard. The steward of this hell on earth, perhaps its Satanic master, is the devious and manipulative lawyer Mr Tulkinghorn. He is 'surrounded by a mysterious halo of family confidences, of which he is known to be the silent depository'.

There are noble mausoleums rooted for centuries in retired glades of parks among the growing timber and the fern, which perhaps hold fewer noble secrets than walk abroad among men, shut up in the breast of Mr. Tulkinghorn.[4]

Dickens introduces mausoleums very deliberately: death and property are the twin themes of his novel, and one particular noble mausoleum dominates its end. It is in the grounds of Sir Leicester Dedlock's gloomy Lincolnshire family seat Chesney Wold. And here we come to the nub of things. Chesney Wold is the house which has the most significant role in the book, and which many of its readers misremember as Bleak House itself; certainly Dickens's tentative titles referred to it, and it is featured as the frontispiece in the first edition. Sir Leicester is 'an honourable, obstinate, truthful, high-spirited, intensely prejudiced, perfectly unreasonable man'. His family is 'as old as the hills, and infinitely more respectable'. He is twenty years older than his proud and beautiful wife Lady Honoria Dedlock, who is whispered to lack family, but who has been floated to the top of the fashionable tree by her marriage to wealth and station. She remains haunted by memories of her lost lover and the daughter she has been told is dead – one thread of *Bleak House*'s intricate, many-layered story is her discovery of the fate of both of them.

A storm that floods the grounds around the house emphasizes its isolation from the modern world; the shutters of the 'old, echoing place' are closed, and all around 'solitude, with dusky wings, sits brooding'. Mrs Rouncewell, its housekeeper of fifty years is unperturbed.

> The house is there in all weathers, and the house, as she
> expresses it, 'is what she looks at'. She sits in her room …
> and the whole house reposes on her mind. She can open it on
> occasion and be busy and fluttered, but it is shut up now and
> lies on the breadth of Mrs. Rouncewell's iron-bound bosom in
> a majestic sleep.[5]

When the Dedlocks are in residence the house wakes up, albeit with a 'dismal grandeur' that daunts the visiting legions of cadging cousins and bickering politicians as much as it impresses them. As in *Seven Gables*, the portraits that hang on the wall are all but animate. When Lady Dedlock takes notice of a pretty servant and makes the girl her own maid in memory of her lost daughter,

> a staring old Dedlock in a panel, as large as life and as dull,
> looks as if he didn't know what to make of it, which was
> probably his general state of mind in the days of Queen
> Elizabeth.[6]

In a later chapter, 'clear cold sunshine' glances through the drawing-room window:

> Athwart the picture of my Lady, over the great chimney-piece,
> it throws a broad bend-sinister of light that strikes down
> crookedly into the hearth and seems to rend it.[7]

Chesney Wold is Dickens's metonym for the aristocracy that gripped England in its dead hand. Everyone in government is related to Sir Leicester, who, 'like a glorious spider, stretches his threads of relationship ... from my Lord Boodle, through the Duke of Foodle, down to Noodle'. Dedlock legal causes always triumph, because his money and influence ensure they will. But in the course of the novel the Dedlocks and Chesney Wold decline and fall. Lady Dedlock dies on the steps of the cholera-ridden burial ground where her old lover 'Nemo' is buried, and Sir Leicester is entombed in his own flesh by a stroke incurred by the shock of her death; both will end up in the mausoleum in their park. The future lies in the industrial north, where Mrs Rouncewell's son Robert is a successful ironmaster. Railways are being planned; change is in the air.

Dickens often visited Rockingham Castle in Leicestershire, the home of his friends Richard and Lavinia Watson, and enjoyed performing in his own plays in its Long Gallery. He wrote to Lavinia in 1853 admitting that 'in some of the descriptions of Chesney Wold I have taken many bits, chiefly about trees and shadows, from observations made at Rockingham'. He noticed a huge portrait of a former Lady Rockingham above the drawing-room chimney piece, and he used the double yew hedge known as the Elephant Walk as the model for his Ghost's Walk. The design of Rockingham's garden still resembles that of Chesney Wold, 'adorned at regular intervals with smooth round trees and smooth round blocks of stone, as if the trees were going to play at bowls with the stones'.

Having shown the bleakness of the law courts and Chesney Wold, Dickens teasingly reveals in his third chapter that the house he actually names Bleak House in his story is a cheerful establishment near St Albans owned by the tale's generous *deus ex machina* John Jarndyce. At this point the narrative switches to the voice of the novel's heroine, Esther Summerson, inherited as a ward by John Jarndyce after the death of her forbidding 'godmother', who has told her only that she was 'her mother's disgrace'. He elects to make her a companion for Ada Clare, another of his wards, who has the misfortune to be tangled up in the 'scarecrow of a suit' that is Jarndyce and Jarndyce, one 'so complicated that no man alive knows what it means'. His third ward, Richard Carstone, is also involved in the suit. These three young innocents represent the 'romantic side' that Dickens promises in his preface, and when they arrive at Bleak House they find 'light, and warmth, and comfort [and the] hospitable jingle, at a distance, of preparations for dinner; with the face of its generous master brightening everything we saw'.

> It was one of those delightfully irregular houses where you
> go up and down steps out of one room into another... Our
> sitting-room was green and had framed and glazed upon the
> walls numbers of surprising and surprised birds, staring out
> of pictures at a real trout in a case, as brown and shining as if
> it had been served with gravy; ... All the movables, from the
> wardrobes to the chairs and tables, hangings, glasses, even to the
> pincushions and scent-bottles on the dressing-tables, displayed
> the same quaint variety. They agreed in nothing but their perfect
> neatness, their display of the whitest linen, and their storing-up,
> wheresoever the existence of a drawer, small or large, rendered it
> possible, of quantities of rose-leaves and sweet lavender.[8]

John Jarndyce tells them that his home had in truth been bleak a generation earlier, when its name was changed from The Peaks by its despondent owner Tom Jarndyce, who was so maddened by the interminable legal labyrinth of the suit that he blew his brains out in a Chancery Lane coffee house. 'When I brought what remained of him home here, the brains seemed to me to have been blown out of the house too, it was so shattered and ruined', mourns the sensibly law-averse John Jarndyce.

He explains that the disputed Jarndyce property includes the 'infernal gulf' of a London slum nicknamed Tom-all-Alone's (perhaps after Tom Jarndyce), 'a street of perishing blind houses, with their eyes stoned out', now the miserable home of many of the hope-deferred victims of Chancery suits. Dickens likens the slum to 'a ruined human wretch' on which 'vermin parasites appear'.

> [T]hese ruined shelters have bred a crowd of foul existence that
> crawls in and out of gaps in walls and boards; and coils itself to

sleep, in maggot numbers, where the rain drips in; and comes and goes, fetching and carrying fever and sowing more evil in its every footprint...

He personifies the place further by simply calling it 'Tom'.

The moon has eyed Tom with a dull cold stare, as admitting some puny emulation of herself in his desert region unfit for life and blasted by volcanic fires; but she has passed on and is gone. The blackest nightmare in the infernal stables grazes on Tom-all-Alone's, and Tom is fast asleep.[9]

Its dead or dying occupants have moribund surroundings. Those in the mysterious Nemo's room are described as decomposing: a 'perishing' hearth-rug, a portmanteau 'collapsed like the cheeks of a starving man', a 'rusty skeleton of a grate', 'gaunt eyes in the shutters'.

Soon after her arrival at Bleak House, Esther is presented with its keys, heralding her guardian's hope that she will be not just Ada's companion, but the mistress of the house, brightening up his own life. Her surname puns on the sunshine she will spread, exactly as the sun-named Phoebe does in *Seven Gables*. Ada and Richard fall in love, but Richard insists on putting all his time and money into the law case, rejecting John Jarndyce's good sense in favour of the hollow promises of the vampirish Mr Vholes. When Esther and Ada visit his chambers, they see Richard's name on the door 'in great white letters on a hearse-like panel'. He becomes 'bloodless and gaunt', eventually dwindling into death.

After the murder of Mr Tulkinghorn, the story develops into a detective mystery, and the action swings like a pendulum between dreary locations (the Dedlocks' houses, the law courts, the slums and their doomed occupants) and a bevy of brighter ones: not only John Jarndyce's restored Bleak House, but Lawrence Boythorn's pretty parsonage house, the briskly run Bagnet household, which 'contains nothing superfluous and has not a visible speck of dirt or dust in it', and the ironmaster Robert Rouncewell's elegant house

Charles Dickens aged 41, photographed in 1863 by Robert Hindry Mason for a *carte de visite*: these small albumen prints were presented to friends and collected in albums.

M. Charles Dickens

in the industrial north, 'a pleasant mixture of the originally simple habits of the father and mother with such as are suited to their altered station'.

Dickens's playfulness over the naming of Bleak House has a purpose. For all the book's prevailing gloom and numerous deaths, he intends optimism to prevail. Good-natured characters outnumber evil ones. The book ends by offering us another model domestic establishment called Bleak House, which John Jarndyce creates in Yorkshire for the benefit of Esther and her future husband Allan Woodcourt:

> a cottage, quite a rustic cottage of doll's rooms; but such a
> lovely place, so tranquil and so beautiful, with such a rich
> and smiling country spread around it… [A]s we went through
> the pretty rooms, out at the little rustic verandah doors,

and underneath the tiny wooden colonnades garlanded with woodbine, jasmine, and honey-suckle, I saw in the papering on the walls, in the colours of the furniture, in the arrangement of all the pretty objects, MY little tastes and fancies, MY little methods and inventions which they used to laugh at while they praised them, my odd ways everywhere.[10]

Most unexpected of all is the way that Sir Leicester Dedlock finally wins our sympathy for his nobility in the face of Lady Dedlock's fate. After she dies, Chesney Wold becomes

a vast blank of overgrown house looking out upon trees, sighing, wringing their hands, bowing their heads, and casting their tears upon the window-panes in monotonous depressions. A labyrinth of grandeur, less the property of an old family of human beings and their ghostly likenesses than of an old family of echoings and thunderings which start out of their hundred graves at every sound and go resounding through the building.

Sir Leicester gives her an honoured place in the family mausoleum, and looks forward to joining her there when his time comes. Until then,

Up from among the fern in the hollow, and winding by the bridle-road among the trees, comes sometimes to this lonely spot the sound of horses' hoofs. Then may be seen Sir Leicester – invalided, bent, and almost blind, but of worthy presence yet – riding with a stalwart man beside him, constant to his bridle-rein. When they come to a certain spot before the mausoleum-door, Sir Leicester's accustomed horse stops of his own accord, and Sir Leicester, pulling off his hat, is still for a few moments before they ride away.[11]

KITCHEN TABLE SOCIETY

Uncle Tom's Cabin and
Harriet Beecher Stowe

The cabin of Uncle Tom was a small log building, close
adjoining … his master's dwelling. In front it had a neat
garden-patch, where, every summer, strawberries, raspberries,
and a variety of fruits and vegetables, flourished under careful
tending. The whole front of it was covered by a large scarlet
bignonia and a native multiflora rose, which, entwisting and
interlacing, left scarce a vestige of the rough logs to be seen.

Harriet Beecher Stowe, *Uncle Tom's Cabin*, 1852[1]

It is essentially domestic and of the family, this book, with
its long discussions, its carefully studied portraits. Mothers
of families, young girls, children and servants can read and
understand it, and men, even the most superior, cannot ignore it.

George Sand, 17 December 1852[2]

The most politically influential dwelling in fiction is also the
smallest: a one-room shack in Kentucky that housed a family of
slaves. Books demanding the abolition of slavery in America were
numerous before the 1852 publication of Harriet Beecher Stowe's
Uncle Tom's Cabin, but none had its instant and lasting impact.
In the nineteenth century it was outsold only by the Bible, and
was translated into over forty languages. Whether or not Abraham
Lincoln (who himself began his days in a Kentucky log cabin) did

The sensational sales of Harriet Beecher Stowe's *Uncle Tom's Cabin* were increased by such publicity bills as this one, which were displayed in bookshops in the 1850s and 1860s.

say 'So you're the little woman who wrote the book that made this great war' when he met Stowe in 1862,[3] the world before and afterwards gave her credit for doing so.

What made the book seize the public imagination was that Stowe rooted her protest in the domestic. 'The worst abuse of the system of slavery is its outrage upon the family', she wrote in her guide to the sources of her novel, *The Key to Uncle Tom's Cabin* (1853). 'It is one which is more notorious and undeniable than any other'. By centring her book on an idyllic little home that is ruined by the greed of a thoughtless owner, Stowe ensured that it appealed

especially to women – and the hands that rocked the cradles succeeded in rocking their husbands too.

Stowe describes Aunt Chlöe's 'own snug territories' in detail.
A table, 'somewhat rheumatic in its limbs', is drawn out in front
of the fire, … displaying cups and saucers of a decidedly brilliant
pattern'. The wall over the fireplace is 'adorned with some very brilliant scriptural prints, and a portrait of General Washington'. Aunt
Chlöe is a cook 'in the very bone and centre of her soul'. While
her two sons are teaching the baby to walk, she is cooking 'her ole
man's supper', 'presiding with anxious interest over certain frizzling
items in a stew-pan'. She is also cook at the Shelby family's house,
and her husband Tom manages their farm. Calling them 'Aunt'
and 'Uncle' emphasizes the affectionate respect in which they are
held by the Shelbys.

Interest in *Uncle Tom's Cabin* was the greater because Harriet and
her sister Catherine already had an established literary following
among the housewives of America. Born in Litchfield, Connecticut,
in 1811, Harriet was the sixth of the Reverend Lyman Beecher and
Roxana Foote Beecher's eleven children, who were all brought up
in the expectation that they would do their best to improve the
world. Both sisters wrote voluminously, expressing strong views
on education, the management of children and domestic arrangements. Harriet excelled at fiction. *The Coral Ring* (1843) was her first
anti-slavery and pro-temperance tract. After moving to Cincinnati,
Ohio, she often met escaped slaves and heard their horrific stories.

Stowe's immediate spur for writing the book was the passing of
the Fugitive Slave Act of 1850. Nicknamed the Bloodhound Law,
it required anyone who came across escaped slaves to return them
to their owners. After the passing of the Fugitive Slave Act in 1850,
her sister Catherine wrote to her saying 'Hattie, if I could use a pen
as you can, I would write something to make this whole nation
feel what an accursed thing slavery is.' That challenge set Harriet
to writing her novel. Her awareness of the plight of slave mothers
was heightened by the fact that she had lost a son to cholera a few

years earlier, and had just given birth again. In a much later letter to her son Charles she wrote:

> I well remember the winter you were a baby and I was writing 'Uncle Tom's Cabin'. My heart was bursting with the anguish excited by the cruelty and injustice our nation was showing to the slave... I remember many a night weeping over you as you lay sleeping beside me, and I thought of the slave mothers whose babes were torn from them.[4]

The right of every human being to a Christian home is the crux of the plot. Hence its title, *Uncle Tom's Cabin*, and the endearing account of garden, kitchen and other internal arrangements offered at length early on in the novel. It comes as a shock when in the opening chapter, sarcastically titled 'The Man of Humanity', we discover that Arthur Shelby, owner of the Kentucky farm on which Tom and Chlöe live, and a man who prides himself on treating his slaves well, has neglected his affairs to such an extent that he is going to tear this happy family apart and sell Uncle Tom, the most valuable of his slaves. Not only that; he agrees to throw in Harry, an engaging little 4-year-old boy, who happens to put his head round the door. Shelby does draw the line at selling Harry's beautiful mother Eliza, whom the slave trader makes a spirited attempt to acquire after she has taken Harry away.

Suspicious of the slave-trader's interest in Harry, Eliza listens at the door and when she discovers that Harry is to be sold resolves to run away, a move condoned by the appalled Mrs Shelby. Eliza's husband George, a 'bright and talented young mulatto man' on a nearby plantation, is also determined to escape, because his owner, suspicious of his invention of a hemp-cleaning machine, reduces him to 'a life of toil and drudgery' in the fields. Stowe makes the new law's inhuman implications vividly clear in the course of Eliza's flight, pursued by bloodhounds, across the ice floes on the Ohio River. Then she lightens the narrative by giving a teasingly ironic twist to the drama in the intimacy of an attractive domestic setting:

The light of the cheerful fire shone on the rug and carpet of a cosy parlor, and glittered on the sides of the tea-cups and well-brightened tea-pot, as Senator Bird was drawing off his boots, preparatory to inserting his feet in a pair of new handsome slippers, which his wife had been working for him while away on his senatorial tour.[5]

Mrs Bird, 'looking the very picture of delight', after admonishing 'a number of frolicsome juveniles', asks her husband if it is 'true that they have been passing a law forbidding people to give meat and drink to those poor coloured folks that come along? I heard they were talking of some such law, but I didn't think any Christian legislature would pass it!'

Just as the senator is pompously explaining why he agreed to the law, a bedraggled and footsore Eliza arrives in their kitchen and collapses. After she reveals that she would have lost her son if she had stayed with her master, the senator realizes how inhumane the new law is. He tells his wife to alter a dress for Eliza, and later that night takes Eliza and Harry to a Quaker household run with 'motherly loving kindness' by Rachel Halliday, supported by her husband Simeon.

Everything went on so sociably, so quietly, so harmoniously, in the great kitchen, – it seemed so pleasant to every one to do just what they were doing, there was such an atmosphere of mutual confidence and good fellowship everywhere, – even the knives and forks had a social clatter as they went on to the table; and the chicken and ham had a cheerful and joyous fizzle in the pan, as if they rather enjoyed being cooked than otherwise…[6]

The Quakers are true to themselves and their faith, ignoring the new law and doing what they can, short of violence, to help refugee slaves like the Harrises. George turns up as well, and looks round wonderingly. 'This, indeed, was a home, – *home*, – a word that George had never yet known a meaning for'.

After a thrilling escape from slave-catchers, the reunited family reach Canada, where they live in 'a small, neat tenement, in the outskirts of Montreal', and George works for a machinist. Stowe describes their home tellingly:

> The time, evening. A cheerful fire blazes on the hearth; a tea-table, covered with a snowy cloth, stands prepared for the evening meal. In one corner of the room was a table covered with a green cloth, where was an open writing-desk, pens, paper, and over it a shelf of well-selected books. This was George's study. [A] zeal for self-improvement ... led him to devote all his leisure time to self-cultivation.[7]

Eventually they are joined by George's sister and Eliza's mother, whose stories also wend their way through the novel. So a traditional family is set up, with children, a grandmother and an aunt. They travel to France, where George takes a degree, and eventually find a future in the West African state of Liberia.[8]

Uncle Tom has no such luck, and is literally 'sold down the river'. On the deck of the paddle steamer that takes him down the Mississippi, he reads his bible and dreams of his

> little cabin overgrown with the multiflora and bignonia. There he seemed to see familiar faces of comrades who had grown up with him from infancy; he saw his busy wife, bustling in her preparations for his evening meals; he heard the merry laugh of his boys at their play, and the chirrup of the baby at his knee...[9]

His luck seems in when he dives overboard to save the life of a little girl; on her urging, her father, Augustine St Clare, buys him. St Clare emerges as a lazily benevolent master, with a streak of cynicism about life. The one person he loves is his only daughter Evangeline, a child of such angelic intensity that she is clearly not long for this world. She and Uncle Tom develop a profound affinity through their shared Christian faith. Little Eva, like Stowe, finds slavery deeply unchristian; Tom, by contrast, submits to it with Christian meekness. He makes a new version of his beloved cabin, a monastic 'cubiculum' over the stables, where he prays for St Clare's careless soul, preaches to his fellow slaves, and sings 'beautiful things about the New Jerusalem' to Little Eva. Stowe was careful to make relatively benevolent slave-owners like the Shelbys, the Birds and the St Clares attractive. 'I shall show the best side of the thing, and something faintly approaching the worst', she explained to her publisher Mr Bailey on 9 March 1851. Southerners often argued that slaves were part of their family, and that it was a 'patriarchal institution'. Stowe shows the hollowness of this idea when adversity strikes.

St Clare's domain is far from perfect. His wife Marie is a spoilt hypochondriac, and the household a 'shiftless' one, especially in Stowe's favourite setting, the kitchen, which is ruled by Dinah, a characterful cook who produces magnificent meals against a background of muddle and waste.

> her kitchen generally looked as if it had been arranged by
> a hurricane blowing through it, … yet, if one would have
> patience to wait her own good time, up would come her dinner
> in perfect order, and in a style of preparation with which an
> epicure could find no fault.[10]

The slovenliness of the St Clare household is exacerbated by being seen through the critical eyes of Ophelia, Augustine's upright sister from Vermont who has come to take over management of the household for Marie and lessen what St Clare derides as its 'hurryscurryation'. By contrast, in the household Ophelia has left, 'all household arrangements move with the punctual exactness of the old clock in the corner'.

> There are no servants in the house, but the lady in the snowy
> cap, with the spectacles, who sits sewing every afternoon
> among her daughters … The old kitchen floor never seems
> stained or spotted; the tables, the chairs, and the various
> cooking utensils, never seem deranged or disordered…[11]

In comparing this with Dinah's creative chaos, Stowe piles on the humour and wit that are evident in the housekeeping manual she later wrote with her sister Catherine, *The American Woman's Home* (1870), a best-seller which presented in lively fictional form the different styles of housekeeping suited to different temperaments.

Besides being another welcome respite from the shocking episodes that dominate the story, the digression reinforces the importance of home and family that permeates the whole novel; it also brings into play the domestic ideal repeatedly described in books and essays by the Beecher sisters: one in which household work, carried out by members of the family rather than abandoned to slaves or servants, is not seen as drudgery but as valuable and rewarding. Domesticity gives women power, increasing as it does their influence over their menfolk. *The American Woman's Home* was dedicated 'To the Women of America, in whose hands rest the real destinies of the Republic'. Women such as Mrs Shelby, Emily, Mrs Bird, Eva, Ophelia, Cassy and Rachel Halliday are all forceful and influential characters. All through the book, they initiate or aid escapes from slavery.[12]

Like Dickens, Stowe understood the potent appeal of children in fiction with a social message. Besides Harry and Little Eva, she offers a character whose cocky resilience and subversive wit seized the public imagination. When Ophelia criticizes the lack of education of the St Clare slaves, Augustine offers her a challenge by giving her a 9-year-old girl called Topsy, making the pertinent point that Northerners were quick to criticize Southern slave-owners, but loth to have anything to do with black people. Ophelia accepts the challenge, but the quicksilver Topsy repeatedly thwarts her. But Stowe mixes the comic aspect of Topsy with horror. In the ultimate family nightmare, she 'had no father, had no mother'; she is a 'speculator's child', one of a legion 'raised for market' by making female slaves pregnant in order to sell their babies.

As time goes by, St Clare puts more responsibility in Tom's hands, just as Shelby did, and Tom begins to inspire others with his

'The dark places of the earth are full of the habitations of cruelty': Stowe quotes Psalm 74 in her description of Tom's degradation at the hands of Simon Legree. Hammatt Billings's illustration shows Cassy tending Tom on his deathbed.

own faith. Eva dies, and her father decides to become a Christian, free his own slaves and work for emancipation. Ophelia writes to the Shelbys to give them the good news, but St Clare's sudden death in a tavern brawl means that all his slaves are sold except for Topsy, who belongs to Ophelia; reformed by Eva's love, Topsy goes north with Ophelia and eventually becomes a missionary in Africa.

Now real adversity hits Uncle Tom. He is sold to the villainous and vicious Simon Legree, and finds himself chained hand and foot, and taken even deeper into the South. The nadir of Tom's story is reflected in the quotation from Psalm 74 that introduces chapter 40: 'The dark places of the earth are full of the habitations of cruelty', a phrase that Joseph Conrad later quoted in *The Heart of Darkness* (1899). Legree's house is in a state of decay, which reflects his character:

> [T]he place looked desolate and uncomfortable; some windows stopped up with boards, some with shattered panes, and shutters hanging by a single hinge, – all telling of coarse neglect and discomfort.[13]

Tom, who had 'been comforting himself with the thought of a cottage, rude, indeed, but one which he might make neat and quiet, and where he might have a shelf for his Bible, and a place to be alone out of his laboring hours', has to share one of several 'rude shells, destitute of any species of furniture, except a heap of straw, foul with dirt'. Matters go from bad to worse. Legree orders Tom to be flogged to death, which he bears with a Christ-like humility that leads to the conversion of the men who beat him.

As he lies dying in his last pathetic home, George Shelby arrives. He is too late to save his life, but Tom's face lights up.

> 'It's all I wanted! They haven't forgot me. It warms my soul; it does my heart good! Now I shall die content! Bless the Lord, on my soul!'[14]

George gives him a decent burial and returns home. He frees all the Shelby slaves to spare them 'the risk of being parted from home', then re-employs them as paid workers. Uncle Tom's humble cabin is made a shrine to Tom.

After the Civil War, absurdly distorted representations of *Uncle Tom's Cabin*'s central characters led to the book being reviled in the twentieth century. Today perceptive critics recognize its subtleties and its formidably massed arguments against slavery. 'Love and protest, maternal duty and political action, compose Stowe's reformulated domestic virtue' writes Gillian Brown.[15] Although Stowe's book is now something of a period piece, it is remarkably interesting, and very easy reading. Tom's humble, flower-bedecked Kentucky log cabin, a potent symbol of the domestic deprivation inseparable from slavery, deserves a prime position among memorable fictional dwellings.

BACHELOR LAIR

221B *Baker Street and*
Arthur Conan Doyle

[T]he old landmarks were all in their place. There were the
chemical corner and the acid-stained, deal-topped table. There
upon a shelf was the row of formidable scrap-books and books
of reference which many of our fellow-citizens would have been
so glad to burn. The diagrams, the violin-case, and the pipe-
rack – even the Persian slipper which contained the tobacco
– all met my eyes as I glanced round me.

> Arthur Conan Doyle, 'The Adventure
> of the Empty House', 1903

Holmes is enclosed by compulsive habits as well as snug quarters,
each time he takes tobacco from his slipper he is reminded of
himself, reliving the whim of the original arrangements and
confirming himself in the privacy of his ways.

> Robert Harbison, *Eccentric Spaces*, 1977[1]

221B Baker Street is the most famous address in detective fiction.
It is Sherlock Holmes's heartland, a springboard to adventure and a
recuperative haven, the scene of quizzical deductions and dramatic
denouements, an experimental laboratory, a central hub for spies
and messengers and one of the intellectual centres of Europe. It
appears in all four of the novels and most of the fifty-six stories that
Arthur Conan Doyle (1859–1930) wrote about Holmes and Watson.

In 'The Adventure of the Empty House' it offers an illusion that is the downfall of one of Sherlock's most dastardly foes.

221B's topographical situation came early on in Doyle's imagining of a brilliant 'consulting detective', as skilled in the art of deduction as was his own medical mentor in Edinburgh, Dr Joseph Bell.[2] Doyle's original jottings for *A Study in Scarlet* (1887) refer to one 'Ormond Sacker, ~~from Soudan~~ from Afghanistan', living at '221B Upper Baker Street' with one 'Sherrinford Holmes', a 'reserved, sleepy-eyed young man – philosopher – collector of Violins'. At the time, Doyle himself was living 2 kilometres east of Baker Street in Montague Place, near the British Museum.[4] Choosing Baker Street, rather than one of the luxurious blocks of mansion flats that were springing up in London's West End in the 1890s, was deliberate. It was respectable but unostentatious, a facade behind which Holmes could lurk discreetly. The gang of street urchins immortalized as the Baker Street Irregulars would not have been welcomed by upper-class neighbours. It was also conveniently placed for the Great North Road and the London railway terminals. Our heroes rarely spend much time in Baker Street once 'the game's afoot', but it is usually the start and end point for the tales, and at times Holmes 'would lie upon the sofa in the sitting-room, hardly uttering a word or moving a muscle from morning to night'. It is, writes Robert Harbison, 'one of the most distilled versions' of the Victorian sense of home. Holmes's enclosure is exaggerated 'because people are missing and ritual fills up every vacant space'.

The layout of the lodgings is described in detail in the second chapter of *A Study in Scarlet*. Watson is invited by Holmes to inspect 'a suite in Baker Street' that he has his eye on.

> We met next day as he had arranged, and inspected the rooms at No. 221B, Baker Street, of which he had spoken at our meeting. They consisted of a couple of comfortable bed-rooms and a single large airy sitting-room, cheerfully furnished, and illuminated by two broad windows.[4]

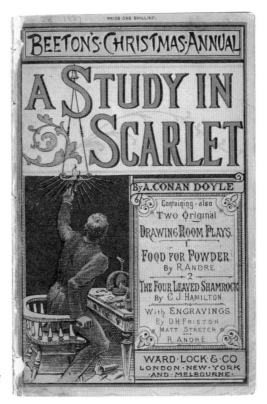

'There's the scarlet thread of murder running through the colourless skein of life, and our duty is to unravel it, and isolate it, and expose every inch of it.' Arthur Conan Doyle's *A Study in Scarlet*, the first story about Sherlock Holmes, was originally printed in *Beeton's Christmas Annual* in 1887.

The rooms are being let out by the discreet and respectable Mrs Hudson, who manages the housekeeping with the help of a maid and a 'buttons', or pageboy. Clues to the contents of both sitting room and bedroom are liberally scattered through the novels and stories that Arthur Conan Doyle wrote between 1887 and 1927, when Holmes did at long last take his last bow. There is a bathroom, unless Watson got Billy the page to bring up a tub in front of his bedroom fire so that he could have the bath he mentions taking in *The Sign of the Four* (1890). Mrs Hudson and the maid cook in the basement, and have bedrooms at the top of the house. In the spacious first-floor sitting room, armchairs flank the bearskin rug that lies in front of the fireplace, there is a wicker chair for visitors, tobacco is secreted in a Turkish slipper and cigars in the coal scuttle. On a deal table in one corner chemical equipment is

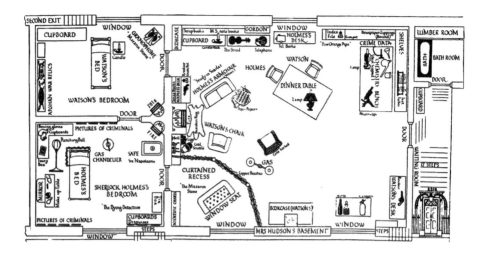

Using details from Doyle's many stories, Ernest H. Short constructed this plan of the living quarters of Sherlock Holmes and Dr Watson at 221B Baker Street for *The Strand Magazine* in 1950; purists will object that Dr Watson's bedroom should be on the floor above.

to hand. Mention is also made of a closet for disguises, a jackknife stabbed through a pile of unanswered letters on the mantelpiece, a 'gasogene' soda siphon, a Stradivarius violin, pipes of all shapes and sizes and much else. All in all, it lives and breathes bachelor heaven.

Holmes's decided preference for the single life and intolerance of any feminine fussing is confirmed in 'The Reigate Squires' (1893), when he agrees to go to convalesce in Surrey only after Watson assures him that Colonel Hayter's establishment 'was a bachelor one'. Holmes also has a virtual retreat in his own mind. Defending his refusal to know anything about subjects he thought irrelevant, he likens a man's brain to 'a little empty attic'.

> [Y]ou have to stock it with such furniture as you choose. A fool takes in all the lumber of every sort that he comes across, so that the knowledge which might be useful to him gets crowded out, or at best is jumbled up with a lot of other things so that he has a difficulty in laying his hands upon it. Now the skilful workman is very careful indeed as to what he takes into his

brain-attic. He will have nothing but the tools which may help him in doing his work, but of these he has a large assortment, and all in the most perfect order. [5]

The adventure in which 221B earns its spurs as a heroic house, and in which it is described in most detail, is 'The Empty House' (1903), the celebrated story which reveals that Holmes did not fall to his death with Moriarty at the Reichenbach Falls, as he seemed to do a decade earlier in 'The Final Problem' (1893). Instead, after three years of living under cover, he reveals himself to Watson and takes him on a lengthy peregrination around London, ending up in the empty Compton House, opposite the rear of their old quarters. From its window, he shows Watson the set-up he has staged in the sitting room of 221B: a silhouetted figure which shifts position occasionally appears to be Holmes himself, seated in a chair. Holmes has calculated that Moriarty's second-in-command Colonel Moran will take the bait and shoot at him, and so he does, revealing his whereabouts. Once Moran is apprehended and packed off to prison, mouthing curses, Holmes and Watson (whose wife has conveniently died while Holmes was absent) take up their bachelor partnership once again:

> Our old chambers had been left unchanged through the supervision of Mycroft Holmes and the immediate care of Mrs. Hudson. As I entered I saw, it is true, an unwonted tidiness, but the old landmarks were all in their place. … There were two occupants of the room – one, Mrs. Hudson, who beamed upon us both as we entered – the other, the strange dummy which had played so important a part in the evening's adventures. It was a wax-coloured model of my friend, so admirably done that it was a perfect facsimile. It stood on a small pedestal table with an old dressing-gown of Holmes's so draped round it that the illusion from the street was absolutely perfect.[6]

Often, when the house is the hero of a book, its housekeeper is its essential interpreter and enabler. Mrs Hudson, Holmes's landlady as well as his housekeeper, is no exception. Behind the scenes at 221B, she orchestrates the household arrangements and meals. As time goes on, she is paid 'a princely sum' to compensate for such untoward happenings as callers at all hours, occasional gunshots, a broken sitting-room window frame, the sacrifice of a sick terrier and sudden invasions by street urchins. Not only does the house belong to her, she frequently plays an important part in the action: it is she who crawls in to shift the wax dummy of Holmes every fifteen minutes in 'The Empty House'.[7]

There is something of the escapism of a Victorian male club in the uncompromisingly masculine character of Holmes's and Watson's home.[8] Enumerating the unorthodox bachelor aspects of the Baker Street household in elaborate detail, insisting on Sherlock Holmes determinedly remaining unmarried, and ruthlessly killing off Watson's wife may have had a little wish fulfilment about it; the eternal longing of a man for a private retreat. Doyle's own domestic life could not have been more different from that of his hero. He liked the role of the classic Victorian paterfamilias, something that his father had never been. He married Louise ('Touie') Hawkins in 1885, and remained loyal to her all her life, despite falling in love in 1897 with the charismatic Jean Leckie, whom he married a year after Touie's death in 1907.

Doyle's extended family included his own and his spouses' brothers and sisters as well as five children, along with a motley mix of dogs, horses and other pets. Closest to his heart was his mother Mary Foley Doyle, recipient of all his confidences by letter, but always refusing to live with him. In his medieval romance *Sir Nigel*, he painted her portrait as Dame Ermyntrude Loring, alongside his own as her son, Sir Nigel. In his childhood he admired her dogged resilience in face of his father Charles's addiction to alcohol and drugs, and was relieved when after Charles's death she found a protector in their lodger, Dr Bryan Waller. Following Waller's example in qualifying as a doctor seemed a sensible way to ensure a good income; he warmed up by taking a job as ship's surgeon on a whaler, then set up his plate in Portsmouth, soon deciding to specialize in ophthalmology – a prescient move for the man who created the world's most observant detective.

Maintaining a family home mattered to Doyle. He lived at various times in three substantial Edwardian houses. The first was 12 Tenison Road in Norwood (1891–94), where he and Touie took vigorous exercise on a tandem tricycle; he made Norwood the setting for *The Sign of the Four* and 'The Adventure of the Norwood Builder'. The second, Undershaw (1897–1907), was built to his specifications at Hindhead in the Surrey hills, a climate that suited Touie's consumptive tendency. Undershaw boasted a miniature monorail electric railway big enough for passengers in its garden and was rich in armorial stained glass: Doyle inherited his mother's pride in her descent from the Plantagenets. His longest-lasting residence was Windlesham Manor, near Crowborough (1906–31), where he moved after his marriage to Jean. He also spent some time at Bignell Wood, near Minstead in the New Forest.

Despite the success of the Sherlock Holmes stories, Doyle himself did not rate them highly. Working on a second series of Holmes stories in 1891, he wrote to his mother on 11 November to say that he thought of 'slaying Holmes in the sixth [story] & winding him up for good and all. He keeps me from better things.' The 'better things' were his historical fictions *Micah Clarke, The White Company, Brigadier Gerard, Rodney Stone* and *Sir Nigel* ('My absolute top!'). What kept Doyle writing about Holmes and Watson was the popular enthusiasm for their adventures that led magazine editors to raise their offers for Sherlock stories from £25 each to £1,000 for a dozen. In April 1893 Doyle did kill off Holmes, but he resurrected him ten years later because the American magazine *Collier's Weekly* offered him the enormous sum of $25,000 for six stories and $45,000 for thirteen, regardless of length. 'I don't see why I should not have another go at them and earn three times as much money as I can by any other form of work', he wrote to his mother in the spring of 1903.[9] Like it or not, he had created a legend and an imaginary residence which has over the years acquired a vast speculative literature. Every step any Doyle character takes in or around Baker Street has been catalogued and questioned; every material object classified with mock scholarly precision. In 1940 real spies moved in. Either chance or an influential spook's sense of humour set up the World War II Special Operations Executive in Baker Street, and Baker Street or Bakerstrasse remains espionage slang for an HQ.

It is a credit to the immediacy of Doyle's writing that so many readers thought he was writing fact rather than fiction, and addressed countless letters to Holmes, in Baker Street, rather than to Doyle. Ironically, the entirely invented premises became established reality in 1951. When Doyle wrote *A Study in Scarlet* in 1897, Baker Street addresses ended at around 100; '221B' was deliberately non-existent, as was 403 Brook Street in 'The Resident Patient', and 427 Park Lane in 'The Empty House'. But Sherlock Holmes's lodgings fascinated the nation to such an extent that, as part of the celebrations for the Festival of Britain, '221B' was re-created in minute detail on an upper storey of the Abbey National Building, which stretched across numbers 219–229 of the extended and renumbered Baker Street. A *Daily Telegraph* leader praised the staged apartment under the headline 'Holmes, Sweet Holmes'. Today Sherlock Holmes societies flourish all over the world, and BBC TV's *Sherlock*, starring Benedict Cumberbatch, has proved immensely popular.

HOUSEHOLD GODS
Poynton and Henry James

Poynton was the record of a life. It was written in great
syllables of color and form, the tongues of other countries and
the hands of rare artists. It was all France and Italy, with their
ages composed to rest. For England you looked out of old
windows – it was England that was the wide embrace.

Henry James, *The Spoils of Poynton*, 1896[1]

his phrases were servants moving
silently about the great house of his prose
letting in sunlight into the empty rooms.

R.S. Thomas, 'Henry James', 1978[2]

Houses fascinated Henry James all his life. He used architectural
metaphors to describe the process of writing in his famous essay 'The
House of Fiction'. They are similarly applied not only to his novels
but to the characters in them. Isabel Archer was, he wrote, 'the single
small cornerstone' on which he erected 'the large building of *The
Portrait of a Lady*'.[3] Conversely, he uses human metaphors to describe
houses. *The Portrait of a Lady* tells of Isabel Archer's life pilgrimage
from familiar New York brownstone to the 'warm, weary brickwork'
of the Thameside mansion Gardencourt, 'with the complexion of
which time and the weather had played all sorts of picturesque tricks',
and finally to Gilbert Osgood's gloomy villa with 'heavy lids, but

Elliott & Fry cabinet card photograph of Henry James, taken in 1884. Larger and thicker versions of the *carte de visite*, they were displayed on stands in cabinets or in albums.

no eyes' in Florence. Ralph Touchett admires Isabel as a 'beautiful edifice'; Osgood says he has the key to turn 'the very complicated lock' of Isabel's intellect; he wants her mind to be to his 'like a small garden-plot to a deer park'. James's most moving architectural analogy is his words about his mother on her deathbed: 'She was our life, she was the house, she was the keystone of the arch. She was patience, she was wisdom, she was exquisite maternity.'[4]

James's tragicomic tale *The Spoils of Poynton* (1896) is constructed around three houses and their contents. First and foremost is Poynton itself, 'early Jacobean, supreme in every part', and filled with the impeccably tasteful fruits of twenty-six years of collecting by Adela Gereth and her husband. These objects are, James writes in his preface, 'the citadel of the interest, with the fight waged around'. The book's working title was *The House Beautiful*,[5] but, after a decorating magazine of that name appeared while he was writing, it was changed when published in serial form in *Atlantic Monthly* to *The Old Things*. That title highlighted the contents of Poynton as the crux of the novel. It was improved to *The Spoils of Poynton* when it appeared as a book.

The second house is the vulgarly ostentatious mansion of Water-bath, 'smothered [in] trumpery ornament and scrapbook art, with strange excrescences and bunchy draperies'. It is the 'intimately ugly' home of the Brigstocks, whose daughter Mona Mrs Gereth's son Owen plans to marry. This will mean Mrs Gereth's banishment to the third house, Ricks, a Cinderella to the grander establishments. Left to Mr Gereth by his maiden aunt, it is still furnished with her things: 'the little worn, bleached stuffs and the sweet spindle-legs'. Owen declares it 'a jolly little place' which 'stands there with open arms' to welcome his mother. Ricks will, ironically, emerge as the house that is the hero of the book, the only place that is true to itself, with neither aesthetic pretension nor vulgarity. The three houses are exactly matched to the three central characters: Mrs Gereth, the dethroned mistress of Poynton; Mona Brigstock, a brash 'New Woman', hot for her rights; and Fleda Vetch, who 'hadn't a penny in the world nor anything nice at home, and whose only treasure was her subtle mind'. Again, it is neither the tempestuous Mrs Gereth nor the implacable Mona who emerges as heroic, but Fleda. Somewhat to James's own surprise, he writes in his preface, she 'planted herself centrally', and let it be seen that 'she had character'.

The Spoils of Poynton was the first novel that Henry James wrote after a succession of failed plays, and its melodramatic structure is a hangover from theatricalities. It opens with the meeting of Mrs Gereth and Fleda, a fellow guest at Waterbath. They shudder together at its ghastliness and watch in dread as Mrs Gereth's son Owen and Mona Brigstock grow close. Mr Gereth died untimely two years ago, after a marriage devoted to the thrills of collecting. The exquisite antique pieces at Poynton represent Mrs Gereth's identity. But 'the cruel English custom of the expropriation of the lonely mother' means that both they and the house now belong to Owen. Mr Gereth had assumed that 'he could depend on Owen's affection' in sharing Poynton's treasures with his mother. He hadn't bargained for Mona Brigstock's insistence on her rights, although she is in truth the right wife for the 'handsome and heavy' Owen, whose room full of guns and whips is out of keeping with the transcendent work of art which his parents made of the rest of Poynton's interior.

Mrs Gereth, still 'fresh and fair and young in her fifties', is horrified at the prospect of Mona taking possession of all she has created at Poynton, ruining the exquisite aura of the house by mixing in 'maddening relics of Waterbath, the little brackets and pink vases, the sweepings of bazaars, the family photographs and illuminated texts, the "household art" and household piety'. Finding an admiring and sympathetic friend in Fleda, she invites her to see Poynton, drawing back its curtains and removing covers as she shows her round:

> The shimmer of wrought substances spent itself in the
> brightness; the old golds and brasses, old ivories and bronzes,
> the fresh old tapestries and deep old damasks threw out a
> radiance in which the poor woman saw in solution all her old
> loves and patiences, all her old tricks and triumphs.[6]

Fleda is overwhelmed by its beauty, dropping into a seat Leda-like, 'with a soft gasp and a roll of dilated eyes'.

Mrs Gereth exults in her reaction, which fortifies her resolve to fight for her treasures. Battle royal is joined when she lives up to the Arthurian resonance of her name and announces in a letter to Fleda that she has 'crossed the Rubicon' and moved to Ricks.

> [H]aving passed the threshold of Poynton for the last time,
> the amputation, as she called it, had been performed. Her leg
> had come off – she had now begun to stump along with the
> lovely wooden substitute; she would stump for life, and what
> her young friend was to come and admire was the beauty of her
> movement and the noise she made about the house.[7]

Fleda discovers what Mrs Gereth meant by her warlike allusion to crossing the Rubicon when she visits her at Ricks and discovers that she has gutted Poynton. The battle imagery of the novel's title is maintained in the text. 'A little army of workers, packers, porters'

Henry James commissioned a photograph of the Small Drawing Room at the Wallace Collection taken from this angle as the frontispiece for the 1908 New York edition of *The Spoils of Poynton*: he specified that the view of the fireplace, with its loaded mantelpiece, be photographed obliquely, showing the flanking armchairs and paintings and damask-hung walls in order to emphasize that the accumulated Wallace 'spoils' and Hertford House itself were as inseparable from each other as Poynton House and its contents.

and even Owen's own 'myrmidons' have loaded up 'mighty vans', and Ricks is 'stuffed with as many as it could hold of the trophies of her friend's struggle'. Their effect on Ricks is 'like a minuet danced on a hearth-rug', not the symphony that was Poynton. Fleda has 'in a flash, the vision of great gaps in the other house … the far-away empty sockets, a scandal of nakedness in high, bare walls'. It is not Mrs Gereth who has undergone amputation, but Poynton itself.

> In the watches of the night she saw Poynton dishonored; she had cared for it as a happy whole, she reasoned, and the parts of it now around her seemed to suffer like chopped limbs.[8]

Fleda's sympathy begins to shift to Owen, who has thus far shown her nothing but trusting kindness, grateful that his mother has a companion. When Mrs Gereth insists on using her as a go-between, sympathy becomes love, especially when Owen, deeply muddled by the intransigence of both his mother and Mona (who has said that the marriage is off without the treasures of Poynton), falls in love with her, 'his impatience shining in his idle eyes as the dining-hour shines in club-windows'. When Owen guesses that she loves him too, she feels 'as if a whirlwind had come and gone, laying low the great false front that she had built up stone by stone'. But Fleda, who has, like Fanny Price in *Mansfield Park*, a powerfully certain, and ultimately self-protective, moral compass, says to Owen that Mona must give him up before they can be united.

Exultant when she divines that Owen is in love with her acolyte, Mrs Gereth impulsively anticipates her victory by sending everything back to Poynton, not realizing that all depended on Mona giving Owen up. But as soon as Mona discovers that the house is restored, she rushes Owen off to a registry office and marries him. When she hears, Mrs Gereth's face becomes 'a dead gray mask. A tired old woman sat there with empty hands in her lap.'

> [L]ike some great moaning, wounded bird, [she] made her way, with wings of anguish, back to the nest she knew she should find empty.[9]

Several weeks later she sends Fleda a letter asking her to keep her company at Ricks. Its wording tellingly emphasizes her obsession with possessions.

> [W]ith nothing else but my four walls, you'll at any rate be a bit of furniture. For that, you know, a little, I've always taken you – quite one of my best finds.[10]

Remembering that she herself had liked 'the blessed refuge of Ricks' from the start, Fleda accepts. To her amazement, her friend has transformed it into a delightful home. She has brought 'the maiden aunt', as they had jokingly called its former furnishings, out of the barn to which they had been banished, and has used 'the little melancholy, tender, tell-tale things' to create what Fleda perceptively calls 'a kind of fourth dimension'.

> It's a presence, a perfume, a touch. It's a soul, a story, a life. ...
> It's not the great chorus of Poynton; but you're not, I'm sure,
> either so proud or so broken as to be reached by nothing but

that… You've only to be a day or two in a place with four sticks for something to come of it![11]

Owen sends Fleda an apologetic letter from Paris, where he and Mona are spending their honeymoon, asking her to take something really precious from Poynton for herself, but when she goes down to find the jewelled Maltese cross she has long admired (religious imagery rivals that of war in the book) she finds that the house is on fire. Poynton, spoils and all, is utterly destroyed. The novel's dramatic conclusion makes us shift our perspective on the three houses. Poynton was a museum of the Gereths' life as collectors rather than a home. Mrs Gereth, whom James repeatedly calls 'poor lady', loved her things more than her son, and fantasized about living at Poynton as 'a custodian who was a walking catalogue and who understood beyond any one in England the hygiene and temperament of rare pieces'. Her ruling passion 'despoiled her of her humanity'. 'There were no ghosts at Poynton', Fleda reflects. 'That was the only fault.' Waterbath, for all its vulgarity, is a cosy place, observing 'household piety' by displaying the family portraits and mementoes of friends, holidays and events that are essential to homeliness. It is oddly reminiscent of Fanny's East Room in Mansfield Park. Mona would have added humanizing elements to the over-exquisite Poynton.

We realize that Mrs Gereth needed, however painfully, to come to terms with the fact that her old life is over, which she does by making Ricks a house perfectly suited to her. 'There's more room than I quite measured the other day, and a rather good set of old Worcester', she concedes. Fleda Vetch, who knew in her heart of hearts that she and Owen were ill-suited, and had always felt a sympathy for the maiden aunt, will be content and far from downtrodden as Mrs Gereth's companion at Ricks. She does need a patron, just as the clinging plant she is named for needs a support, but she has stood up for what she felt to be right against her friend's machinations several times, most memorably after Mrs Gareth berates her for sending Owen back to Mona.

'You simplify far too much. You always did and you always will. The tangle of life is much more intricate than you've ever, I think, felt it to be. You slash into it', cried Fleda finely, 'with a great pair of shears, you nip at it as if you were one of the Fates!'[12]

Mrs Gereth has to accept Fleda's 'independence of character'. From now on they will be 'yoke-fellows' rather than martial goddess and admiring minion.

The inspiration for *Poynton* came three years before it was written, when at a Christmas Eve dinner party, Henry James heard talk of how

> a good lady in the north, always well looked on, was at daggers drawn with her only son, ever hitherto exemplary, over the ownership of the valuable furniture of a fine old house just accruing to the young man by his father's death.[13]

James had visited many such fine houses since he decided to settle in England in 1876. He declared in his travelogue *English Hours* (1905) that

> of all the great things that the English have invented and made a part of the credit of the national character, the most perfect, the most characteristic, the one they have mastered most completely in all its details, so that it has become a compendious illustration of their social genius and their manners, is the well-appointed, well-administered, well-filled country house.[14]

He was a connoisseur of the ways such houses were furnished, and a fascinated observer of 'that most modern of our current passions, the fierce appetite for the upholsterer's and joiner's and brazier's work, the chairs and tables, the cabinets and presses, the material odds and ends, of the more labouring ages'.[15] Nouveau riche taste was guided by the pretentious style magazines of the kind that Mrs Brigstock gives Mrs Gereth, only to get it hurled back at her.[16] More discriminating collectors sought out genuine

An early postcard of Lamb House, Rye, which Henry James furnished as meticulously and tastefully as Mrs Gereth did her final home, the 'blessed refuge' of Ricks.

antiques, actually made in 'the more labouring ages'. James's own taste, was for eighteenth-century Italian and French pieces rather than the Nordic and Teutonic Arts and Crafts style that reached its apogee in William Morris's Kelmscott Manor in Oxfordshire. James inclined more to the ideas in Clarence Cook's book *The House Beautiful* (1878), Edith Wharton's *The Decoration of Houses* (1897) and Candace Wheeler's *Household Art* (1893).[17] Mrs Gereth's genius for creating atmosphere exactly echoes Wheeler's description of the 'mysterious charm, a nameless something, an attractive ghost of harmony and tranquillity' that makes poetry of well-chosen objects in a room.[18] James was moreover writing at the time that the fate of the fabulous Wallace Collection in Hertford House was being disputed by lawyers, a connection he emphasized by choosing a photograph of a room there filled with 'well-chosen objects' for the frontispiece of the 1908 New York edition of the novel.

One reason for Henry James's interest in what made a congenial home was that he was himself eager to create one. He lived in lodgings near Green Park when he first moved to London, then in a mansion flat near Kensington Gardens. But after the humiliation of his failed plays, he yearned for a retreat from London. *Poynton* was largely written while he was staying in Point Hill House, looking over the little red-roofed town of Rye. Exploring Rye, he came across Lamb House, and fell in love with it; a year later he got the opportunity of taking a twenty-one-year lease on it. Finally, he bought it outright. 'I have lived into my little old house and garden so thoroughly that they have become a kind of domiciliary skin, that can't be peeled off without pain', he wrote a decade later.[19]

The way he chose to furnish Lamb House revealed his own position on interior decorations. His friend Louisa, Viscountess Wolseley, who had something of Mrs Gereth about her in her talent for tasteful acquisitions, helped him choose some elegant Georgian mahogany furniture for his sitting room; book cases were built in, and there were pictures which reflected his personal taste – a Burne-Jones, an inscribed photograph of his friend the French writer Alphonse Daudet, a small portrait of Flaubert, some illustrations from an edition of *Daisy Miller* and a Whistler etching. Elsewhere in the house he hung family portraits, and a picture of his close friend Constance Fenimore Woolson, the American novelist who fell to her death in Venice in 1893. When he came to write *The Awkward Age*, he implicitly damns both Waterbath and Poynton, and portrays Lamb House, his own version of Ricks, exactly as Mr Longdon's house.

> Mr Longdon had not made his house, he had simply lived
> it, and the 'taste' of the place … was just nothing more than
> the beauty of his life. Everything on every side had dropped
> straight from heaven, with nowhere a bargaining thumb-mark,
> a single sign of the shop.[20]

PROPERTY

Robin Hill and John Galsworthy

Without a habitat a Forsyte is inconceivable – he would be like a novel without a plot, which is well-known to be an anomaly.

> John Galsworthy, *The Man of Property*, 1907[1]

Robin Hill is not a substitute for a personal story, it's an open and erasable canvas for its unfolding. … Such a house respects and reinforces inhabitants' passions and supports their self-expression.

> Svetlana Nikitina, 2011[2]

In his 1922 preface to a new edition of *The Man of Property*, the first novel in the trilogy he retrospectively called *The Forsyte Saga*, John Galsworthy (1867–1933) justifies describing the three novels as a saga by pointing out that in ancient times 'tribal instinct was even then the prime force, and "family" and the sense of home and property counted as they do to this day'. He would later add several linking novellas and another six novels to his fictions about the Forsytes and their ilk.

Pickled in these pages, the upper middle class lies under glass for strollers in this wide and ill-arranged museum of letters to gaze at. Here it rests, preserved in its own juice.[3]

Opening in the mid-1880s and closing in the early 1930s, the books span some fifty years, a pageant of England through high Victorian complacency, the successive shocks of the Boer War and the First World War, and the cynicism of the post-war years. In none is a house more symbolically important than in the first book of the series, *The Man of Property*. Property, inanimate and animate, is its theme. Robin Hill, an airy hill-top mansion, is the linchpin of the novel and its sequels.

The Forsyte fortunes were made from property. In 1821 'Superior "Dosset" Forsyte', a stonemason of West Country farming stock, moved to London and began buying land and building houses. When the story begins in 1886, his six sons, who have 'inherited a talent for bricks and mortar', are established in dignified houses 'placed at stated intervals' around Hyde Park 'like sentinels'. They and their sisters, children, in-laws and grandchildren criss-cross the park to visit each other.

> The Forsytes are the middlemen, the commercials, the pillars of society, the cornerstones of convention; everything that is admirable![4]

The opening chapter of the novel, '"At Home" at Old Jolyon's', reveals the family as both a safety net and a hive of gossip. Although devoted to Forsyte interests, its members are riven with spite and envy. Their tartly voiced opinions function like a Greek chorus, predicting, condemning and regretting. Through the decades they exhibit, for all their feuds, 'a tenacious unity' in face of London's 'terrible call to individualism'. Their homes are protective shells

> composed of circumstance, property, acquaintances, and wives, which seem to move along with them in their passage through a world composed of thousands of other Forsytes with their habitats.[5]

Galsworthy makes a point of tailoring homes to their occupants, and uses buildings as both nests and cages. Characters look

John Galsworthy at his writing desk in 1929: he was then still at work on short stories about the Forsytes, whose saga he began with *The Man of Property* in 1907.

longingly up at, or out of, windows, and doors repeatedly close or indeed slam. Old Jolyon is the senior member of the family, and his Stanhope Gate mansion is a mix of past and present. The great drawing-room is

brocaded up to the frieze, full of furniture from Baple and
Pullbred's [and] in the huge gilt mirror were reflected those
Dresden china groups of young men in tight knee breeches,
at the feet of full-bosomed ladies nursing on their laps pet
lambs...[6]

But old Jolyon is also ready to take on the future: Stanhope Gate is
one of the first houses in London to be lit by electric light. By contrast Timothy, the youngest of the older Forsytes, lives in a house
more mausoleum than home; he is a remote oracle, ministered to
by his spinster sisters.

The most overtly successful member of the second London
generation of Forsytes is the 'man of property' of the novel's title.
Soames Forsyte is a shrewd 31-year-old lawyer who manages most of
the family's affairs. A connoisseur and collector of fine art, especially
paintings, 'the tragedy of [his] life is the very simple, uncontrollable
tragedy of being unlovable, without quite a thick enough skin to
be thoroughly unconscious of the fact'.[7] The person who loves him
least is his enigmatic, hauntingly beautiful wife Irene.

The gods had given Irene dark brown eyes and golden hair,
that strange combination, provocative of men's glances... [T]he
full soft pallor of her neck and shoulders, above a gold-coloured
frock, gave to her personality an alluring strangeness.[8]

Ever since their marriage, she has regretted giving way to the
'stealthy tenacity' with which he courted her for two years; she
now loathes the sense that he effectively owns her. Soames, like *The
Spoils of Poynton*'s Mrs Gereth, is a cold fish. He 'loves deeply, but
his buried feelings run only in the deep channel of possession',[9] and
of all his possessions Irene is the one he values most.

Their house in Montpelier Square is exquisitely tasteful, and far
more contemporary in feel than the abodes of other Forsytes.

It owned a copper door knocker of individual design, windows
which had been altered to open outwards, hanging flower
boxes filled with fuchsias, and at the back (a great feature) a

little court tiled with jade-green tiles, and surrounded by pink hydrangeas in peacock-blue tubs.

Outward perfection masks inward discontent. At Montpelier Place,

> two kinds of fastidiousness were at war. There lived here a mistress who would have dwelt daintily on a desert island; a master whose daintiness was, as it were, an investment, cultivated by the owner for his advancement…[10]

There is no room there for Soames's collection of pictures, which are, arrestingly,

> nearly all landscapes with figures in the foreground, a sign of some mysterious revolt against London, its tall houses, its interminable streets, where his life and the lives of his breed and class were passed.[11]

Irene wants to leave Soames, but he refuses her the separation he promised as an option if their marriage didn't work. Instead, he decides to build a house in the country to remove her from the many men who admire her. There will be space for his pictures at last. It also suits his business instincts, aware as he is that Londoners were becoming hungry for fresh air. He snaps up a hilltop site south of Richmond Park with glorious views as far as Epsom and the North Downs. His choice of architect combines aesthetic inclination with family solidarity: a rising young architect 'of the new school' called Philip Bosinney, who is engaged to his niece June. Bosinney insists on dictating the interior decorations and furnishings because he follows the fashionable Glasgow School's creed of seeing the house and its interior as a whole. Charles Rennie Mackintosh and his followers were concerned with both form and atmosphere. Their ground plans were models of practicality and comfortable, convenient planning. Much influenced by James McNeill Whistler, they also aimed for a highly charged atmosphere 'of a mystical, symbolic kind… Repose is achieved by broad, unarticulated forms and a neutral background colour such as grey.' Patterned material was taboo, and decorative objects sparse, 'mildly unexpected in the great, restful whole'.[12]

Bosinney is 'an anomaly' in Forsyte eyes, 'like a novel without a plot' because he has no proper home. He lives in a top-floor flat in Sloane Street (then a Bohemian quarter); his sitting room is a mere recess in his office, 'screened off to conceal the necessaries of life – a couch, an easy chair, his pipes, spirit case, novels and slippers'. What Soames doesn't bargain for is the attraction that arises between Bosinney and Irene, an attraction that intensifies as they discuss the plans and the decor of the startlingly unusual Robin Hill. Bosinney has the equally unusual Irene in mind as he designs and fits out the house, rejecting the gabled cosiness of the Arts and Crafts style, and 'the way we load our houses with decoration, gimcracks, corners, anything to distract the eye'.

> On the contrary the eye should rest; get your effects with a
> few strong lines. The whole thing is regularity – there's no
> self-respect without it.[13]

Self-respect is what Bosinney sees that Irene lacks. Robin Hill is a two-storeyed rectangular house designed round a covered-in court. A conduit rather than a cage, it is at one with its airy, hilltop setting. Its huge-windowed freedom is what Irene's heart cries out for, rather than the physical and emotional captivity of being Soames's wife. It is utterly foreign to Soames, who is uneasy outside the ordered arrangements of the London Forsyte homes. However, as a connoisseur of beauty, he is impressed.

> The decoration was really in excellent taste. The dull ruby
> tiles that extended from the foot of the walls to the verge of a
> circular clump of tall iris plants, surrounding in turn a sunken
> basin of white marble filled with water, were obviously of the
> best quality. He admired extremely the purple leather curtains
> drawn along one entire side, framing a huge white-tiled stove.
> The central partitions of the skylight had been slid back, and
> the warm air from outside penetrated into the very heart of the
> house.[14]

Behind the leather curtains is the picture gallery where Soames will be able to hang his paintings. 'Excellent apartments' are provided for servants rather than 'the usual garrets'. Earlier, Galsworthy emphasizes Irene's slave status by saying that 'servants were devoted to Irene, who, in defiance of all safe tradition, appeared to recognise their right to a share in the weaknesses of human nature'; at Robin Hill they too are to be given self-respect.

Soames is, however, nervous that his new house will 'look like a barrack'. He complains that 'there's a lot of room cut to waste'. He also resents the cost of the house and its fittings rising from £8,000 to over £12,000, and the fact that Bosinney is unapologetic, flaring up like a prima donna when his work of art and love is criticized. Hostility mounts between the 'man of property' and Bosinney, who rates integrity of artistic creation far above value for money. Although in Forsyte eyes he appears to 'have no habitat', it is in fact Soames, cocooned in wealth and calculated comfort, who is profoundly homeless.

When Soames realizes that Bosinney and Irene are in love, perhaps having an affair, he sues Bosinney for overspending on Robin Hill, despite the fact that he knows the lawsuit will ruin the impoverished architect. He then 'asserts his rights' over Irene, invading her bedroom to rape her. Now we understand the novel's opening epigraph, 'You will answer / The slaves are ours': part of Shylock's insistence on his pound of flesh in *The Merchant of Venice*. Soames sees Irene as his property. When Bosinney, who has just lost the lawsuit, hears of Irene's rape, he wanders through the London fog utterly distraught, and falls, perhaps throws himself, under the wheels of a carriage.

The Forsytes close ranks after Bosinney's death. Soames puts Robin Hill up for sale, and old Jolyon buys it as a home for himself and his son, young Jolyon and his family. Irene, emotionally shattered, packs and leaves Montpelier Square, but then has no option but to return.

Huddled in her grey fur against the sofa cushions, she had a strange resemblance to a captive owl, bunched in its soft feathers against the wires of a cage. The supple erectness of her figure was gone, as though she had been broken by cruel exercise; as though there were no longer any reason for being beautiful, and supple, and erect.[15]

With circular elegance, the novel that opened '"At Home" at Old Jolyon's' ends with young Jolyon calling on Soames, glimpsing Irene in the doorway of the drawing room, eyes 'wild and eager', hands outstretched in pleading, and Soames slamming the door in his face, and snarling 'we are not at home'. The conventional phrase is literally true.

Before he published *The Man of Property*, Galsworthy had already written two long stories involving members of the Forsyte family, with whom he identified more than a little. His own family was strikingly similar to the Forsytes, with origins in the West Country. His father had a good eye for houses, moving out of a substantial house in London's Portland Place to Parkfield, on Kingston Hill, just before John was born, and buying a fine airy site high on nearby Coombe Hill large enough for the three capacious country houses which he built and occupied successively. The site resembled that of Robin Hill, on a natural terrace close to a coppice of ancient oak trees, with views over woods and fields to the North Downs. John lived in the first, Coombe Warren, until he was 8, in the second, Coombe Leigh, until he was 15, and in the third, Coombe Croft, until he was 19, at which point, in 1886, the whole family moved back to London.

It was perhaps these frequent domestic changes that focused Galsworthy's interest on the importance of a house suiting its occupants. Certainly, his childhood on Coombe Hill created in him a love for the country that endured throughout his life. Old Jolyon, with his sense of fairness and fondness for small children, is a portrait of Galsworthy's father, whom he adored. He was less close to his mother, a fastidious and class-conscious woman obsessed by 'externalities'. Moving frequently is often a sign of something wrong in a marriage, and Galsworthy's parents were indeed ill-suited. His friend Ford Madox Ford wrote: 'There was something pixy-ish and hard about both those old people, the father ferocious, the mother young for her age, flighty, with bright-coloured bonnet ribbons.'[16] They separated in old age.

Unhappy marriages are a recurring theme in Galsworthy's novels, and Irene's plight closely resembled that of his own wife Ada Pearson, who first married his cousin Arthur Galsworthy. John and Ada fell in love, and she was his mistress and muse (he credited her with suggesting he became a writer) for almost a decade before they finally married after Arthur's death. The delay was because John could not bear the idea of his father knowing of the affair. This deceit was in contrast to the openness with which, in *The Man of Property*, young Jolyon incurs the deep disapproval of his father when he divorces his first wife and marries the children's governess. The price of his honesty is that he loses touch with both his father and his children.

A secondary storyline in *The Man of Property* tells of how old Jolyon, lonely after June's engagement to Bosinney, reconnects with his son. Galsworthy, who had originally intended *The Man of Property* as a stand-alone book, wrote a short sequel, *Indian Summer of a Forsyte*, in 1918. It tells how Irene leaves Soames and becomes a music teacher; when she visits Robin Hill to mourn Bosinney, she is befriended first by Old Jolyon and then by the now widowed young Jolyon, who falls in love with her. A new novel, *In Chancery* (1920), deals with Irene's divorce from Soames and marriage to Young Jolyon; they live in Robin Hill.

Galsworthy drew up meticulously detailed drawings of the facade of Robin Hill, its downstairs and upstairs layouts, and a view of the central glass-roofed hall. The house was evidently intensely real to him, and he enjoyed imagining it becoming at last the home of the woman for whom it was built. A studio for Jolyon is added on, and his painting 'deepened and improved'. Once their children are

'The whole thing is regularity – there's no self-respect without it.' Galsworthy drew up meticulously detailed drawings (now in the British Museum) of Robin Hill, the house he imagined Bosinney designing to give Irene Soames the freedom she craved. This is a view of the central glass-roofed hall.

born, the house becomes even more of a home. Nikitina argues that Robin Hill 'helps to reconstitute a family on different terms of intimacy than those that existed in more fashionable quarters of London'.

Robin Hill houses long memories, anchors strong attachments and helps face life's difficulties. It fits all lives together like flagstones on a terrace. Husband and wife, children and parents seem to reside on the same horizontal plane, on the same level – the realm of mutual love with transparent walls and the ceiling ready to receive and share the light.[17]

In strong contrast to the tall, vertically arranged London houses, which shut their occupants away from each other in prescribed spaces, Robin Hill allows connection between the people living in the house and the natural world all around. Frank Lloyd Wright saw such an 'extended horizontal line' as 'the true earth-line of human life, indicative of freedom'.[18] Wright also believed in the unity of house, furnishings and fittings:

> Make a human dwelling-place a complete work of art, in itself expressive and beautiful, intimately related to human life and fit to live in, lending itself more freely and suitably to the individual needs of the dwellers as itself an harmonious entity.[19]

Although Galsworthy published *The Man of Property* three years before Wright's *Studies and Executed Buildings* appeared with German publisher Wasmuth in 1910–11, he was clearly in sympathy with his ideas.

The idea of home, which opens and closes *The Man of Property*, arches over *The Forsyte Saga*. In *To Let* (1921), the third novel, young Jolyon and Irene's son Jon, and Soames and his second wife Annette's daughter Fleur fall in love. But when after his father's death Jon is told of his mother's previous marriage to Soames, and how he raped her, he realizes he must give Fleur up. Standing under the great oak tree that has sheltered three generations of Jolyons at Robin Hill, he and Irene decide to emigrate to Canada, and Robin Hill is let out.

> They stood a few minutes longer under the oak-tree – looking out to where the grand stand at Epsom was veiled in evening. The branches kept the moonlight from them, so that it only fell everywhere else – over the fields and far away, and on the windows of the creepered house behind, which soon would be to let.[20]

The final scene of *To Let* has Soames, the unlovable but oddly touching backbone character of the series, sitting near the family vault on Hampstead Hill and reflecting on the passing of 'the Forsyte age and way of life, when a man owned his soul, his investments, and his woman, without check or question'. In the harsh new world, 'the State had, or would have, his investments, his woman had herself, and God knew who had his soul'. The 'waters of change' were foaming in, he reflects, but he wouldn't resist them. '[T]hey would lapse and ebb, and fresh forms would rise based on an instinct older than the fever of change – the instinct of Home.'

ANCHORAGE

Howards End and E.M. Forster

The novel rises like a piece of architecture before us. It is all
bricks and timber, but it is mystery, idealism, a far-reaching
symbol.

R.A. Scott-James, 1910[1]

My best novel and approaching a good novel. Very elaborate
and all pervading plot that is seldom tiresome or forced, range
of characters, social sense, wit, wisdom, colour. Have only just
discovered why I don't care for it: not a single character for
whom I care… Perhaps the house in H.E., for which I once did
care, took the place of the people.

E.M. Forster, May 1958[2]

'*Howards End* is a hunt for a home' E.M. Forster reflected in 1958.[3]
It is also a wistful love song to a real house: a revisiting of the
profound loss Forster experienced when he left his childhood home
of a decade in 1889. Rooks Nest, the Hertfordshire farmhouse that
he immortalized as the romantically vine-hung and rose-garlanded
Howards End, takes centre stage on the first page of the novel.
Helen Schlegel, a liberal-minded intellectual who is visiting the
Wilcoxes, whom she and her sister Margaret met on holiday,
describes it in a letter home.

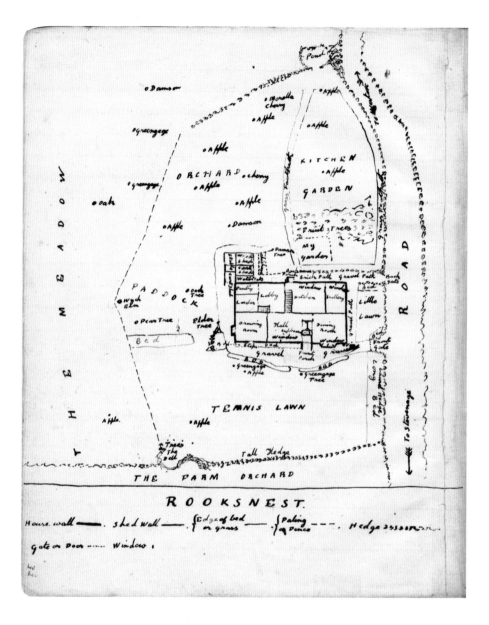

Among the pages of E.M. Forster's autograph manuscript memoir of his childhood home Rooks Nest is a lovingly detailed reconstruction of the layout of the house and its grounds. It is now preserved in the Forster Archive in his last home, King's College, Cambridge. Notice the part of the kitchen garden which he labels 'My Garden' and the damsons, greengages and morello cherry in the orchard.

It is old and little, and altogether delightful – red brick. We can scarcely pack in as it is, and the dear knows what will happen when Paul (younger son) arrives to-morrow. From hall you go right or left into dining-room or drawing-room. Hall itself is practically a room. You open another door in it, and there are the stairs going up in a sort of tunnel to the first-floor. Three bed-rooms in a row there, and three attics in a row above. That isn't all the house really, but it's all that one notices – nine windows as you look up from the front garden. Then there's a very big wych-elm – to the left as you look up – leaning a little over the house, and standing on the boundary between the garden and meadow. I quite love that tree already.[4]

A day later, Helen and Paul kiss 'under the column of the vast wych-elm'. Her next letter announces she is in love, rapidly followed by a telegram to say that it is 'all over'. Paul exits to work for his father's rubber company in Africa, and Helen returns to London and the tall thin house in Wickham Place in which she and Margaret and their brother Tibby have lived all their lives.

Howards End 'fades into Limbo'. It remains, however, of profound importance to Paul's mother Ruth, a 'Holy of Holies'. She was born there, and belongs 'to the house, and to the tree that overshadowed it'. She married Henry Wilcox in order to save it from being pulled down. When the Wilcoxes acquire a London mansion flat overlooking Wickham Place, Ruth, now terminally ill, has a chance encounter with Margaret. Hearing that her family home Wickham Place is to be demolished to build flats, she is shocked: 'To be parted from your house, your father's house – it oughtn't to be allowed', she says. 'It is worse than dying.' She secretly decides to leave Howards End to her. After Ruth's death, the Wilcoxes find a pencilled note to this effect that she scrawled on her deathbed, but agree to ignore it. 'To them Howards End was a house: they could not know that to her it had been a spirit, for which she sought a spiritual heir.' The house goes to Charles, their eldest son, now married to a feather-brained woman aptly called Dolly.

But Fate, or perhaps Ruth Howard's tenacious ghost, intervenes. When his daughter Evie gets engaged, Henry begins to pursue Margaret. Helen disapproves, especially when the career advice that Henry gives to their would-be cultured protégé Leonard Bast ends in Bast losing his job. But Margaret admires Henry's decisive, all-enabling masculinity, and agrees to marry him. She begins a gentle campaign to make him aware of his inner self, hoping to bridge the materialism of the Wilcox outlook and her sister Helen's idealism.

> Only connect! That was the whole of her sermon. Only
> connect the prose and the passion, and both will be exalted,
> and human love will be seen at its height.[5]

Forster, to whom love of home was paramount, uses houses to symbolize both prose and passion. Howards End is the central jewel in a carefully devised setting of other houses, each of them a reflection of character and values. Most of them belong to the Wilcoxes, who acquire houses for prestige and profit. They 'collect houses', quips Helen.

> They have, one, Ducie Street; two, Howards End, where my
> great rumpus was; three, a country seat in Shropshire; four,
> Charles has a house in Hilton; and five, another near Epsom;
> and six, Evie will have a house when she marries, and probably
> a pied-à-terre in the country – which makes seven. Oh yes, and
> Paul a hut in Africa makes eight.[6]

Theirs is the 'civilization of luggage', of furnishings imported wholesale from Maples or the Army & Navy Stores. They drive their cars too fast, and have no sense of the Howards End wych-elm's 'primitive magic', desecrating it by building a garage among its roots for the car that replaces the pony that once grazed in the paddock. After Ruth's death, they rent the house out. When Margaret says, 'Why, I thought of you … as anchored there for ever', Henry replies, 'We like it in a way, but now we feel that it is neither one thing nor the other. One must have one thing or the other.' When Margaret says, 'Houses are alive', Henry answers, 'I'm out of my depth.'

Henry's South Kensington house in Ducie Street is imperiously masculine. Maroon leather armchairs squat in its paved hall for the men to smoke in. 'It was as if a motor car had spawned', thinks Margaret. The dining room has a 'sumptuous dado' and 'gilded wall-paper, amid whose foliage parrots sang'. With its 'heavy chairs', and 'immense side-board loaded with presentation plate', the room is all male.

> Margaret, keen to derive the modern capitalist from the
> warriors and hunters of the past, saw it as an ancient guest-hall,
> where the lord sat at meat among his thanes. Even the Bible –
> the Dutch Bible that Charles had brought back from the Boer
> War – fell into position. Such a room admitted loot.[7]

She accepts Henry, but feels much more at ease in his Shropshire house, Oniton, 'a grey mansion, unintellectual but kindly … the sort of mansion that was built all over England in the beginning of the last century, while architecture was still an expression of the national character'. She is becoming increasingly aware of the importance of living in a house related to both its setting and its occupants. Although aware that the huge house 'would take some digesting', she is determined 'to create new sanctities among these hills'.

She has been more affected than she had expected by the loss of Wickham Place, the house in which the Schlegel siblings were born and in which they have spent all their lives. They had been too busy living 'a life of cultured but not ignoble ease, … swimming gracefully on the grey tides of London', to recognize its value. Margaret realizes that its loss 'had taught her more than its possession'. She now values its lining of the family's books and furniture:

> Round every knob and cushion in the house sentiment
> gathered, a sentiment that was at times personal, but more
> often a faint piety to the dead, a prolongation of rites that
> might have ended at the grave.[8]

Linings matter. Howards End's original furniture has been installed in Oniton, one reason that Margaret finds it congenial. She visits the old farmhouse for the first time when its tenant absconds. Even though it is empty and filthy and neglected she can see that its many rooms could be filled with children playing and friends finding shelter. She admires the 'peculiar glory' of the wych-elm, superstitiously studded with pigs' teeth, towering protectively over the house, 'a comrade, bending over the house, strength and adventure in its roots, but in its utmost fingers tenderness'. She even fancies that she hears 'the heart of the house beating, faintly at first, then loudly, *martially*'. The noise is in fact Mrs Avery, a neighbour who had been a close friend of Ruth and deeply in tune with her, descending the hidden staircase. 'I took you for Ruth Wilcox', she says to Margaret, 'You had her way of walking.' She returns to London, happily musing on the sense of space at Howards End, its 'ruddy bricks' and 'flowering plum-trees' that seem the essence of England. After Wickham Place is demolished, Henry offers Howards End as a warehouse for the Schlegels' belongings. So 'the bulk of the things went country-ways, and were entrusted to the guardianship of Miss Avery.'

The domestic circumstances of the Schlegels and the Wilcoxes reflect their wealth. 'You and I and the Wilcoxes stand upon money as upon islands', Margaret says to Helen. 'It is so firm beneath our feet that we forget its very existence. It's only when we see some one near us tottering that we realise all that an independent income means.' The Basts are severely compromised by their poverty. Their basement flat is south of the river in Camelia Road, in a block of flats 'constructed with extreme cheapness'. Stuffed with ugly rented furniture, its draped mantelpiece 'bristling with Cupids', only these, the books and a photograph frame belong to Leonard. '[I]t struck that shallow makeshift note that is so often heard in the modem dwelling-place.' Leonard, who met the Schlegels after Helen accidentally took his umbrella away after a performance of Beethoven's Fifth Symphony, is a touchingly honest failed hero. He has cultural aspirations. He reads Ruskin's *The Stones of Venice*, plays Grieg, and spends a whole night walking out of London into the country, in part in emulation of his literary heroes George Borrow, Richard Jeffries and Robert Louis Stevenson, in part because his own roots are among country folk. But he loyally stands by the vulgar wife who caused his respectable family to cut ties with him.

Disaster strikes when Helen gatecrashes Evie's Oniton wedding with the Basts to appeal for help for them, and it turns out that Leonard's wife Jackie was Henry's mistress ten years earlier. She and the Basts are hustled away. Soon afterwards, Helen leaves for Germany after asking her brother Tibby to send half her fortune to the Basts. Leonard refuses to accept it, and the Basts continue to sink financially. Nothing is heard of Helen for eight months, by which time Oniton has been sold and Margaret and Henry are married and planning a house in Sussex. Helen, still refusing to meet Margaret, returns to England, and goes to Howards End to collect her books, only to discover that Mrs Avery, mystically in tune with Ruth's wish that Margaret should live there, has unpacked their furniture and made a home of the house for them. She has put an old cradle in one bedroom and hung the family sword over the fireplace. Need for the loved relics of home and her books is what brought Helen back from Germany to Howards End, and when she sees their furniture lining the house with memories her first impulse is to improve on Miss Avery's arrangements.

The novel rises to a climax when Margaret ambushes Helen at Howards End, and discovers that she is expecting Leonard Bast's baby. In an angry confrontation with Henry, Margaret defends the Schlegels' spiritual and liberal values against the bully-boy hypocrisy of the Wilcoxes, and tells him she is going back to Germany with Helen. She stays the night with Helen at Howards End; as if foreseeing this, Mrs Avery had earlier sent a boy with milk. Next morning, just as Charles Wilcox arrives to expostulate with the Schlegels, a sick and weary Leonard turns up in an attempt at atonement.

At the sight of Helen's 'seducer', Charles grabs the Schlegel family sword to thrash him with, but before he does Leonard keels over, pulling a bookcase full of books over himself, and dies of a heart attack. Charles is convicted of manslaughter and imprisoned for three years. Shamed and broken, Henry accepts Margaret's loving care and lives with her, Helen and the new baby at Howards End, having made his children accept that he is leaving the house to Margaret in the first instance and then to Leonard's baby. At this point, Dolly lets the cat out of the bag:

> It does seem curious that Mrs. Wilcox should have left
> Margaret Howards End, and yet she gets it after all.[9]

Later, Margaret asks Henry about this, and when she hears the story of the scribbled note, 'something shook her life in its inmost recesses'. Ruth's will has somehow driven events. The novel ends at the time of year in which it began, with Helen and her baby rejoicing as the meadow is cut for hay.

Making Leonard Bast's son the heir to Howards End emphasizes Forster's sympathy with aspiring working men (he taught in the Working Men's College in Great Ormond Street between 1902 and 1911). Margaret voices his longing for a return to the ancient rhythms and rootedness of country life.

> In these English farms, if anywhere, one might see life steadily
> and see it whole, group in one vision its transitoriness and its
> eternal youth, connect – connect without bitterness until all
> men are brothers.[10]

Howards End, now lived in by people who cherish it, and with an heir whose ancestors lived a rural life, symbolizes hope.

E.M. Forster (1879–1970) was affected all his adult life by a sense of being displaced, of lacking a real home. He liked nothing better than houses connected in some way with his family. 'A house gives security. It is an anchorage', he wrote to Faith Culme-Seymour.[11] Nicola Beauman expands on this in her 1993 biography:

E.M. Forster was affected all his adult life by a sense of being displaced, of lacking a real home. Here he poses shyly in a lane near Garsington Manor, in 1910, for his redoubtable hostess Lady Ottoline Morrell, a keen amateur photographer.

Disappearing houses, people displaced from their normal surroundings, the importance of an ancestral home, the genius loci, spirit of the place, and the need to cherish it are a constant theme in his work.[12]

He also lacked a father. Eddie Forster, an architect, to whom houses and families were as important as they would be to his son, died when Morgan was twenty months old. The family was then living in London in Melcombe Place, a house similar to the Schegels' Wickham Place. After his father died his mother Lily embarked on a round of visits, which must have been unsettling for the little boy. When he was 4 they had to leave Melcombe Place as it was to be demolished to make way for the building of Marylebone railway station. Lily, whose entire life revolved around her son, decided to move out into the country. In 1879 she took a lease on a house near Stevenage called Rooks Nest. Its original name was Howards, after the family that had once lived there, A small house, without mains water or electricity, it left an indelible impression on Forster. He claimed that it formed his 'middle-class and atavistic' attitude to life and society. It certainly gave him stability during that most formative of life's decades, the years between 4 and 14.

> I took it to my heart and hoped ... that I should live and die there. We were out of it in ten years. The impressions received there remained and still glow – not always distinguishably, always inextinguishably.[13]

The first piece of sustained writing that he undertook was a nine-page description of his childhood at Rooks Nest, written soon after he and Lily left it, when he was at Tonbridge School. He details its floor plan with the exactness of an estate agent, describing the red and blue stone squares on the kitchen floor, the yellow bricks on that of the larder, the unexpectedness of the stairs behind one of the doors in the hall (something Margaret is struck by at Howards End), the generously sized upstairs rooms, and the 'mingled odour of apples, mice and jam' in the upstairs store cupboard and the three attics. He longed to own the house, but the Postons, who also owned the neighbouring farm, refused to sell what was in truth their family home. He remained faithful to it all his life, fighting a 1946 proposal to build the London satellite town of Stevenage, which he felt would fall like a meteorite on 'the ancient and delicate scenery of Hertfordshire'. On one of several visits he made to Rooks Nest in later life, when it was the home of the composer Elizabeth Poston, he wrote:

> This house is my childhood and my safety. The three attics preserve me. Only a little of my passion and irrationality was used up in *Howards End*.[14]

Today a sculpture inscribed 'Only Connect', the most famous line in *Howards End*, marks the entrance to Forster Country, a path leading from St Nicholas Church to a panorama of fields and hedges. The fame of Forster's novel has ensured the preservation of both the house and its immediate setting.

The last significant house in Forster's life was West Hackhurst, the house at Abinger designed for his aunt Laura Forster by his father; it in turn was inspired by the layout of Eddie and Laura's family home, Stisted Rectory. After Laura's death in 1925, Forster and his mother moved there, and stayed until Lily's death in 1945. At this point, aged 66, he moved into King's College, Cambridge, where he remained until his death in 1970. Furniture from the Rooks Nest drawing room – a many-shelved overmantel made by his father, a fender, a carpet and a writing desk – had followed him and his mother from house to house. They were installed in his rooms in King's. I had tea with him there in 1965. He talked of dreams, and how he recorded his own immediately on waking. Aged 86, he resembled a benevolent tortoise, permanently sheltered in a shell resonant with his past.[15]

COLOSSAL ILLUSION
West Egg and F. Scott Fitzgerald

There was music from my neighbor's house through the
summer nights. In his blue gardens men and girls came and
went like moths among the whisperings and the champagne
and the stars.

F. Scott Fitzgerald, *The Great Gatsby*, 1925[1]

The central role of Gatsby's house in his dream of Daisy
becomes increasingly clear: it has to prove to her that he has
attained her exclusive world of great wealth and now has a 'real
right to touch her hand'.

Kathleen Parkinson, 1988[2]

From the very beginning of *The Great Gatsby*, Francis Scott Fitzgerald (1896–1940) emphasizes the spectacularly artificial and un-
homely nature of the dwelling that dominates the story. A crazy
hotchpotch of architectural styles on the north side of 'slender,
riotous' Long Island, east of New York City, its 'feudal silhouette'
resembles a turreted Normandy Hôtel de Ville, 'with a tower
on one side, spanking new under a thin beard of raw ivy, and
marble swimming pool and more than forty acres of land'. Inside
it has 'Marie Antoinette music rooms and Restoration salons'. An
'important-looking door' leads into 'a high Gothic library, panelled
with English oak, and probably transported complete from some

ruin overseas'. To the amazement of an 'owl-eyed' drunk who is swaying on the edge of a huge table, the books are real. 'What thoroughness! What realism!' he observes admiringly. 'Knew when to stop too – didn't cut the pages.' Upstairs there are 'period bedrooms swathed in rose and lavender silk … dressing rooms and poolrooms and bathrooms with sunken baths'. Jazz throbs from its windows when it is gaudily lit up for parties.

The 1920s were riotous times. 'The whole upper tenth of a nation living with the insouciance of grand dukes and the casualness of chorus girls', Scott Fitzgerald wrote in a 1931 article; 'the Jazz Age now raced along under its own power, served by great filling stations full of money.'[3] West Egg is a vibrant symbol of the degeneracy and excess of the Jazz Age, a term Scott claimed he coined. The mysterious and immensely wealthy Jay Gatsby's palace was built ten years earlier 'in the "period" craze'. It has every possible luxury, but no home comfort, and Gatsby's relationship with it is at arm's length. It is a tool. He chose it because it could be seen and he hopes admired by the love of his life, Daisy Fay, who lives with her husband Tom Buchanan and their 3-year-old daughter across the bay on the twin promontory of East Egg. White colonial mansions along their shore signal it as the home of old money, 'the staid nobility of the countryside'. West Egg is, by contrast, full of 'spectroscopic gaiety', a mix of bootleggers, dubious financiers and film producers. To capture Daisy's interest, Gatsby regularly lights up his palatial residence like a funfair and fills it with partying people. After they leave, he wanders down to the shore and gazes across the water at the distant green light which shines from the jetty of Daisy and Tom's house.

Gatsby's pretentious monstrosity of a house is presented in a succession of different moods in the course of the novel. It looms over the book's restless central characters: Gatsby, Daisy and Tom Buchanan, the narrator Nick Carraway (initially critical of Gatsby but finally admiring) and the cool, self-contained Jordan Baker, with whom Nick has a tepid affair. They are mid-western Americans (like Fitzgerald himself), lured to New York because that is where the action is socially and financially. Home is a place to show off in. They are constantly on the move by car or train between Long Island and Manhattan. Gold and green, the colours of money, recur in descriptions of the Buchanans; Gatsby is associated with silver, stars and moonlight. He is wildly unrealistic about Daisy. She is the fairy-tale princess in a tower, his grail quest.

Dividing the glitzy seaside suburb and New York is a 'valley of ashes' created by the vast waste-burning operation of Flushing Meadows, the grey desert home of the underclasses, 'where ashes take the forms of houses and chimneys and rising smoke' and 'ash-grey men swarm up with leaden spades'. Fitzgerald, much influenced by T.S. Eliot's *The Waste Land* (1922), uses it to signal the hollowness at the heart of divided American society; it also evokes Eliot's 'The Hollow Men' (1925), and the entrance to hell in Dante's *Inferno*.

A faded oculist's hoarding showing blue eyes gazing over this 'solemn dumping ground' through a giant pair of spectacles obsesses

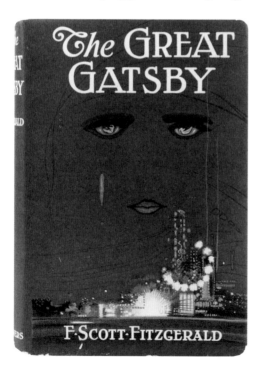

The Spanish artist Francis Cugat designed the unforgettable original cover of *The Great Gatsby* while the book was being written: it combined a vision of the unattainable Daisy, whose disembodied face appears to drift above the spectacular funfair of Gatsby's palatial West Egg mansion, and Scott Fitzgerald's powerful image of giant eyes on an oculist's billboard brooding over the wasteland between West Egg and New York.

George Wilson, the 'anaemic' and 'spiritless' garage owner whose vibrantly alive wife Myrtle is Tom Buchanan's mistress. Wilson believes that the hoarding shows God is watching and judging them; at the tragic climax of the novel he carries out what he thinks is God's sentence on Gatsby.

We see the characters through the eyes of Nick Carraway, cousin of Daisy Fay and neighbour of Gatsby. His 'weather-beaten cardboard bungalow' is crammed between Gatsby's house and another huge mansion. When Gatsby discovers through Jordan Baker that Nick knows Daisy, he invites him to one of his parties. He meets Jordan again, and eventually Gatsby himself, 'an elegant young rough-neck a year or two over thirty, whose elaborate formality of speech just missed being absurd', but whose rare smile had 'a quality of eternal reassurance in it'. After the party, the guests ebb away 'in a caterwauling crescendo'.

> A sudden emptiness seemed to flow now from the windows and
> the great doors, endowing with complete isolation the figure
> of the host, who stood on the porch, his hand up in a formal
> gesture of farewell.[4]

Nick notes the pretentious mongrel names of those who accept Gatsby's hospitality during the summer (the Stonewall Jackson Abrams, Mrs Ulysses Swett, Eckhart and Clive Cohen, Clarence Endive and the virtually resident Klipspringer). He finds they pay Gatsby 'the subtle tribute of knowing nothing about him'.

> 'He's a bootlegger,' said the young ladies, moving somewhere
> between his cocktails and his flowers. 'One time he killed
> a man who had found out that he was nephew to Von
> Hindenburg and second cousin to the devil.'[5]

Gatsby offers Nick a patently untrue version of his past as he drives him through the valley of ashes to have tea with Jordan in the city.

> I lived like a young rajah in all the capitals of Europe – Paris,
> Venice, Rome – collecting jewels, chiefly rubies, hunting big

game, painting a little … trying to forget something very sad that had happened to me long ago.[6]

Nick discovers from more reliable sources that Gatsby is entirely self-made: initially the protégé of Dan Cody, a yachtsman smuggler, later involved in scams with Meyer Wolfsheim, a professional gambler. But he sympathizes with him more and more, especially when Jordan tells him that three years ago Daisy had tried to back out of her wedding to Tom when she heard that Gatsby, her first lover and something of a war hero, had returned from Europe. Jordan adds that Daisy is far from happy with Tom and that Gatsby has asked her to get Nick to invite Daisy to tea, so that he can happen by and invite her to see his mansion, and how much he can offer her.

When Nick returns to West Egg that night, he sees Gatsby's house 'lit up from tower to cellar' as if for a party. But when he strolls over, nobody is there except Gatsby himself; he has been 'glancing into some of the rooms', anticipating Daisy's visit. He had thrown himself into 'the colossal vitality of his illusion' with 'creative passion, adding to it all the time, decking it out with every bright feather that drifted his way'. When Daisy eventually visits, the house is splendid but weirdly unpeopled; they troop through the numberless rooms, with Daisy uttering 'enchanting murmurs'. They end up drinking Chartreuse in Gatsby's own strikingly simple apartment, a Robert Adam-style study and a bedroom only adorned with a toilet set of pure, dull gold.

> He hadn't once ceased looking at Daisy and I think he
> revalued everything in the house according to the measure of
> response it drew from her well-loved eyes. Sometimes, too, he
> stared around at his possessions in a dazed way, as though in
> her actual and astounding presence none of it was any longer
> real. Once he nearly toppled down a flight of stairs.[7]

Nick leaves them gazing at each other, 'possessed by intense life'.

Over the next few weeks, Tom Buchanan's suspicions mount. He calls on Gatsby, makes enquiries about his background, and discovers the dubious sources of his wealth. Resentful of Daisy's frequent absences, he goes with her to Gatsby's next party. The house's atmosphere sours. It has 'the same profusion of champagne, the same many-coloured, many-keyed commotion', but also 'an unpleasantness in the air, a pervading harshness'. Tom refuses to be impressed by the celebrities of whom Gatsby boasts, and Daisy is increasingly uneasy about the vulgarity of the guests. '[T]he whole caravansary had fallen in like a card house at the disapproval in her eyes.' Nevertheless, her love affair with Gatsby flowers, and he ordains a new, party-less era for the house. She visits him in the afternoons, and to lessen gossip new servants are taken on.

Then Gatsby takes his siege a step further, visiting Tom in the Buchanans' own house, a restrained and elegant white mansion. Both men are taken aback: Gatsby by the way Daisy's home is so right for her and by the sight of her little daughter, Tom by the realization that Daisy is in love with Jay. They hide from the situation in a wild drive in each other's cars to New York; as they drive past the Wilsons' garage, Myrtle sees Tom at the wheel of Gatsby's distinctive yellow car. In the neutral ground of a suite in the Plaza Hotel, Gatsby makes his bid for Daisy and, despite her refusal to deny that she had ever loved Tom, thinks he has won her. They return to Long Island, with Daisy at the wheel of Gatsby's car. Myrtle dashes out to it to escape her jealous husband and is hit by the car, but Daisy doesn't stop; Tom, following with Nick and Jordan, stops to find Myrtle is dead, assumes that Gatsby was driving, and vengefully tells Wilson where to find him.

Motor cars are both prestigious and dangerous in *Gatsby*, sweeping characters from one stage set of a house to another, imperilling life. Similarly restless movement was imprinted in Scott Fitzgerald from childhood. His wealthy mother was never satisfied for long with the same house in Saint Paul, Minnesota, often only moving a few streets away. The chronology of Fitzgerald's life at the end of Andrew Turnbull's biography reveals that he rarely spent more than a year in any one place.[8] He was ceaselessly going on holiday, shifting hotels

Gatsby's palatial mansion in West Egg closely resembles the spectacular Gothic fantasy of Beacon Towers. Built at Sands Point on the shore of Long Island Sound for the millionairess Alva Belmont, it was in its heyday when Scott Fitzgerald and Zelda were living in nearby Great Neck. It was demolished in 1945.

frequently. 'With people like us, our home is where we are not', says Monsignor D'Arcy to Amory Blaine in Fitzgerald's first book, *This Side of Paradise* (1920), a fictional version of his years at Princeton. He returned home to write it in the attic of the most permanent of his parents' St Paul homes, 599 Summit Avenue, 'a mausoleum of American architectural monstrosities'.

He was then in love with Zelda Sayre, a Southern belle, in July 1918, whom he met while serving as a second lieutenant at Camp Sheridan in Montgomery, Alabama. Although she was as much in love with him as he was with her, she hesitated at the idea of marrying when his income was so uncertain. The success of *Paradise* gave Fitzgerald the wherewithal to marry. Zelda was utterly undomesticated, and as eager for change as he was. 'I hate a room without an open suitcase in it; it seems so permanent', she is reputed to have said. Scott and Zelda moved house often; they were, he wrote in a memoir of New York entitled 'My Lost City' (1935), 'like small children in a great, bright, unexplored barn'. In October 1922 they moved to 6 Gateway Drive in Great Neck, Long Island, the rail head of the New York and Flushing Railway. Great Neck was the junction point of a pair of promontories, Kings Point and Sands Point, and the area was an expensive suburb of Manhattan. Zelda called the house 'a nifty little Babbitt-home',[9] and it was more like Nick Carraway's modest bungalow than Tom Buchanan's colonial mansion or Gatsby's hybrid palace. Neither Scott nor Zelda ever became domestic, but they came closest to it at Gateway Drive, employing a couple to keep house for them and a nurse for their baby daughter Scottie, who was born on 26 October 1922.[10]

Life in Great Neck led Fitzgerald to plan 'something new – something extraordinary and beautiful and simple and intricately patterned'. He began work on *Gatsby*. Daisy Fay Buchanan was inspired by Scott Fitzgerald's first love, a Chicago debutante called Ginevra King. They had been passionately close for two years before her father warned Scott off with words that would appear in *The Great Gatsby*: 'poor boys shouldn't think of marrying rich girls'. Scott saved her letters all his life, and phrases from them recur in his books. The Points were re-created as vulgar West Egg and upper-crust East Egg. Gatsby's house was inspired in part by a monstrous turreted folly on the shore of Sands Point called Beacon Towers. Built in 1917 for the wealthy socialite Alva Belmont, it was later owned by William Randolph Hearst.[11] In May 1924 the Fitzgeralds crossed the Atlantic, and *Gatsby* was largely written on the Riviera while Zelda was having an affair with a young French pilot; a situation that added to the ferocity of Tom Buchanan's jealousy.

After the tragic accident at the Wilsons' garage, Nick is waiting for a taxi on the Buchanans' East Egg drive. Gatsby looms out of the darkness and tells him that he has arranged for Daisy to signal to him if Tom 'tries any brutality' after the 'unpleasantness'. But when Nick peers in through a window, he sees husband and wife around a supper table in the kitchen, Tom's hand on Daisy's.

There was an unmistakable air of natural intimacy about the picture and anybody would have said that they were conspiring together.[12]

Gatsby maintains his 'vigil' until the lights are extinguished, then returns to his deserted mansion. Nick, unable to sleep, calls by and finds him alone and dejected.

His house had never seemed so enormous to me as it did that night when we hunted through the great rooms for cigarettes... There was an inexplicable amount of dust everywhere and the rooms were musty... 'Jay Gatsby' had broken up like glass against Tom's hard malice, and the long, secret extravaganza was played out.[13]

As Gatsby tells Nick of how he first met and fell in love with Daisy, describing her beautiful family home in detail, we realize that she will never take the gamble of giving up her privileged world for his rackety one. But 'he had committed himself to the following of a grail ... He felt married to her.' When Nick leaves, he turns to see Gatsby, utterly alone, waving with 'a radiant and understanding smile..., his gorgeous pink rag of a suit a bright spot of colour against the white steps'.

The final image of Gatsby sees him lying on an inflated mattress in his swimming pool among fallen autumn leaves, with 'an ashen, fantastic figure gliding toward him through the amorphous trees'. George Wilson shoots him through the heart, then shoots himself. After the funeral, attended only by Nick, Jay's father (who reveals much about Jay's boyhood ambitions to 'get ahead'), and the 'owl-eyed man' who so admired the library, the house, now notorious and defaced with graffiti, is left deserted, weeds and wilderness encroaching. Going down to the beach, Nick imagines 'the inessential houses' melting away, and the return of 'the old island here that flowered once for Dutch sailors' eyes – a fresh green breast of the new world'.[14] He broods on Gatsby's tragic failure to achieve his dream, ambivalent about such efforts to stretch out arms to the future. 'So we beat on, boats against the current, borne back ceaselessly into the past.'

Gatsby is determined to turn the tide of time when he creates his honeytrap for Daisy. Fitzgerald must frequently have wished to do the same, as he descended into a decadent cycle of drinking and partying that destroyed his and Zelda's physical and mental health; she developed schizophrenia in 1930, and spent most of the rest of her life in care. He used this experience in the fine but bleak *Tender Is the Night* (1934), and that of his later years in Hollywood in the unfinished *The Last Tycoon* (1941). In 1940 he died of a heart attack aged only 44. Zelda, who developed into a remarkable painter, but became increasingly manic, outlived him by only six years.

Houses never became homes for Scott Fitzgerald. In a curious little 1936 essay written for *Esquire* magazine entitled 'Author's House', he sustains an extended metaphor of a house which represents his own life and psyche. In its dark and damp cellar is 'everything I've forgotten … all the complicated dark mixture of my youth and infancy that made me a fiction writer instead of a fireman or a soldier'. He points to a dark corner and says: 'That is where I buried my first childish love of myself, my belief that I would never die like other people, and that I wasn't the son of my parents but a son of a king, a king who ruled the whole world.'

He meanders through the house until he reaches the attic, stuffed with hoarded school books, magazines, maps and letters. 'This is a sort of a library in its way, you see – the library of a life', he announces. 'And nothing is as depressing as a library if you stay long in it.' Finally he takes his visitor up to the rooftop turret, an echo of his parents' St Paul house.

> 'I lived up here once,' the author said after a moment.
>> 'Here? For a long time?'
>> 'No. For just a little while when I was young.'
>> 'It must have been rather cramped.'
>> 'I didn't notice it.'
>> 'Would you like to try it again?'
>> 'No. And I couldn't if I wanted to.'
> He shivered slightly and closed the windows.[15]

Sales of *The Great Gatsby* were disappointing in Fitzgerald's lifetime, but it is now rightly reckoned to be his masterpiece. The book's intensity and elegance, and the economy of its writing, are unforgettable. 'There are pages so artfully contrived that one can no more imagine improvising them than one can imagine improvising a fugue', wrote the respected literary critic H.L. Mencken. 'They are full of little delicacies; charming turns of phrase, penetrating second thoughts. … They are easy and excellent reading – which is what always comes out of hard writing.'[16]

THE QUEEREST SENSE
OF ECHO

Knole, Virginia Woolf & Vita Sackville-West

> Suppose Orlando turns out to be Vita and it's all about you ...
> suppose there's the kind of shimmer of reality which sometimes
> attaches itself to my people, as the lustre on an oyster shell...
> shall you mind?
>
> Virginia Woolf to Vita Sackville-West, 9 October, 1927[1]

> Knole was like a lover to her, and that is why houses and the
> idea of inheritance play such an important part in her books.
>
> Nigel Nicolson, 1966[2]

The best-known appearance in fiction of the magnificent Tudor
palace of Knole, near Sevenoaks in Kent, is in Virginia Woolf's
exuberant magical realist fantasy *Orlando* (1928), an affectionate
tribute to her friend Vita Sackville-West (1892–1962). Vita was
obsessed by Knole. She would have inherited it had it not been
entailed in the male line. She repeatedly celebrated it in her own
writings, especially her novel *The Edwardians* (1930). The different
purpose to which the great house is put in the two novels can only
be understood in the context of the intense and rewarding friendship between Virginia and Vita which began in 1922.

Although the great house in *Orlando* is never given a name, there
is no doubt that it is based upon Knole, informed by Vita's lively

history *Knole and the Sackvilles* (1922), which Virginia borrowed soon after meeting her. Its '365 bedrooms' suggest that, like Knole, it is a calendar house, designed with seven courts, twelve entrances, and fifty-two staircases. Knole is also recognizably the great house of Chevron in *The Edwardians*, 'spread out like a medieval village with its square turrets and its grey walls, its hundred chimneys sending blue threads up into the air'. Vita's descriptions of Knole in her history and of Chevron in her novel are all but interchangeable; those in her history are if anything more imbued with romance. She describes the house as 'gentle and venerable', with

> the deep inward gaiety of some very old woman who has always been beautiful, who has had many lovers and seen many generations come and go, smiled wisely over their sorrows and their joys, and learnt an imperishable secret of tolerance and humour.[3]

Vita was the only child of Lionel Sackville-West, 3rd Baron Sackville. She was born at Knole in 1892, and it remained her home until 1913, when she was married in its chapel to the diplomat Harold Nicolson (1886–1968). It was always more of a person to her than a house, an ever-present source of comfort into which she could escape her formidable, ruthless and critical mother Victoria, who 'wounded and dazzled and fascinated and charmed me by turns'.[4] She roamed its 26 acres of buildings and gardens and the thousand-acre estate, and read avidly in her father's library. Constantly scribbling, she had written (though not published) five novels (one in French) and five plays by the time she was 18, all tucked away in an elaborate inlaid cabinet given to her by her mother.

Her writings are haunted by her lost inheritance. *The Heir*, published in 1922, is a delightful tale of wish-fulfilment rather in the style of H.G. Wells. A Wolverhampton insurance salesman finds that he has inherited an ancient house in Kent. At first he goes along with everybody's assumption that he will simply sell it, but recklessly rebels at the eleventh hour against doing so. His credo, and Vita's, comes in the last chapter:

The Cartoon Gallery at Knole, named for its copies of Raphael's cartoons for the Sistine Chapel tapestries. This 1844 watercolour by Joseph Nash shows its elaborately carved fireplace and the delicate plasterwork of its ceiling; figures in Elizabethan dress re-create life in the age of Elizabeth. It hung at Knole when Virginia Woolf explored it for inspiration for *Orlando*.

To know what one really wanted, what one really cared for, and go for it straight. Wasn't that a good and simple enough worldly wisdom?[5]

In 1923, she published her edition of the diaries of her ancestress by marriage Lady Anne Clifford, a strong-minded woman who fought effectively to inherit her Westmorland estates despite being a woman. Vita also wrote poetry singing Knole's praises. She had her own garden at Knole, and was a gifted plantswoman, passionately sensitive to nature.

Although forced to face the fact that Knole could never be hers, Vita found solace in acting the ideal heir. Her glamorous, mannish persona was irresistible to men and women alike. Before she married Harold, she had turned down two heirs to dukedoms, and continued having liaisons with women throughout her life. She

Conversations – about life, literature, love, sex, friendships and families – were the most important part of the friendship of Virginia Woolf and Vita Sackville-West. They provided mutual literary inspiration: both wrote books centring around Vita's home, the Tudor mansion of Knole, Sevenoaks, Kent. They are seen here on the lawn of Monks House, near Lewes, in 1933.

first met Virginia Woolf (1882–1942) in 1922 at a supper given by Virginia's brother-in-law, Clive Bell. Virginia was 40, esteemed for her writings in highbrow literary circles but little known beyond them. Vita was 30 and widely fêted as the author of several popular novels and collections of poetry. 'I simply adore Virginia, and so would you', she wrote to her husband Harold. 'She is utterly unaffected. She dresses atrociously. I've rarely taken such a fancy to anyone.' Virginia, awed but cagey, was less fulsome, describing

Vita in her diary as 'florid, moustached, parakeet-coloured, with all the supple ease of the aristocracy, but not the wit of the artist'. She was 'not much to my severe taste', and made her feel 'virgin, shy, & schoolgirlish'. However, Virginia was in need of a new female literary sounding-board after the unexpectedly sudden death of Katherine Mansfield, with whom she had had 'an oddly complete understanding'.

> A woman caring as I care for writing is rare enough I suppose to give me the queerest sense of echo coming back to me from her mind the second after I've spoken.[6]

Vita had a quite differently shaped gap in her life left by the ending of her long and tempestuous affair with the flamboyant Violet Trefusis. It had involved many escapades and much cross-dressing, produced two novels, and survived both their marriages. It finally burnt out in 1921, when Denys Trefusis and Harold Nicolson flew out to Amiens to confront the runaways. Although Vita would continue to have what Harold referred to as 'muddles' with other women, writing better books became her primary ambition, and she found Virginia a discriminating mentor.

Written and spoken conversations – about life, literature, love, sex, friendships and families – were the most important part of their relationship. Virginia was fascinated by the echoes of her own difficulties with parents and siblings in Vita's exaggerated and exotic confessions. She soon perceived that Vita was

> a pronounced Sapphist, & may, thinks Ethel Sands, have an eye on me, old though I am. Nature may have sharpened her faculties. Snob as I am, I trace her passions 500 years back & they become romantic to me, like old yellow wine.[7]

Increasingly appreciative of Vita's physical beauty, flattered by her admiration, dazzled by her aristocratic nonchalance, intellectually interested, emotionally moved, and always interested in experiment that might make good copy, Virginia wrote flirtatious letters to her new confidante, and received much more explicit epistles in return. The relationship trembled on the brink of physicality, but their 'affair', even at its height, was, Vita assured Harold, 'a mental thing, a spiritual thing ... an intellectual thing', because she was well aware of Virginia's fragile mental state and her nervousness about sex.[8] They shared a bed on a few occasions, but all the experience did was confirm Virginia's belief that she was not a lesbian, but rather 'a eunuch ... someone who pulls the shade over the fury of sex'.[9] Physical passion subsided into 'a warm-slipper friendship'.[10]

The friendship cooled somewhat when Virginia's snobbery led to her resentment at being seen as one of Vita's Sapphic coterie.[11] However, the intimate and fruitful conversation between them continued for over a decade, a decade in which both produced the bulk of their best work.

In 1926 came the publication of Vita's long poem *The Land*, a celebration of the Weald of Kent past and present in winter, spring, summer and autumn. It was awarded the prestigious Hawthornden Prize for imaginative literature in 1927. Later that year Virginia, who had just finishing writing *To the Lighthouse* (1927), mused in her diary about writing

> a biography beginning in the year 1500 & continuing to the present day, called *Orlando*: Vita; only with a change about from one sex to another.[12]

So was born the book that Vita's son Nigel called 'the longest and most charming love letter in history', in which 'she explores Vita, weaves her in and out of the centuries, tosses her from one sex to the other, plays with her, dresses her in furs, lace and emeralds, teases her, flirts with her, drops a veil of mist around her, and ends by photographing her in the mud at Long Barn, with dogs'.[13]

Virginia had visited Vita at Knole on several occasions. The first, on 5 July 1924, is described in her diary with a combination of mystified admiration and socialist resentment:

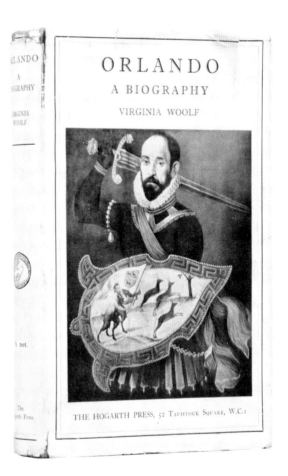

To emphasize the relationship of Virginia Woolf's *Orlando* to the great house of Knole, the cover of the first edition of the book reproduced a photograph of a portrait of a Tudor nobleman, then in the Worthing Art Gallery, sadly destroyed by a bomb during World War II. The novel was an instant success, selling 11,000 copies in its first year.

His lordship lives in the kernel of a vast nut. You perambulate miles and miles of galleries; skip endless treasures – chairs that Shakespeare might have sat on, tapestries, pictures, floors made of the halves of oaks & penetrate at length to a round shiny table ... [where] one solitary peer sits lunching by himself ... his napkin folded into the shape of a lotus flower.[14]

In October she told Vita of her plans for *Orlando*, a novel about 'a nobleman afflicted with a love of literature', and said that she was rereading *Knole and the Sackvilles*, adding (conflating person and house), 'Dear me; you know a lot: you have a rich dusky attic of a mind.' She began writing, with a fluidity and speed that astonished her. The lovely but coarse Muscovite princess with whom Orlando falls in love is Violet Trefusis; the hare-like Archduchess Harriet is Vita's ducal suitor Lord Lascelles, and the dashing explorer Marmaduke Shelmerdine Bonthrop is Harold Nicolson.[15] But the spine of the novel is the house, to which Orlando returns time and again for reassurance and literary inspiration, just as Vita did.

> [W]hen the door was shut, and he was certain of privacy, he would have out an old writing book, stitched together with silk stolen from his mother's workbox, and labelled in a round schoolboy hand, 'The Oak Tree, A Poem'.[16]

'The Oak-Tree' is the fictional equivalent of Vita's prize-winning poem *The Land*, a literary expression of her love of nature.

Virginia was still working on the last chapter of *Orlando* when the sudden death of the 61-year-old Lord Sackville was announced, and Vita had to accept the loss of her childhood home and her dreams. Virginia wove a message of comfort into a chapter elliptically referring to the funeral: 'An organ boomed. A coffin was borne into the chapel … some church clock chimed in the valley', then describing Orlando, now a woman, albeit dressed in whipcord breeches and a leather jacket, striding into the dining room with her elk hounds, accepting the congratulations of the assembled poets (whose portraits then hung on the walls of Knole's dining room) on winning the two-hundred-guinea Burdett Coutts prize for 'The Oak Tree'. It was a message to Vita that Knole's lasting legacy to her is the inspiration it has provided for her writing. Orlando tours the house, fancying

> that the rooms brightened as she came; stirred, opened their eyes, as if they had been dozing in her absence. She fancied, too, that, hundreds and thousands of times as she had seen them, they had never looked the same twice…

Day slips into night, and as she climbs the hill above the house the moon rises.

Its light raised a phantom castle upon earth. There stood the great house with all its windows robed in silver. Of wall or substance there was none. All was phantom. All was still. All was lit for the coming of a dead Queen. Gazing below her, Orlando saw dark plumes tossing in the courtyard, and torches flickering and shadows kneeling. A Queen once more stepped from her chariot.

Orlando is there to welcome her.

'The house is at your service, Ma'am,' she cried, curtseying deeply. 'Nothing has been changed. The dead Lord, my father, shall lead you in.'[17]

Midnight strikes. Orlando/Vita abdicates, exiting aloft with Shelmerdine/Harold and a wild goose, its quills a metaphor for the literary creativity that, Virginia is telling her friend, is far more worthwhile than remaining chained to a lost past. Vita loved *Orlando*. 'You made me cry with your passages about Knole, you wretch', she wrote.

Orlando spurred Vita into writing her own book about her own changed relationship with Knole, thanks to Virginia's influence. *The Edwardians*, published in 1930, featured a fictional heir close kin to her in character. He and his sister are archly named Sebastian and Viola (who cross-dresses in Shakespeare's *Twelfth Night*). It begins in 1906, a few years after *Orlando* ended. Its hero is sitting high on the roofs of his inheritance, the great house of Chevron, recognizably the Knole of Vita's childhood.

Acres of red-brown roof surrounded him, heraldic beasts carved in stone sitting at each corner of the gables. Across the great courtyard the flag floated red and blue and languid from a tower. Down in the garden, on a lawn of brilliant green, he could see the sprinkled figures of his mother's guests, some sitting under the trees, some strolling about; he could hear their laughter and the tap of the croquet mallets.[18]

Instead of being exiled from Knole, as was Vita's mother Victoria, Sebastian's mother Romola Cheyne is the unchallenged chatelaine of Chevron, revelling in sumptuous parties. Sebastian tolerates his mother's entertaining, but finds in the time-hallowed continuity of the below-stairs world of Chevron and the estate 'a vitality of an order different from the brilliant excitement of his mother's world'.

> The whole community of the great house was humming at its
> work. In the stables, men were grooming horses; in the 'shops',
> the carpenter's plane sent the wood-chips flying, the diamond
> of the glazier hissed upon the glass; in the forge, the hammer
> rang upon the anvil and the bellows windily sighed.[19]

After the visitors leave, one atypical guest remains, a famous explorer with distinctly anarchic leanings called Leonard Anquetil (his Christian name hints at his affinity with the ideas of Leonard and Virginia Woolf). He challenges Sebastian to break away from the destiny custom has ordained for him: life in a 'splendid tomb' in 'suffocating surroundings, lethal for all their beauty', their tyranny 'disguised under a mask of love', in short 'an atrophy of the soul'. Sebastian and his sister Viola take Anquetil for a candlelit tour of Chevron's great rooms of state, never used now. Quivering in the flicker of candles, the old rooms and their ancient furnishings seem less museum-like, and Anquetil (as was Virginia) is moved despite himself.

> The old rooms, in the candlelight, inspired him with a
> tenderness he would not by daylight have credited. Their
> beauty, which he had thought to be exterior, became significant;
> they were quickened by the breath of some existence which
> they had once enjoyed... Warring emotions tore him; he
> was determined not to sink under enchantment, ... the only
> inhabitant of the palace of Sleeping Beauty able to stick pins
> into his flesh and startle himself from the overtaking sleep.[20]

He warns Sebastian that the days of houses like 'mellow, majestic Chevron' are numbered. The house is 'dying from the top'. In the attics, its bones were 'stripped to their flesh', 'the silvery galleries recalled the pallor of a skeleton'. Sebastian risks carrying the house and his great name to the grave, 'tied onto him like so many tin cans to the tail of a poor cat'.

But Sebastian has just become fascinated by his mother's vampish friend Lady Roehampton, and follows in his forebears' footsteps, returning to Chevron for comfort when bruised by rejection or self-disgust. Signs of change increase. The head carpenter Wickenden's son refuses to follow his father into the Chevron carpentry shop, opting instead to 'go into the motor trade'. Motor cars, as in *Howards End*, *The Great Gatsby* and indeed *Orlando*, are harbingers of a new age, destructive of the old closed safe world of home. Sebastian himself 'bought the fastest motor on the market and drove it himself' (Vita too loved driving fast). Disillusioned after a succession of unsatisfactory affairs, he prepares to get engaged to the highly suitable Alice, dull and plain but with 'a profound understanding of Chevron', and plays his part in the ultimate aristocratic ritual: carrying a tiny piece of the royal regalia to the Coronation of George V.

> The long line of his ancestors rise up and stand about him like ghosts, pointing their fingers at him and saying that there was no escape... He was like a piece in a game of chess; he must move, woodenly, to the square next prescribed for him.[21]

On his return from Westminster Abbey, he catches sight of Anquetil, returned from six years abroad, and looking 'hard and healthy' and 'extraordinarily happy'. He has been corresponding with Viola ever since he left, and is going to marry her in three years' time, after his next adventure. He repeats the offer he made long ago on the roofs of Chevron.

> 'Come with me, and learn that life is a stone for the teeth to bite on... You may perhaps come back with a sense of proportion... You'll be a better master to Chevron.'
> 'Alright,' said Sebastian. 'I'll come.'[22]

The Edwardians ends right there, but we glimpse Anquetil, Viola and Sebastian some twenty-five years later as minor characters in Vita's next novel, *Family History* (1931). Socialist and pacifist in politics, Anquetil and Viola now exactly resemble Leonard and Virginia Woolf (apart from having two children) and live a 'rational and enlightened' life among like-minded friends in London. Sebastian, 'an unhappy man', has never married; he spends half the year being a good landlord on his Chevron estates, and half the year abroad. *The Edwardians* reflects not only Vita's passion for her ancient home, but her acceptance that the days of such houses are over. Her uncle Charles Sackville-West, who inherited it, agreed. He gave it to the National Trust in 1947.

Happily, soon after finishing *The Edwardians*, Vita found a substitute for Knole in the ruined Elizabethan great house of Sissinghurst, which she and Harold acquired early in 1930. Over the next decade they transformed it into a characterful, unpretentious home embellished with furniture from Knole, including the cabinet that had once held her teenage writings. Its garden, which merges into the unspoilt countryside of Kent, and her atmospheric tower writing room became Vita's preferred places. She had achieved stability thanks to Virginia's good advice and the steadfast constancy of her husband Harold. The three great loves of her life, she had told Harold in the early days of their marriage, were Knole, her writing and him – in that order. As time went on, she told him that he had first place in her heart.

SHEER FLAPDOODLE

Cold Comfort Farm and Stella Gibbons

*** Under the ominous bowl of the sky a man was ploughing the sloping field immediately below the farm, where the flints shone bone-sharp and white in the growing light. … Every now and again … he glanced up at the farm where it squatted on the gaunt shoulder of the hill, and something like a possessive gleam shone in his dull eyes.

'I think I have much in common with Miss Austen. She liked everything to be tidy and pleasant and comfortable about her, and so do I.'

Stella Gibbons, *Cold Comfort Farm*, 1932[1]

Cold Comfort Farm or A Good Woman's Influence is the story of the Cinderella-like transformation of a dysfunctional rural farm and family by a competent young *dea ex machina*. 'Let other pens dwell on guilt and misery' runs its introductory epigraph. The quotation from *Mansfield Park* is doubly apposite. Not only is *Cold Comfort Farm* an essentially merry book; it is also about restoring order to a spectacularly tumbled house. Flora Poste could not be more different from Fanny, but both act as catalysts, transforming the fortunes of the houses on which they descend. *Cold Comfort Farm* also deserves comparison with *The House of the Seven Gables* in the way that the farm initially lives and breathes malevolence ('crouched like a beast, about to spring, under the bulk of Mockuncle Hill'), but is eventually 'gay and cheerful' for the joyful wedding finale.

Stella Gibbons (1902–1989) set her novel in a 'near future' in which television-phones have been invented and air taxis are commonplace. It is a razor-sharp parody both of the then fashionable 'loam and lovechild' regional novels of Mary Webb and Sheila Kaye-Smith and of the Freudian fixations of D.H. Lawrence (voiced by Mr Mybug, a fine caricature of a Bloomsbury intellectual[2]). The story bounces off the starting blocks and never flags. Orphaned at the age of 20, and inheriting only 'from her father a strong will and from her mother a slender ankle', Flora Poste resolves to live off her relatives and collect material for a novel, confiding to her cosmopolitan friend Mrs Smiling that

> When I have found a relative who is willing to have me, I shall take him or her in hand, and alter his or her character and mode of living to suit my own taste. Then, when it pleases me, I shall marry.[3]

She elects to live in deepest Sussex with her father's cousins the Starkadders, unable to resist either the promise of their address (Cold Comfort Farm, Howling, Sussex) or the brooding menace of the letter she receives from Judith Starkadder ('Child, child, if you come to this doomed house, what is to save you?'). Her hopes are fulfilled when she sees the house, 'a sluggish animal light' shining from its 'dormers and mullions and scullions'. The architectural variations of the past are 'like ghosts embedded in brick and stone … mute history'. A three-page description of its layout quickly degenerates into absurdity. 'The front door of the farm faced a perfectly inaccessible ploughed field', and 'a long corridor ran half-way through the house on the second storey and then stopped. One could not get into the attics at all. It was all very awkward.'

Gibbons then moves to the farm's bleak setting and its warring occupants, thoughtfully using asterisks, Baedeker style, to signal particularly fine passages to readers 'who are not sure whether a sentence is Literature or ... sheer flapdoodle':

> *** His huge body, rude as a wind-tortured thorn, was printed darkly against the thin mild flame of the declining winter sun that throbbed like a sallow lemon on the westering lip of Mockuncle Hill... High up, a few chalky clouds doubtfully wavered in the pale sky that curved over against the rim of the Downs like a vast inverted pôt-de-chambre. Huddled in the hollow like an exhausted brute, the frosted roofs of Howling, crisp and purple as broccoli leaves, were like beasts about to spring.[4]

Possession of the remote Sussex farm is at the heart of matters. 'There have always been Starkadders at Cold Comfort' is the family mantra, repeated like a tolling bell. But which Starkadder? Ruling the roost from her well-appointed bedroom is Aunt Ada Doom, who lives off the fat of the land, issuing oracular pronouncements and descending only on high days and holidays. Downstairs her children squabble tempestuously: Amos and his wife Judith, Reuben (the ploughman above), their children Seth and Elfine, two half-brothers of Amos (Luke and Mark) and five cousins (Micah, Urk, Ezra, Caraway and Harkaway). Four hired men and numerous put-upon womenfolk fatalistically reiterate the cursedness of the house at odd intervals. Notable among them is the aged cowherd Adam Lambsbreath, who dotes on 'liddle Elfine, wild as a marshtigget', and Meriam Beetle the hired girl, a regular recipient of Seth's 'mollockings' and so just as regularly in labour 'in the wretched hut down at Nettle Flitch Field', where she 'housed the fruits of her shame'.

So begins Flora's immersion in matters rural. After curtly tele-gramming Mrs Smiling ('Worst fears realised darling seth and reuben too send gumboots'), she faces her Herculean task. In the ragged garden 'mallow, dog's-body and wild turnip were running riot'; in the cowsheds, Graceless, Pointless, Feckless and Aimless wait their turn to be milked, and in the 'clammy darkness of his cell' Big Business the bull wakes to another day with a 'tortured bellow'. In the filthy kitchen, a bubbling 'snood of porridge' hanging over a sullen fire gives 'an ominous, leering heave':

> it might almost have been endowed with life, so uncannily did its movements keep pace with the human passions that throbbed above it.[5]

Among the passions are those of Judith, ranting with 'eyes dark as imprisoned cobras' at her libertine son Seth, whose proudly displayed diaphragm muscles 'heaved in rough rhythm with the porridge'; of Amos, a hot-gospeller who threatens them all with the 'reeking red pits of the Lord's eternal wrathy fires'; of Elfine, who 'like a kingfisher streaked across the kitchen in a glimmer of green skirts and flying gold hair'; and of foxy-eared Urk, a 'red, hard-bitten man' who is promised to Elfine and sneaks up the apple tree outside her window to watch her going to bed.

Flora shrewdly calculates the potential of each of her rustic relatives and manipulates them into achieving it. She inspires Amos with the idea of touring the world in a Ford van to terrify the unrighteous into repentance, passing on his rights in the farm to Reuben, who will run it well. She invites down a Hollywood producer who signs up the broodingly handsome and already movie-mad Seth. Fey Elfine, who spends her time roaming the moors like a latter-day Cathy Earnshaw in the hopes of captivating young Richard Hawk-Monitor, the local squire, is introduced to *Vogue* magazine and *Persuasion*, warned not to mention poetry, and given a smart haircut and a sensationally simple evening dress for Richard's coming-of-age party; by the end of the evening she is engaged to marry him.

Aunt Ada is wooed with the prospectus of the Hotel Miramar in Paris, and a tempting role model in the glamorous septuagenarian actress Fanny Ward, 'who looked so much younger than she really was'. A splendid climax sees her abandoning her iron grip on the family and obsession with the nasty thing she once saw in the woodshed, and using the wealth she has cannily accumulated to take to the air in an elegant black leather flying suit and begin a life of luxury in France. Cousin Judith's unhealthy adoration for her son Seth is transferred onto a fascinated London psychoanalyst. Big Business is given his freedom, Meriam is instructed in birth control, and she and Urk move into an all-mod-cons villa called 'Byewaies'. Adam Lambsbreath is given a job as cowherd to the Hawk-Monitors, taking his own deformed but beloved herd with him.

The once comfortless farm is transformed into a rural paradise for Elfine and Richard's wedding reception.

> [H]ow gay and cheerful the farm looked, with the awning all bravely white and crimson in the sun, and the wreaths of flowers and the rosy clouds of peonies shining out of the darkness of the kitchen, through the open door.[6]

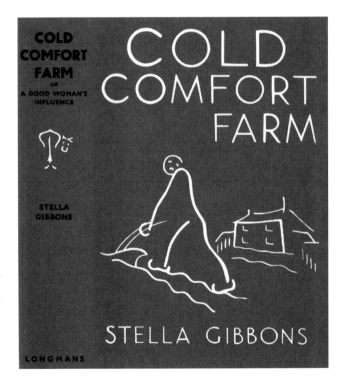

Iconic cover artwork showing Reuben Starkadder ploughing among fanged flints economically conveyed the atmosphere of Stella Gibbons satirical masterpiece *Cold Comfort Farm*. The spine is embellished by the rump of Big Business.

For the first time in their lives the Starkadders are 'having a nice time, and having it in an ordinary, human manner... Not having it because they were raping somebody, or beating somebody, or having religious mania or being doomed to silence by a gloomy, earthy pride...'

What of Flora herself? Deftly redirecting the sex-obsessed Mr Mybug on to Rennett, another of the hired girls, and politely refusing Reuben's wistful proposal of marriage, she summons a far more eligible relative in the shape of her second cousin Charles, who descends in his Twin Belisha Bat plane *Speed Cop* II and whisks her off to live happily ever after in a final scene straight out of a regional romance.

> She glanced upwards for a second at the soft blue vault of the midsummer night sky. Not a cloud misted its solemn depths. To-morrow would be a beautiful day.[7]

Flora Poste was a wistfully idealized portrait of her creator. Stella was the only well-balanced member of a family that was almost as histrionic as the Starkadders. She was well acquainted with ranting and rutting men (both her grandfather and her father were tempestuous drink-prone serial adulterers, despite being well respected in their professions of engineer and doctor respectively), quivering and despairing females (her governesses were frequently seduced by her father), and a herd of histrionic, constantly interfering uncles and aunts. She and her two brothers lived in London's then down-at-heel Kentish Town, where their father had his surgery. Like Robert Poste, he was a 'large man who had been serious about games and contemptuous of the arts'; like Robert Poste, his death in 1926 'was not regretted by his child'. Her mother's, in the same year, was: she had provided a steady point of love through the chaos, sending Stella to North London Collegiate School, which suggested she took a two-year journalism course set up at University College for the benefit of returning soldiers. After working as a cable decoder for British United Press, she moved first to the *Evening Standard* and

Instant success greeted journalist Stella Gibbons's first foray into fiction at the age of 30: sadly the fame of *Cold Comfort Farm* has overshadowed the many other fine novels that she wrote after it.

then *The Lady*, where she established its books page as a source of discerning literary criticism.

In 1928, while she was working for the *Standard*, the prime minister, Stanley Baldwin, delivered a speech at the Royal Society of Literature honouring the legacy of Mary Webb, who had died a year earlier, and whose novels had fallen out of fashion since the move towards modernism of such writers as T.S. Eliot, Virginia Woolf and Dorothy Richardson. The times were ripe for rural nostalgia. Baldwin's encomium reminded readers of the sheer readability of the regional novel, and Webb's novels, especially *Gone to Earth* (1917), became all the rage. Loam literature reached a zenith of absurdity with *Gay Agony* (1930) by Harold Manhood, which was set in a village called Thrust-on-the-Moor, with such biblically named characters as Micah and Rebecca, and culminates with the feisty Lynah 'demasting' the rape-prone villain. Two quotations from it are enough to justify the belief that Gibbons, who reviewed it in *The Lady*, had it in mind when she penned *Cold Comfort Farm*:

> A few clouds of equal shape were gathered low in the west, grouped like thirsty animals with heads turned towards the well-mouth of the sun...
>
> The smell of chamomile daisies came strongly, a sour stench that was like the afterbreath of lust.[8]

It was, however, Mary Webb's books that Gibbons had most in her sights when she began *Cold Comfort Farm*.[9] The *fs* of the alliterative opening sentence of Webb's *Gone to Earth* ('Small feckless clouds were hurried across the vast untroubled sky – shepherdless, futile, imponderable – and were torn to fragments on the fangs of the mountains, so ending their ephemeral adventures with nothing of their fugitive existence left but a few tears') are aped in *Cold Comfort Farm*'s 'fields fanged with flints', and a cow called Feckless. *Gone to Earth* has a house grander but every bit as anthropomorphized as Cold Comfort.

> Undern Hall, with its many small-paned windows, faced the north sullenly. It was a place of which the influence and magic were not good. … The front door was half glass, so that a wandering candle within could be seen from outside, and it looked inexpressibly forlorn, like a glow-worm seeking escape from a chloroform-box or mankind looking for the way to heaven.[10]

Webb's *The House in Dormer Forest* (1920) tells of 'Oolert's Dingle', a house 'with a malignant air, as of an old ruler from whom senility takes the power, but not the will, for tyranny'; its personality hangs 'like a haunting demon, from the old roof-tree'.

Cold Comfort Farm was enthusiastically received both in Britain and in America. *Punch* hailed Gibbons's 'devilish skill' in mocking 'a certain type of much-read, earthy, passionate novel', written by authors 'whose roots run so deep into the sad soil that their thoughts have grown consequently limited to the inevitability of gloom and reproduction'. 'The most brilliant satire of the season' wrote M.E. Harding in *The Saturday Review of Literature*. 'It is a masterpiece – the sort of thing that happens about once in ten years. It is outrageously funny, it is angry, it is necessary. Buy this book and keep it.'

The fame of her first novel has veiled the fact that Gibbons wrote twenty-five novels after it, as well as publishing poetry, children's books and short stories; her last novel, *The Woods in Winter*, was published in 1970. Modest and retiring, she shunned celebrity and never courted publicity. In this she followed her foremost literary inspiration, Jane Austen. Stella Gibbons admired her hugely, knew her books backwards and quoted her in the epigraphs of several novels. Flora's initial hopes of Cold Comfort Farm echo Catherine Morland's Gothic imaginings of Northanger Abbey. 'When I am fifty-three or so I would like to write a novel as good as *Persuasion*, but with a modern setting, of course', she confides to Mrs Smiling. When baffled as to what to do about Aunt Ada Doom, she 'opened *Mansfield Park* to refresh her spirits'. Gibbons gives a final nod to *Emma* at the end of the book, parodying its opening sentence when Flora posts Aunt Ada off to Paris, 'emphasizing what a pleasant life could be had in this world by a handsome, sensible old lady of good fortune, blessed with a sound constitution and a firm will'.

Austen remained Gibbons's guiding star all her literary life. But whereas Jane was preoccupied with the gentry, Stella specialized in the middle classes' lower echelons. Her settings are always telling. In *Westwood* (1946), the novel she was most proud of, she pilloried the Hampstead literati:

> Each house looked as if it had been designed by a border-line gnome. Towers, gables, rustications, lanterns, dormers and leaded panes abounded, and so did angles, bright tiles and horizontal windows, the gnomes having combined Pseudo-Tudo with Lutyens-Functional.[11]

Chaotic families recur, as do enduring and supportive friendships between women. Her endings are often unsettling, resigned rather than romantic. She continued to mock literary genres: *Bassett* (1946) satirized the post-war fashion for books about exploring the countryside. Gibbons's high contemporary reputation was reflected in her election to the Royal Society of Literature in 1950, and in 1954 Malcolm Muggeridge asked her to write regularly for *Punch*.

She revisited Cold Comfort Farm in 1940 with a very funny short story, 'Christmas at Cold Comfort Farm', which tells of pre-Flora times. The Farm appeared again in a full-length book, *Conference at Cold Comfort Farm* (1949), a spirited sequel that deserves to be better known. It is a prescient critical broadside against the National Trust, then turning away from preserving land to acquiring country houses in lieu of death duties. Thinly disguised as the Weavers' Whim Trust, it has taken over the Farm and transformed it into a nightmare of whimsy.

> There were typical farmhouse grandfather clocks ticking all
> over the place, and ... a Welsh dresser all over peasant pottery.
> In the Lytel Scullerie there were fifteen scythes arranged in a
> half-moon over the sink; there were horse-brasses all round the
> Greate Inglenooke and all round the Lytel Fire-places.[12]

For good measure, it satirises both the post-war conference intent on saving the world (an opportunity to resurrect Mr Mybug as its (dis)organizer), and the pretentiousness of modern writers, artists and sculptors. Deciding that she needs to put her 1932 improvements into reverse, Flora summons back the unreconstructed Starkadder menfolk from South Africa to toss out the doilies and the dainties. Big Business is towed home behind their airliner in a glider.

Cold Comfort Farm was adopted as a set text for schools in 1978, and put on the A-Level syllabus in 2001. Still high in the current listing of the 100 best novels written in English, it has remained loved by many, including Libby Purves, who interviewed Gibbons on Radio 4 in 1981. Talking of her famous satire, Gibbons said:

> I think, quite without meaning to, I presented a kind of
> weapon to people, against melodrama and the overemphasizing
> of disorder and disharmony, and especially the people who
> rather *enjoy* it. I think the book could teach other people not to
> take them seriously, and to avoid being hurt by them.

The subtleties and social importance of her other novels are now being recognized by literary scholars and many have been reprinted.[13] She abhorred dogmatism, and was, wrote her nephew Reggie Oliver in *Out of the Woodshed* (1998), his fine biography of his aunt, 'like all interesting people, a mass of contradictions'.

HOUSE OF SECRETS

Manderley and Daphne du Maurier

> The house possessed me from that day, even as a woman holds her lover.
>
> Daphne du Maurier, *The Rebecca Notebook*, 1981[1]

> Rebecca is the story of two women, one man, and a house. Of the four, as Hitchcock once observed, the house, Manderley, is the dominant presence.
>
> Sally Beauman, 2002[2]

Granddaughter of an eminent artist, and daughter of a popular actor, Daphne du Maurier (1907–1989) became in the long run better known than either. Her most famous book is the macabre thriller *Rebecca* (1938), in which the great Cornish house of Manderley first acts as a sinister instrument and finally is destroyed. Ironically, its model was Menabilly, a house on the Gribben peninsula a few miles west of Fowey, which became, eleven years after *Rebecca* was written, the most loved house of du Maurier's life. Seat of the Rashleigh family ever since it was built in the Elizabethan era, it was rebuilt in Georgian times, and given a six-bay front and a central courtyard. Its nineteenth-century owner Jonathan Rashleigh (1820–1905) planted its extensive grounds thickly with trees – pines, cedars, eucalyptus and beech; he also introduced rhododendrons and bamboos. It had been shut up and neglected for almost thirty years when Daphne discovered it in April 1929, walking up through its by then fantastically tangled woods from its beach in Pridmouth Cove. She had rowed over from Fowey, where she often took refuge from the bustle of London life and her overbearing father in Ferryside, her family's holiday house.

From the moment she saw Menabilly, she imagined it as a person as much as a place:

> The house, like the world, was sleeping … Menabilly would sleep on, like the sleeping beauty of the fairy tale, until someone should come to wake her.
>
> I watched her awhile in silence… She was, so it seemed to me, bathed in a strange mystery. She held a secret – not one, not two, but many – that she withheld from many people but would give to one who knew her well.[3]

What she loved most was its hidden quality, its remoteness from the world. She sought and received permission to wander around the estate, and for over a decade knew it only from walks up from the beach and occasional illicit explorations of its shuttered and cobwebby interior. Its deserted condition inspired her 1932 ghost story 'The Happy Valley'. In it, time trips. A woman on a honeymoon walk discovers the house, looks through the windows and sees her husband in a decade's time, stooped and sad. Then she is shown her own untimely grave by a boy, who she realizes is the son they have not yet had.

Gossip variously had it that Menabilly's then owner Dr John Rashleigh neglected it either because of the misery of the orphaned childhood he spent there with his guardian or because he found his wife in the arms of her lover there.[4] A more likely reason was that it was inconveniently large and damp, but the rumours contributed to *Rebecca*. Menabilly becomes Manderley, a house as formidably beautiful and faithless as its former mistress, Rebecca. Lost at sea when her yacht was wrecked, she was the first wife of Maxim de Winter, whose family had occupied it for centuries, just as the Rashleigh family had occupied Menabilly. The threatening role of

An early dust jacket for Daphne du Maurier's dark thriller *Rebecca* shows the sunny side of the magnificent but malevolent house of Manderley; it was set on the Cornish coast near Fowey.

the house is built up gradually, beginning with seductive references, like drops of rain before a storm. It is famous enough to feature on picture postcards; the never-named heroine remembers buying one when on holiday in Cornwall as a child. Now the much-bullied companion of a wealthy American woman, she meets the widowed Maxim in Monte Carlo. Escaping with him on drives, she listens to him talk longingly about its gardens and woods. After a whirlwind courtship, they marry, returning after a blissful Swiss honeymoon to Manderley. Her optimism falters as their car winds along its tortuously long drive, 'twisting and turning like an enchanted ribbon through the dark and silent woods', and through a tunnel of blood-red rhododendrons, 'showing no leaf, no twig, nothing but the slaughterous red, luscious and fantastic, … monsters, rearing to the sky, massed like a battalion, too beautiful I thought, too powerful'.

She finds the house itself is 'a thing of grace and beauty, exquisite and faultless, lovelier even than I had ever dreamed'. But, gazing into 'the great stone hall, the wide doors open to the library, the Peter Lelys and the Vandykes on the walls, the exquisite staircase leading to the minstrels' gallery, she immediately feels unsuited to it, 'a slim, awkward figure in my stockinette dress'. Arriving is made the more daunting by the army of servants gathered to greet her, 'a sea of faces, open-mouthed and curious, gazing at me as though they were the watching crowd about the block, and I the victim with my hands behind my back'. Foremost among them is the sinister Mrs Danvers, once Rebecca's nanny, now a supremely efficient housekeeper and intent on demoralizing the vulnerable young girl Maxim has chosen to marry. She had worshipped Rebecca, and been her most intimate confidante. Now she dedicates herself to making the dead woman uncannily alive. There is a sense of the living dead about Danvers herself: du Maurier refers no fewer than eight times to her 'skull's face'; Beauman calls her 'the ghastly spirit of the house itself'.[5]

First-person narration emphasizes the distorted point of view of the heroine. Although comforted by the library, where she wistfully imagines growing old with Max, their children running in and out, she is demoralized by the scale of the house, and feels desperately lonely.

> How vast the great hall looked now that it was empty. My feet rang on the flagged stones, echoing to the ceiling, and I felt guilty at the sound, as one does in church, self-conscious, aware of the same constraint.

Insecure, constantly losing her bearings in Manderley's maze of passages, she is repeatedly assaulted by evidence of Rebecca's omnipresent personality: her household routines, the vases she used, her stationery in her desk, her scent on a handkerchief left in a raincoat pocket. Even in the library, she 'shivered as though someone had opened the door behind me and let a draught into the room', realizing that

> I was sitting in Rebecca's chair, I was leaning against Rebecca's cushion, and the dog had come to me and laid his head upon my knee because that had been his custom, and he remembered, in the past, she had given sugar to him there.[6]

The interior of the house lives and breathes its former mistress. It was she who created the splendours of its furnishings and garden. Scents, especially those of flowers, are potent reminders of Rebecca.

Maxim has thoughtfully opened up and redecorated the peaceful east wing of the house, but his over-imaginative bride can't resist exploring Rebecca's old domain in the west wing. She discovers that Rebecca's bedroom, the finest room of the house, is still exactly as it was when Rebecca was alive; her brushes on the dressing table, her clothes in the wardrobe. Groping inside the monogrammed nightdress case on the bed, she discovers that her haunting perfume still clings to the creased nightgown inside. Mrs Danvers finds her there. 'Triumphant, gloating, excited in a strange unhealthy way', she urges her to 'feel it, hold it,'

> how soft and light it is, isn't it? I haven't washed it since she wore it for the last time. I put it out like this, and the dressing-gown and slippers, just as I put them out for her the night she never came back, the night she was drowned.'[7]

The second Mrs de Winter assumes that everyone, including Maxim, adored Rebecca. She cringes from taking any part in domestic arrangements, and tries to hide from visitors; time and again the house or its servants find her out. 'I was an interloper, wandering in rooms that did not know me, sitting at a desk and in a chair that were not mine.'

The grounds and the sea around the 'secretive and silent' house are equally animate. The heroine dreams of the way 'the beeches with white, naked limbs leant close to one another, their branches intermingled in a strange embrace'; 'squat oaks and tortured elms' straggle 'cheek by jowl' with them; 'gnarled roots' look like 'skeleton claws', and 'a naked eucalyptus tree stifled by brambles looked like the white bleached limb of a skeleton'. Unchecked, the hydrangeas 'had gone native now, rearing to monster height without a bloom, black and ugly.

> The rhododendrons stood fifty feet high, twisted and entwined with bracken, and they had entered into alien marriage with a host of nameless shrubs…. A lilac had mated with a copper beech, and to bind them yet more closely to one another the

malevolent ivy, always an enemy to grace, had thrown her tendrils about the pair and made them prisoners.[8]

The sea 'has a mournful harping note' which 'plays a jagged tune upon the nerves.' As the new bride gazes at it, it changes colour, 'becoming black, and the white crests with them very pitiless suddenly, and cruel, not the gay sparkling sea I had looked on first'.

Manderley, Rebecca and Mrs Danvers unite against the luckless heroine in the climax of the novel, a fancy-dress ball given in her honour. As elaborate preparations are made for the party,

> The house began to wear a new, expectant air. ... The old austerity had gone. Manderley had come alive in a fashion I would not have believed possible. It was not the still quiet Manderley I knew. There was a certain significance about it now that had not been before. A reckless air, rather triumphant, rather pleasing. It was as if the house remembered other days, long, long ago, when the hall was a banqueting hall indeed, with weapons and tapestry hanging upon the walls, and men sat at a long narrow table in the centre laughing.[9]

She is tricked by Mrs Danvers into ordering a dress copied from the portrait of Maxim's ancestress Caroline de Winter which hangs in the Long Gallery, so becoming one with both the house and Rebecca, who had worn just such a dress in the last ball held at Manderley. She stands at the top of the staircase, heart fluttering, excited and proud, but is greeted by shocked silence, and an abrupt command from Maxim to change her dress before the guests arrive. Devastated, she runs to her room 'stunned and stupid like a haunted thing', only to see Mrs Danvers at the open door of the west wing, 'her face loathsome, triumphant. The face of an exulting devil.' Struggling to keep up appearances in a substitute dress, she feels like 'a dummy-stick of a person ... a prop who wore a smile screwed to its face', her initial enchantment with her new home twisted by its malevolent sorcery.

Again and again the rockets sped into the air like arrows, and the sky became crimson and gold. Manderley stood out like an enchanted house, every window aflame, the grey walls coloured by the falling stars. A house bewitched, carved out of the dark woods.[10]

At dawn, mist descends and the heroine reaches her nadir. Head swimming, she is tempted by Mrs Danvers to hurl herself out onto the terrace below Rebecca's window. But a siren signalling a wrecked ship breaks Manderley's malign spell. Later a diver exploring the wreck finds Rebecca's lost yacht – with her body in its closed cabin. When Maxim confesses to her that he murdered Rebecca because she had made him hate her, his young wife is more elated than shocked. She feels that 'Rebecca's power had dissolved into the air, like the mist had done', and that it would never again haunt her.[11]

> Ashes to ashes. Dust to dust. It seemed to me that Rebecca had no reality any more. She had crumbled away when they had found her on the cabin floor. It was not Rebecca who was lying in the crypt, it was dust. Only dust.[12]

From now on she stands up to Mrs Danvers. Manderley recedes from the novel's narrative, although one senses it crouching expectantly as Maxim struggles to escape accusations of murder.

It makes one last dramatic appearance, morphing into Rebecca, whose preferred colour was red, whose lifeblood was shed by Maxim. Driving home through the night from London after Maxim has escaped prosecution, they top a hill.

> The road to Manderley lay ahead. There was no moon. The sky above our heads was inky black. But the sky on the horizon was not dark at all. It was shot with crimson, like a splash of blood. And the ashes blew towards us with the salt wind from the sea.[14]

Nor is that the last of it. Despite its destruction, 'memories of Manderley … will not be denied'. The book famously opens with the heroine dreaming of the house, and finding it a burnt-out ruin. Its spirit is as inimical as ever:

> Moonlight can play odd tricks upon the fancy, even upon a dreamer's fancy. As I stood there, hushed and still, I could swear that the house was not an empty shell but lived and breathed as it had lived before.[15]

Rebecca was Daphne du Maurier's best-selling novel. It tapped into many themes about which she felt deeply: jealousy (she once found a bunch of letters from her husband's sophisticated first fiancée tucked in one of his drawers), feelings of inadequacy stemming from her middle-daughter position in the family, the imbalance of relationships between men and women (such as she witnessed between her father and mother), and most of all a sense of place. Her son Kit has said that she was fonder of places than of people. When Alfred Hitchcock came to direct *Rebecca*, he is on record as saying that he saw the house as the most important element, and in the film camera angles repeatedly emphasize the way it dominates the heroine. She is dwarfed by the arch of a fireplace, by a great mullioned window, and by the portrait of Caroline de Winter. Mrs Danvers is repeatedly silhouetted ominously larger than life against features of the house.

The fictional Manderley had Menabilly's setting, but was altogether grander. Du Maurier told Martin Shawcross that Milton Hall, a Cambridgeshire mansion she visited several times as a child, inspired the interiors, the numerous domestic staff and the formal household routines of *Rebecca*. Cannon Hall, in Hampstead, the detached house to which her parents moved when she was 9, has a suitably grand staircase. Another, more local, influence may have been Trelowarren, the home of her friends the Vyvyans, which was certainly the setting for *Frenchman's Creek* (1941), her next novel.

The real Menabilly continued to haunt du Maurier. In 1943, fourteen years after she first saw it, and five years after the publication of *Rebecca*, she achieved her dream. The Rashleighs allowed her

Daphne du Maurier

Mrs. F. A. M. Browning and Her Children in Cornwall

With Her Children in the Grounds of Their Lovely Home

Mrs. Browning Relaxing in Her Study

● Mrs. Browning is the wife of Lt.-Gen. F. A. M. Browning. She is the well-known writer Daphne du Maurier, whose best-seller, *Rebecca*, which was first dramatised, was followed by *Jamaica Inn* and *Frenchman's Creek*, all of which were filmed with such success; her lovely and unusual play *The Years Between* is running in London now. The daughter of the late Sir Gerald du Maurier, she married Lt.-Gen. Browning, Chief of Staff S.E.A.C. in 1932. Her husband was formerly Deputy Commander, First Allied Airborne Army, and landed with his men at Arnhem. The Brownings have three children, two girls and a boy

On the Steps with Tessa, Flavia and Christian

Photographs by Compton Collier

On 4 July 1945 *Tatler and Bystander* devoted a page to Daphne du Maurier's romantic home Menabilly, the house on the Gribben peninsula which inspired her to write *Rebecca* (1938). Although the house was neglected and deserted while she was writing, five years later she rented it from its owners and it became her family's beloved home for twenty-five years.

to rent Menabilly on a long lease; for twenty-five years it was her and her family's much-loved home. *The King's General*, written in 1945, two years after they had moved in, is set in the house during the Civil War. It was inspired by a secret room, in which tradition had it that the body of a man in cavalier dress was found when Victorian alterations were made. When du Maurier finally had to leave Menabilly in 1965, she moved to Kilmarth, a few miles away at Par, near the village of Tywardreath. Still fascinated by the local history, she wrote a time-shifting novel about Kilmarth entitled *The House on the Strand* (1969); the title is a literal translation of the Cornish Tywardreath. Her last novel, *Rule Britannia* (1972), is also set in Kilmarth, where a doggedly independent grandmother very like the 65-year-old Daphne masterminds rebellion against the taking over of Britain by the Americans.

It is easy to see why Menabilly so obsessed du Maurier. Walking the coast path from Fowey to Gribben Head, you still only occasionally glimpse it, lurking behind its protective woods, but it has a unique allure. The path winds past a little beach house that is instantly recognizable as Rebecca's love nest. The house is privately owned, but two holiday houses on the estate are available to rent.

A HOUSEHOLD
OF THE FAITH

Brideshead Castle and Evelyn Waugh

[H]e had spoken a name that was so familiar to me, a
conjuror's name of such ancient power, that, at its mere sound,
the phantoms of those haunted late years began to take flight.

Evelyn Waugh, Prologue, *Brideshead Revisited*, 1945

Like Keats's urn, Brideshead is an unravished bride not only
because it is a work of art eminently beautiful, but also because
it is Christ's Church which is eminently true.

Rodney Delasanta and Mario L. D'Avanzo, 1965[1]

Written in the last months of the Second World War, *Brideshead
Revisited: The Sacred and Profane Memories of Captain Charles Ryder*
is regarded by most of its readers as an elegy for the passing of a
particular way of life. Evelyn Waugh endorsed this view fifteen
years later:

> It was impossible to foresee, in the spring of 1944, the present cult
> of the English country house. It seemed then that the ancestral
> seats which were our chief national artistic achievement were
> doomed to decay and spoliation like the monasteries in the
> sixteenth century. So I piled it on rather, with passionate sincerity.[2]

But it has a hidden purpose. The vast Palladian edifice, set in 'an
exquisite man-made landscape', is much more than the family seat

of the dysfunctional Flyte family. Waugh's original title was *A Household of the Faith: A Theological Novel*. In his first preface, he wrote that his 'ambitious, perhaps intolerably presumptuous' aim was 'nothing less than an attempt to trace the workings of the divine purpose in a pagan world, in the lives of an English Catholic family, half-paganized themselves, in the world of 1923–39'. These are the 'sacred and profane memories' of its rarely remembered subtitle.

Its background is the most important experience of Waugh's life: his conversion to Catholicism in 1930, a year after the failure of his first marriage. 'The book is about God', he wrote in a letter to Nancy Mitford soon after it was published.[3] Brideshead, a constant in the story, is presented as a divided realm, both pagan Arcadia and lost Eden. Catholic emblems recur. It lies 'couched among the lime trees like a hind in the bracken'; the deer is a Christian symbol of piety. Its prominent dome is a heavenly tent kin to Rome's St Peter's, and high up inside it the Flyte children's all-forgiving Nanny Hawkins sits, rosary in hand, an oleograph of the Sacred Heart on her mantelpiece. The exuberantly baroque Italian fountain on the terrace which 'seemed always to draw us to itself for comfort and refreshment' has connotations both of baptism and of the Eucharist. Scenes around the fountain recur: moonlit silver under an indigo sky when Charles arrives for his first long visit to the house, painted by him time and again, moonlit once more as the scene of Julia's despair at her sinfulness. Its dried-up appearance in the epilogue suggests, wrongly it will emerge, that faith has died at Brideshead.

At the heart of the house is the chapel, created for Lady March-main as a wedding gift from her husband, at the height of his enthusiasm for her, because 'she brought back my family to the faith of their ancestors'. Its decoration shows that Lord Marchmain was well aware of his wife's fondness for kitsch prettiness rather than great art.

> Angels in printed cotton smocks, rambler-roses, flower-
> spangled meadows, frisking lambs, texts in Celtic script, saints
> in armour, covered the walls in an intricate pattern of clear,
> bright colours. There was a triptych of pale oak, carved so as to

The first edition of *Brideshead Revisited* (1945) sported an elegantly rococo dust jacket and gave its full title, a hint that it was, as he wrote to Nancy Mitford in January 1945, 'about God'.

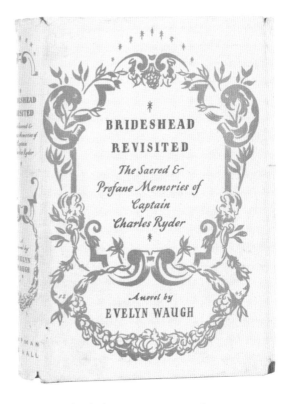

give it the peculiar property of seeming to have been moulded in Plasticine. The sanctuary lamp and all the metal furniture were of bronze, hand-beaten to the patina of a pock-marked skin; the altar steps had a carpet of grass-green, strewn with white and gold daisies.[4]

'Golly' is all Ryder can say when Sebastian shows it to him. He copies his host's dip of fingers in the holy water stoup and genuflects, explaining the gesture away as 'just good manners'. It is in fact a prediction that one day he will genuflect in earnest.

In the novel's prologue, set in 1943, Captain Charles Ryder, 'homeless, childless, middle-aged, loveless', is relocated with his regiment to Brideshead Castle, in Wiltshire, a house that he knew well in his early twenties, and returned to in his early thirties. The house and the family who lived there had a cathartic effect on him. Now 39, he goes into a long reverie – the bulk of the book – about his relationship to them. Soon after arriving in Oxford in 1923 he meets the 'entrancing' Sebastian Flyte, who has 'that epicene beauty which in extreme youth sings aloud for love and withers at the first cold wind'. In Sebastian's case, the first cold wind was desertion by his father, who moved to Venice with his mistress, leaving Sebastian uncertain of his own purpose and undefended against the manipulations of a controlling mother. Teddy bear clutched in his arms, he is determined not to graduate from childhood while in Oxford. Charles is fascinated by him, especially when Sebastian sweeps him away to visit Brideshead, his home. He realizes the degree to which his new friend is alienated from his family when Sebastian says

> 'I'm not going to have you get mixed up with my family. They're so madly charming. All my life they've been taking things away from me. If they once got hold of you with their charm, they'd make you their friend not mine, and I won't let them.'[5]

Charles's initial focus of affection is Sebastian, but when he is invited to stay at Brideshead during the long vacation it shifts to the magnificent house – both the place and the family. In the course of the novel, Brideshead will endow Ryder with three gifts, graded in their importance.

The first gift is an Arcadian setting, where he can play in the company of Sebastian at being the child he was never allowed to be.

> I was being given a brief spell of what I had never known, a happy childhood, and though its toys were silk shirts and liqueurs and cigars and its naughtiness high in the catalogue of grave sins, there was something of nursery freshness about us that fell little short of the joy of innocence.[6]

Knitting in the attic nursery, Nanny Hawkins clucks delightedly that they are 'a pair of children'. Deeply devout, she is also kin to one of the classical Fates, emphazising Waugh's twinning of Arcadia and Eden.

The second gift is a vocation: the splendours of Brideshead channel Charles's hitherto vague artistic ambitions into architectural painting.

> It was an aesthetic education to live within those walls, to wander from room to room, from the Soanesque library to the Chinese drawing-room, adazzle with gilt pagodas and nodding mandarins.[7]

He paints a romantic landscape in a rococo plaster panel, and 'by luck and the happy mood of the moment, [I] made a success of it. The brush seemed somehow to do what was wanted of it.' He goes on to produce 'a very passable echo of Piranesi' in a painting of the great fountain. As he paints, he 'felt a whole new system of nerves alive within me, as though the water that spurted and bubbled among its stones was indeed a life-giving spring'. On leaving Oxford he goes to art school in Paris, returning in 1926 to be asked by Bridey, Sebastian's older brother, to paint four views of the family's London home Marchmain House. The commission makes his name, and he becomes fêted as an architectural painter. Waugh was deeply interested in architecture, and liked to call the process of writing architectural rather than creative. 'What makes a writer, as distinct from a clever and cultured man who can write, is an added energy and breadth of vision which enables him to conceive and complete a structure.'[8]

Brideshead's third and greatest gift to Charles is religious faith. Sebastian, the most attractive character in the book, succinctly sums up the Flytes' religious differences:

> Brideshead [the oldest son and heir] and Cordelia are both
> fervent Catholics; he's miserable, she's bird-happy; Julia and
> I are half-heathen; I am happy, I rather think Julia isn't;
> mummy is popularly believed to be a saint and papa is
> excommunicated.[9]

His flippant summary is too crude. His younger sister Cordelia's comments are more pertinent, especially on the subject of vocation. An ardent believer, she wishes that she had one herself so that she could become a nun, but knows that she hasn't. She is, however, loving and selfless, central to the family and as warm-hearted as her namesake in *King Lear*. She perceptively describes her mother, Lady Marchmain, as 'saintly, but not a saint', despite being named for the Spanish mystic Teresa of Avila. Having lost his own mother at an early age, Charles is initially charmed by the attention Lady

Marchmain pays him. He enjoys invitations into her sitting room, a distinctively feminine space which contrasts sharply with the 'august, masculine atmosphere' of the main house. Its ornaments reveal her character:

> potted with innumerable little water-colours of fond
> association; the air was sweet with the fresh scent of flowers
> and musty potpourri; her library in soft leather covers,
> well-read works of poetry and piety, filled a small rosewood
> bookcase; the chimney-piece was covered with small personal
> treasures – an ivory Madonna, a plaster St Joseph, posthumous
> miniatures of her three soldier brothers.[10]

Those three brothers, about whom she is having a memorial book prepared, are implicit reproaches to the unmartial Marchmain menfolk; a minor theme of the novel is the stifling of the guilt of the post-war generation in a whirl of fast living.

Lady Marchmain tries to convert Charles to Catholicism. 'We had many little talks together during my visits when she delicately steered the subject into a holy quarter.' Flattered at first, he soon comes to realize that he is being 'suborned'; Lady Marchmain's real interest is in using him to control the errant Sebastian, who has begun drinking heavily. When Charles won't cooperate, she accuses him of being 'wantonly cruel', 'callously wicked'. Charles leaves Brideshead, as he thinks for good.

> I felt that I was leaving part of myself behind, and that
> wherever I went afterwards I should feel the lack of it... A door
> had shut, the low door in the wall I had sought and found in
> Oxford; open it now and I should find no enchanted garden.[11]

Sebastian too leaves the Arcadia of his childhood to wander in the Levant. Cordelia 'used to think Sebastian had [a vocation] and hated it'; by the end of the novel we realize she was right all along. Sebastian has deep feelings of inadequacy because he is a younger son, of whom nothing is expected. Babied by both nanny and mother, not seriously interested sexually in either men or women, he longs to look after people rather than be looked after. Hence his careful parenting of his teddy bear Aloysius (St Aloysius was a high-born Spanish Jesuit who died caring for victims of an epidemic), and his acting as a Good Samaritan to the maimed German soldier Kurt in a little house that he makes distinctively his own in Fez. Ryder visits him.

> Under the stars in the walled city, ... where the dust lay thick among the smooth paving stones and figures passed silently, robed in white, on soft slippers or hard, bare soles; where the air was scented with cloves and incense and wood smoke – now I knew what had drawn Sebastian here and held him so long.[12]

The last we hear of him is Cordelia's descriptions of his efforts to become a lay brother, punctuated by episodes of drunkenness, 'living on, half in, half out of the community ... a great favourite with the old fathers, something of a joke to the novices'.

The glamorous and amorous Julia's faith is the most complex. Nanny Hawkins scoffs at the idea of making a nun out of her, and she seems to do exactly what she likes regardless of propriety, including embarking on an affair with Charles when both are married. But, as is hinted by Waugh's arrestingly weird choice of words in his description of the affair's first consummation, Charles's relationship with her is sinisterly bound up with his feelings for her home.

> It seemed as though a deed of conveyance of her narrow loins had been drawn and sealed. I was making my first entry as the freeholder of a property I would enjoy and develop at leisure.[13]

However, at a deep level Julia is agonized both by their affair and by her – in Catholic terms – bigamous marriage. She is tortured by the idea that her mother died 'with my sin eating at her, more cruelly than her own deadly illness'. This emerges with shocking suddenness after the stonily correct Bridey announces that as she is living in sin with Charles, he cannot invite his prospective wife to meet her. She sobs out her sense of guilt to Charles as they sit in a dark bay of clipped box beside the ancient fountain. She is living in sin, 'a word from so long ago, from Nanny Hawkins stitching by the hearth and the nightlight burning before the Sacred Heart', and there is 'no way back; the gates barred; all the saints and angels posted along the walls'.

The nightlight evokes the sanctuary lamp that once burnt in the chapel, its flame an enduring symbol of faith. Its extinction at the death of Lady Marchmain and Bridey's closing of the chapel makes it seem as if the Flytes have finally turned away from their religion, but Cordelia correctly predicts that 'God won't let them go for long, you know'.

> 'I wonder if you remember the story mummy read us the evening Sebastian first got drunk – ... "Father Brown" said something like "I caught him" (the thief) "with an unseen hook and an invisible line which is long enough to let him wander to the ends of the world and still to bring him back with a twitch upon the thread".'[14]

'A Twitch on the Thread', as the G.K. Chesterton story is called, is the title Waugh gave to the third book of the novel. In it, Charles witnesses Lord Marchmain's return to Brideshead to die, and his confounding of Bridey's expectations by bequeathing the house to Julia ('so beautiful always; much, much more suitable') because he finds Bridey's wife Mrs Muspratt vulgar. However, just as Charles begins to hope that he has won not only the princess but her castle, his world collapses about his ears. Despite his attempts to prevent the dogged little Catholic priest Father Mackay from administering the last sacrament to Lord Marchmain, he finds himself kneeling beside Julia and Cordelia, and praying, like them, that the dying man will make a sign of contrition. When Marchmain slowly makes the sign of the cross, it decides Julia against a marriage that will not be recognized by her Church. Charles's relationship with her and all at Brideshead is curtly ended.

Evelyn Waugh in 1942, looking every inch Captain Charles Ryder, narrator of *Brideshead*. Converted to the Catholic faith in 1930, he put much of himself into the novel, as well as thinly disguised portraits of friends.

Evelyn Waugh explicitly describes Brideshead as being modelled on Castle Howard. When an excerpt of the book appeared before publication in the November 1944 edition of *Town & Country* magazine, he approved it being headed by an illustration by Constantin Alajalov which showed Captain Ryder standing in front of the ancient seat of the Catholic Howard family. This was in part because Waugh felt its architectural style suited his story, but it was also an attempt to divert attention from Waugh's close friends the Lygons, whose family seat was Madresfield, near Malvern. The moated red-brick Tudor house has attic nurseries (where Waugh wrote *Black Mischief* after his marriage collapsed) and an Arts and Crafts chapel exactly like the one Waugh describes at Brideshead. The Lygons were not Catholics, but they did have an exiled father who lived in Italy, an uptight heir, a younger son with a drinking problem and two characterful daughters, who were very fond of Evelyn. Having him to stay, recalled Lady Dorothy Lygon, was 'like having Puck as a member of the household'.[15] Waugh, whose thwarted childhood meant that he often fell in love with families, also borrowed elements from the Plunket Greenes, the Pakenhams (staunch Catholic families) and the Mitfords. A disclaimer that prefaced the first edition of the novel firmly stated (perhaps primarily for the eyes of the Lygons),

I am not I; thou art not he or she;
they are not they.
    E.W.

The action of *Brideshead* reprises Waugh's earlier literary career. The college rags and the hooligans of *Decline and Fall* (1932) and 'Winner Takes All' (1936) appear again in its Oxford scenes; another great country house is added to the earlier fictional edifices of King's Thursday, Anchorage Hall, Doubting Hall, Hetton Abbey, Boot Magna and Malfrey; the bright young things of *Vile Bodies* (1930) are re-presented, albeit to altered effect. The disillusion with the army Waugh expressed in *Put Out More Flags* (1942) heralds Ryder's cynicism in the Prologue to *Brideshead*. In 1943, two other significant events influenced the imagining of his new novel: his father died, freeing him to express his childhood sense of deprivation, and he persuaded the family of his friend Hubert Duggan, a lapsed Catholic, to call a priest to his deathbed.

Lord Marchmain's deathbed return to the fold leads not only to his prodigal daughter Julia's sacrifice of her sinful relationship with Charles but, offstage, quite how or when we are not told, to Ryder's own conversion. This is conveyed so subtly that many readers of the novel are unaware that it has taken place. It is, however, forecast both in the Prologue, when his platoon commander Hooper describes the service going on in the 'sort of R.C. church' attached to Brideshead as 'more in your line than mine', and in the fourth chapter of Book I, when Ryder muses on his first visit to Brideshead:

perhaps the Beatific Vision itself has some remote kinship with this lowly experience; I, at any rate, believed myself very near heaven, during those languid days at Brideshead.[16]

Its inevitability is suggested when, waking in the night after Cordelia's description of Sebastian in Morocco, he has an image

> of an arctic hut and a trapper alone with his furs and oil
> lamp and log fire; everything dry and ship-shape and warm
> inside, and outside the last blizzard of winter raging and the
> snow piling up against the door. Quite silently a great weight
> forming against the timber; the bolt straining in its socket…[17]

The image recurs after he witnesses Lord Marchmain's final devout gesture of acceptance, but now 'the avalanche was down, the hillside swept bare behind it; the last echoes died on the white slopes; the new mound glittered and lay still in the silent valley'. Ryder's conversion is finally confirmed when, visiting the chapel in the Epilogue, he says a prayer, 'an ancient, *newly-learned* [my stress] form of words'.

Names matter in Waugh's novels. Most of the Flytes are in flight from their ancient faith. Ryder's name hints at a knight on a quest. Sebastian is named for the saint who concealed his faith, Cordelia means warm-hearted, Julia has associations with pagan Rome. Brideshead, 'a conjuror's name of ancient power', is freighted with theological reference – the Bride of Christ, Head of the Church. Arching over the novel are invocations of the lament 'Quomodo sedet sola civitas' ('How lonely the city stands') made by the prophet Jeremiah when the temple of the Jews was destroyed, and also used in Tenebrae, the liturgical office that mourns Christ's death. Cordelia utters it at the deconsecration of the Brideshead chapel, and Ryder remembers it as, in the book's last pages, he wanders through the ruined gardens of Brideshead, despoiled by latrines and random roads, the fountain trapped in barbed wire and polluted with cigarette butts, and all about to be reduced to an assault course and mortar range: a lonely city indeed.

The builders did not know the uses to which their work would descend; they made a new house with the stones of the old castle; year by year, generation after generation, they enriched and extended it; year by year the great harvest of timber in the park grew to ripeness; until, in sudden frost, came the age of Hooper; the place was desolate and the work all brought to nothing.[18]

But, he realizes when he visits the chapel, the Flytes' home is not desolate.

Something quite remote from anything the builders intended has come out of their work, and out of the fierce little human tragedy in which I played; something none of us thought about at the time; a small red flame – a beaten-copper lamp of deplorable design, relit before the beaten-copper doors of a tabernacle; the flame which the old knights saw from their tombs, which they saw put out; that flame burns again for other soldiers, far from home, farther, in heart, than Acre or Jerusalem. It could not have been lit but for the builders and the tragedians, and there I found it this morning, burning anew among the old stones.[19]

At the end of the novel, Bridey, Julia and Cordelia are all in Palestine, as close on earth as they can be to the fount of Christianity. All the Flytes have 'returned to the faith of their ancestors'. Charles Ryder has joined them; his life is now concerned not just with beauty but with truth.

THE SORCERER'S TOWER

I Capture the Castle and Dodie Smith

How one knows the castle! Did you draw plans? …
I particularly liked the big kitchen… I think this is a book that
will be very much lived in by many people, because you can
live inside it, like Dickens.

Christopher Isherwood,
letter to Dodie Smith, 26 October 1948[1]

I have just had another look at the tower. The moon is shining
full on it now. I had a queer feeling that it was more than
inanimate stones. Does it know that it is playing a part in
life again – that its dungeon once more encircles a sleeping
prisoner?

Dodie Smith, *I Capture the Castle*, 1948[2]

Admirers of *I Capture the Castle* are legion, and as disparate as
Christopher Isherwood, Joanna Trollope, Armistead Maupin, Julian
Barnes, Jacqueline Wilson and J.K. Rowling, who declared Cassandra Mortmain 'the most charismatic narrator I have ever met'.
Seventy years after publication it remains high in lists of the nation's
favourite books; I have always loved it, and it was one of the first
books to come to mind when I began thinking about dwellings
that dominated a story. To my astonishment, I discovered that,
despite being deeply knitted into the Suffolk countryside, it was

largely written in a Malibu beach house. At the time Dodie Smith (1896–1990) was, like its heroine's father, suffering from writer's block. Lured to California by the prospect of easy money writing Hollywood scripts, she was out of touch with her roots, unable to turn out the hit plays she had been famous for, and desperately nostalgic for England. So she re-created her 1930s' heartland in a novel.

It is the story of the churchmouse-poor Mortmain family. James Mortmain wrote a highly rated modernist novel entitled *Jacob Wrestling* in the early 1920s, but has been unable to settle down to writing ever since he went to prison for three months for brandishing a cake knife at his wife and assaulting an interfering neighbour. In search of solitude after he came out, he acquired a forty-year lease on Godsend, a dilapidated Suffolk castle with Tudor additions. He set it to rights enthusiastically, filling it with beautiful antiques. But when the story begins, money is tight and everything of value has been sold. Mortmain, his temper perhaps too firmly under control, roosts in his gatehouse study reading whodunnits and making up crossword puzzles, emerging only for meals and oblivious of practical realities. The family is held together by Topaz, whom he married five years after the death of the children's mother. Then a famous artists' model with an immense sense of style, she has dedicated herself to Mortmain and his family with extraordinary domestic resource, though a little histrionically. Her occasional earnings as a model and the contributions of the equally devoted Stephen, their former housekeeper's son, are the only income the family have. Fifteen-year-old Thomas is still at school, and the story is told by 17-year-old Cassandra ('Jane Eyre with a touch of Becky Sharp', pronounces the vicar). Throughout the novel, the castle is a constant, both backdrop and actor. It imposes its massive, uncompromising bulk on their lives, a source of romance for Cassandra, an impediment to progress to her beautiful 20-year-old sister Rose, though it is the means of attracting the suitors she longs for, one of whom will inspire James to write again, though not until he is enwombed in its ancient tower.

The first edition dust jacket of Dodie Smith's *I Capture the Castle* (1949) shows its heroine Cassandra Mortmain and her adored dog Heloïse strolling towards Godsend, her romantic castle home, with the even more ancient Belmotte Tower beyond it.

Cassandra revels in Suffolk ('flat country seems to give the sky such a chance') and the romance of her semi-derelict home, but Rose 'sees nothing romantic about being shut up in a crumbling ruin surrounded by a sea of mud', and is 'very bitter at life because she never meets any eligible men'. Rose resolves to save the family by marrying a rich man, and has herself hoisted up on the kitchen airer to make a pact with the devil in the shape of an ancient gargoyle. The result is frighteningly quick: two young Americans knock at the door asking for help with their car, which has stuck in the muddy lane; they turn out to be Simon Cotton (who sports a suspiciously pointy beard) and his half-brother Neil. Simon is the new owner of the estate on which the castle stands, and is a great admirer of *Jacob Wrestling*. They invite the Mortmains to their luxurious Elizabethan manor Scoatney, a place where Cassandra feels the past 'is like a presence, a caress in the air' and the luxurious bathrooms reduce Rose to tears. Mrs Cotton's directness about James's failure to write galvanizes him into eccentric paths of research, but hours in Scoatney's library and frequent trips to London appear to be yet more distractions. The young Cottons react to the castle in different ways. Neil 'wanted to know all about defending castles – he was particularly taken with the idea of a trébuchet slinging a dead horse over the walls'. Simon is the 'Henry James kind of American, who falls in love with England'.

> As we walked through the courtyard garden, Simon looked up at the mound. 'How tall and black Belmotte Tower is against the starry sky,' he said. I could see he was working himself into a splendidly romantic mood.[3]

He falls in love with Rose, who is much more interested in his money than him. Secretly her heart is set on Neil, 'who thinks England is a joke' and whose first reaction to Godsend is 'What is this place – the House of Usher?' His ambition is a cattle ranch and the wide open spaces of the West. As events unfold, there is much moonlight cavorting in and around the castle walls, skinny-dipping in the moat and falling in love 'in a follow-my-leader game of second-best', with Stephen longing for Cassandra, Cassandra for Simon, whose literary tastes are her own, and both Simon and Neil for capricious and enchanting Rose. General heartache obtains until, with a few deftly constructed twists, all is (almost) set to rights.

'How We Came to the Castle', an eight-page digression in the third chapter, describes the sense Cassandra has of it being alive, aware and magical.

> [We crawled along with the brambles clawing at the car as if trying to hold it back – I remember thinking of the Prince fighting his way through the wood to the Sleeping Beauty. ... Once through, we were in the cool dimness of the gatehouse passage. That was where I first felt the castle – it is the place where one is most conscious of the great weight of stone above and around one. I was too young to know much of history and the past, for me the castle was one in a fairy tale; and the queer heavy coldness was so spell-like that I clutched Rose hard.[4]

Various parts of the castle influence events. 'How I could work in this room!' Mortmain declares when he first explores the gatehouse. Nothing comes of it. Gatehouses are linking places: this one's stone-mullioned windows overlook both the lane at the front and the courtyard at the back: Mortmain is physically removed from the family, but constantly distracted by it, as well as by casual visitors and the detective novels brought to him by their devoted local librarian. As his name suggests, his writing hand is dead.

The book's first line famously describes its heroine Cassandra catching the last of the daylight sitting on the kitchen windowsill with her feet in the sink, wrapped in a blanket against the cold, and scribbling in her journal 'to teach myself how to write a novel – I intend to capture all our characters and put in conversations'. Both kitchen and sink are significant. Kitchens are traditionally seen as the heart of a home, and Godsend's has a glorious hearth.

> The firelight glows steadily through the bars and through the round hole in the top of the range where the lid has been left off. It turns the whitewashed walls rosy; even the dark beams in the roof are a dusky gold. The highest beam is over thirty feet from the ground. Rose and Topaz are two tiny figures in a great glowing cave.[5]

Smith brings this romantic vision firmly down to earth with the smell of carbolic from the sink in which Cassandra has her feet and the rain dripping through the leaky roof. She is setting down events in the first of three writing journals: a sixpenny one (March) given to her by the vicar, a shilling one (April and May) given to her by Stephen and a two guinea one (June to October) sent by Simon.

The three journals give *I Capture the Castle* the structure of a three-act play, full of lively dialogue and devastating one-liners, a reflection of the fact that 53-year-old Dodie Smith was a renowned playwright. Her upbringing had been unusual. Her father died when she was 2, and she and her pretty, timid mother lived with relations in a large and eccentric Manchester household with three pianos and four sitting rooms; she had baths Cassandra-style, in front of the kitchen range. Adored by a bevy of theatre-loving grandparents, aunts, uncles and cousins, she was the star of family productions. When she was 13 her mother remarried an unpleasant waster called Alec Gerald Seton-Chisholm; they moved to London and a Battersea flat and Dodie went to St Paul's Girls' School. She was a great reader, loving E. Nesbit and Sherlock Holmes, but hating *Wuthering Heights*. After the death of her mother when she was 18, she shared a bedsit with a friend and tried her hand first at being an actress, and then working in the legendary Tottenham Court Road furniture emporium W.H. Heal's, where she was soon running the prints and toys gallery, developing an idiosyncratic style of dress and domestic decor, and carrying on a secret affair with the store's married owner, Ambrose Heal. Still in love with the theatre, she tried her hand at writing plays, and achieved a record five box-office sell-outs in a row, beginning with *Autumn Crocus* in 1929 and ending with *Dear Octopus* in 1938. James Drawbell, editor of *Woman's Own*, felt that they succeeded because she was 'much closer to the hearts of the ordinary people than most of her fellow playwrights'.

She eventually married Alec Beesley, advertising manager of W.H. Heal's, seven years her junior and matinée-idol handsome. He remained devoted to her interests all his life, a perceptive critic, clever financial manager and domestically attentive helpmeet. Dodie and Alec longed for a country retreat where she could write in peace, and one of their favourite occupations was exploring old houses, and fantasizing about doing them up and living in them. On a Whitsun 1934 drive through Suffolk, they came across Wingfield Castle, a few miles east of Diss. The fifteenth-century seat of the de la Pole dukes of Suffolk, its glories had faded when their cause collapsed under the Tudors, and what was left of the castle – a fine south front with gatehouse, an unpretentious Tudor house stitched onto its western walls, and an encircling moat – was for sale for £3,000. Its cost, its distance from London and its dilapidation made Wingfield too much of a challenge.[6]

They focused instead on Essex, and one day discovered Finchingfield, 'an astonishingly beautiful village'.

The setting of *I Capture the Castle* was inspired by the crumbling splendour of Wingfield Castle, the moated fifteenth-century seat of the de la Pole Dukes of Suffolk. Dodie Smith looked over it when it was for sale in 1934, then re-created it fifteen years later in her novel.

> Five roads led to a green and a pond, surrounded by old houses
> and cottages ... there was an indescribable rightness about
> the whole composition of the place ... also, to me, there was
> a mysterious touch of unreality, as of something seen in a
> dream.[7]

They explored The Barretts, an isolated cottage. Dodie took against it at first after finding 'a bundle of rags and straw where tramps must have slept', exactly as Cassandra does when the Mortmains first explore Godsend. But she was converted to its charms once they had lit a fire in the huge fireplace in its barn, and discovered an orchard and a pond.

In 1939 they rented out The Barretts and went to America, ostensibly to watch over the New York launch of *Dear Octopus*, but in fact with a mind to stay there if war was declared because Alec, a committed pacifist, would otherwise have been imprisoned as a conscientious objector. The move profoundly altered the course of

Dodie's career. She was lured to Hollywood to work on screenplays, but she longed to return to England. Nostalgia brought Wingfield Castle to mind, and she began to plan a novel about an impoverished family living in a romantic but a dilapidated Suffolk castle; a once-famous author father wasting his talent on trivia (just as she was); a motherless young heroine who loved the idea of romance but had a severely pragmatic streak (again like Dodie). But she soon abandoned it. It was not until 1948, after the war was over, that she turned back to her castle idea. Gazing out at the Pacific, she began again on *I Capture the Castle*. Wingfield was lovingly reimagined as Godsend Castle, and given a cosy village around it reminiscent of Finchingfield.

However, neither Wingfield nor Finchingfield had the feature which is crucial to the novel: 'Belmotte Tower, all that remains of an even older castle'. Mysterious and atmospheric, the sight of it looming above the flat Suffolk landscape is what leads the Mortmains to Godsend in the first place. Smith gives it a much more ominous personality than the crumbling castle at its foot, endowing it with magical, even necromantic, overtones. The vicar's theory is that Belmotte's name is linked to the Phoenician sun god Bel, and every year the Mortmain girls celebrate midsummer there with a votive fire and ritual chants and dancing. When Rose first sees it, she is reminded of 'the tower in *The Lancashire Witches* where Mother Demdike lived'. Smith had loved W.H. Ainsworth's *The Lancashire Witches: A Romance of Pendle Forest* as a child, and borrowed 'stern solitary' Malkin Tower, 'circular in form and very lofty, ... a landmark to the country round', for Belmotte.[8] Both are motte-and-bailey castles, originally built by the Saxons. Both have an entrance 25 foot above the base, accessible in Malkin Tower's case only by ladder after Mother Demdike has the outside steps removed. Smith reverses these features: Belmotte has steps outside, but only a ladder down from the door on the inside.

This feature makes it ideal for the novel's hilarious climax: curing Mortmain's writer's block. Rose and Topaz go to London to choose a trousseau for Rose's marriage to Simon. Thomas and Cassandra, inspired by a psychologist's theory that a new imprisonment might cancel out the inhibiting effect of the old one, secretly furnish Belmotte with all their father's needs, lure him inside, and then haul the ladder up – an apt detail since a ladder was a distinctive element in *Jacob Wrestling*, his literary masterpiece. Their tough love works. A spell of solitude and a chance remark of Cassandra's come together to provide Mortmain with inspiration for another revolutionary literary innovation, even though his imprisonment is prematurely ended by Topaz's return with the dramatic news that Rose has abandoned Simon and eloped with Neil.

Belmotte is particularly important to Cassandra. It is the place where she hides her journals, and she frequently leans against it to write. She 'captures' the castle as well as its occupants in words, and she herself is captivated by it. All her significant meetings with Simon take place there. When Simon turns up to help Cassandra with the Midsummer rites, they go to collect wood from inside it.

> As we came to the tower he stood still for a moment, looking up at its height against the sky.
>   'How tall is it?' he asked. 'It must be seventy or eighty feet, surely.'
>   'Sixty,' I told him. 'It looks taller because it's so solitary.'
>   'It reminds me of a picture I once saw called "The Sorcerer's Tower".'

After they get the wood, Simon helps her out, saying: 'Look – there's magic for you.'

> The mist from the moat was rolling right up Belmotte; already the lower slopes were veiled. ... A carpet of mist had crept to within a few feet of us, then crept no further – Simon said I must be putting a spell on it. Down by the moat it had mounted so high that only the castle towers rose clear of it.[9]

In the final chapter, Simon sits beside Cassandra at the foot of Belmotte, and offers to take her to America with him. Wisely, although 'something about the way he spoke my name made me sure that if I said yes, he would ask me to marry him', she demurs, knowing 'it was only an impulse ... a mixture of liking me very much and longing for Rose'. She also turns down his offer to send her to university. 'I only want to write. And there's no college for that except life.'

Much ink has been spent speculating on what happens to Cassandra in the end. Does she marry Simon? I don't think so, despite that maudlin reiteration of 'I love you.' He is in love with England, not her. Since she is such a recognizable portrait of her creator as a young woman, my money is on Stephen, who is inescapably reminiscent of Dodie's adoring husband Alec; both were given screen tests because of their good looks, and both were well equipped to surround the object of their at first unrequited love with lifelong practical and intellectual support.

Charming, acerbic and steely-willed, Dodie never wanted to share a bedroom or have children. Instead, she and Alec had a succession of Dalmatian dogs: Pongo, Folly and Buzz, and the litter of fifteen that would inspire her best-known book, *The Hundred and One Dalmatians* (1956). It was written three years after they returned to England and The Barretts, where they spent the rest of their lives. Dodie Smith lived to the ripe old age of 94. She left an extraordinary legacy: two utterly different books that continue to enchant readers decades after her death, one for its spotted dogs, the other for its unforgettable castle. It was one she had predicted in *I Capture the Castle*:

> The originators among writers – perhaps, in a sense, the
> only true creators – dip deep and bring up one perfect work;
> complete, not a link in a chain. Later, they dip again – for
> something as unique.[10]

VAST SHAMBLES

Gormenghast and Mervyn Peake

It was as though the castle was recovering from an illness, or was about to have one ... as though the labyrinthian place had woken from its sleep of stone and iron and in drawing breath had left a vacuum, and it was in this vacuum that its puppets moved.

Mervyn Peake, *Gormenghast*[1]

Gormenghast ... is at once the image of the mind, an inspiration to tender nostalgia, a breeding place for insurrection because of its autocratic power, and a terrible warren of the unpredictable.

Lesley Glyn Marx, 1983[2]

No dwelling in modern fiction is as unambiguously personified as Gormenghast Castle, the ancient home of the Earls of Groan. The role it plays in the Titus Groan books is both more powerful than and quite different from that of any of the other significant dwellings so far considered. It is a personification of the past, of childhood and memory. Its decayed state when we are introduced to it reflects its declining power. It was once very different. While exploring, Titus comes across an 'old circus-ground of bygone colours' where the floorboards must once have been a deep and glowing crimson, and the three walls the most brilliant of yellows. The banisters were alternately apple-green and azure, the frames of the doorless doorways being also this last colour.[3]

Now, 'withdrawn and ruinous it broods in umbra', rising from its mountain

> in immemorial defiance of the changing airs, and skies. ...
> Stone after grey stone climbed. ... Stone after grey stone; and
> a sense of the heaving skywards of great blocks, one upon
> another in a climbing weight, ponderous and yet alive with the
> labour of dead days.[4]

Peake's metaphors emphasize Gormenghast's sentience. The book's characters are described as 'the Castle's breath'. Its walls are 'pocked with windows', ivy lies 'across the face of that southern wing like a black hand', the Tower of Flints arises

> like a mutilated finger from among the fists of knuckled
> masonry and pointed blasphemously at heaven. At night the
> owls made of it an echoing throat; by day it stood voiceless and
> cast its long shadow.[5]

There are recurrent references to 'the body of the castle' and to its tangled passages as arteries. Voices grind from its 'lungs of granite'. In summer 'the masonry sweated and was horribly silent'; when autumn comes, 'the crumbling castle, looming among the mists, exhaled the season, and every cold stone breathed it out'.

> Strung across the capstone jaws of its great head a hundred
> windows, the size of teeth, reflected the dawn. There was less
> the nature of glass about them than of bone.[6]

'Acres of ivy' like 'millions of heart-shaped eyelids winking wetly' flutter on its walls 'like the long hair of some corpse'. An exiled character gazes longingly at 'the long, broken line of Gormenghast's backbone'. Its ancient voice is 'endlessness of endlessness', grinding at night 'from lungs of granite'. Tradition demands that

Titus obey 'the voice of stones heaped up into grey towers' until he dies.

> Drear ritual turned its wheel. The ferment of the heart, within these walls, was mocked by every length of sleeping shadow. The passions, no greater than candle flames, flickered in Time's yawn, for Gormenghast, huge and adumbrate, out-crumbles all.[7]

In his 1956 radio play of *Titus Groan*, Peake further emphasized the personification of the Groans' ancestral home by making Gormenghast's 'animated spirit' the narrator.

> I draw my breath through the interstices
> Of innumerable stones.
> I am a world of masonry. I am
> The bones and blood of it...
> And the dreams that shroud it.[8]

Jungian archetypes – rebirth, the trickster, spirit – thread through the books. Sullen and incalculably vast, the castle is an inescapable Great Mother, and, fittingly, it is Titus's massive mother the Countess Gertrude – a name that teasingly evokes *Hamlet*, another tortured prince in a castle – who is most profoundly identified with Gormenghast. She reclines 'hugely and motionlessly', her dark red hair, woven into a knotted structure on her head, casting an enormous 'umbrage'. A furlong of white cats trails after her. A bullfinch has a nest in her red hair. She is the Countess Gertrude 'of huge clay'; her love for Titus is 'as heavy and as formless as loam'.

The saga has been called a Gothic fantasy, but it is closer to a medieval quest or a pilgrim's progress – the epigraph of the first book is a line from Bunyan – in which Titus struggles to separate himself from his mother, pursues his elusive foster-sister, and struggles to throw off the shackles of his destiny. It shifts form. *Titus Groan* (1946) is a scene-setter which introduces the Groans and their grotesque attendants: the stick-insect-like valet Flay, the effete but effective Dr Prunesquallor and the grossly obese cook Abiatha Swelter. Steerpike, 'a solitary Satan', begins his rise to power, charming all the castle's women except the ponderous Countess, making himself useful to its men, and striking at its heart by setting fire to the library, the loss of which sends Titus's father Lord Sepulchrave mad, and gives Steerpike a grip 'on the very entrails of Gormenghast'.

Steerpike's rise continues in *Gormenghast* (1950), while Titus, now 77th Earl of Groan, rebels against the traditional chains that bind his present and his future, and asserts his identity as an individual by escaping from the castle into the thrilling world of the forest in passionate pursuit of his foster-sister the Thing. For this he is punished by incarceration in the Lichen Fort, locked in a womb within a womb. After the discovery of Steerpike's crimes, which include poisoning Nanny Slagg, starving the Earl's demented twin sisters to death in a remote apartment, and causing Titus's sister Fuchsia's death, Flay, Prunesquallor and Titus band together to entrap him. But he murders Flay and disappears into the furthest recesses of the castle. He is, however, no match for the combined forces of Gormenghast and Gertrude.

The most spectacular vision of the castle as corporeal entity occurs when the castle is lit up while the fiendish Steerpike is being hunted:

> Long before any message could have been couriered across the
> body of Gormenghast, there was not a limb, not a digit that
> had not responded to the universal sense of suffocation, not the
> merest finger joint of stone that had not set itself alight. ...They
> swam, those walls, with the hues of hell, with the tints of Zion.
> The breasts of the plumaged seraphim; the scales of Satan.[9]

A 'black and endless deluge' washes through the castle like a ferocious purge, turning it into an island; everybody takes refuge in its uppermost storeys, and Gertrude orchestrates a fleet to search everywhere still above water. It is in the end Titus who finds and eliminates Steerpike, falling on him through tangles of ivy like an avenging angel. Yet Titus does not act to save Gormenghast, only to avenge the death of Fuchsia and Flay. Ironically, Steerpike, serial killer though he was, would have served the castle as meticulously as any former earl. Titus seeks only escape.

> What do I care if the castle's heart is sound or not? …
> I want to be myself, and become what I make myself, a person,
> a real live person and not a symbol any more. … To hell with
> Gormenghast.[10]

He is not going to be the 77th Earl of Groan but the first of a new line. He deserts Gormenghast's and his mother's suffocating influence and rides away to find a self of his own.

> A kind of power climbed through him like sap. Not the power
> of Gormenghast, or the pride of lineage. These were but dead-
> sea fruit. But the power of the imagination's pride.[11]

The ambitious, confused grotesqueries of the Gormenghast books are better understood when we know about its creator's life journey. Mervyn Peake (1911–1968) was a brilliant draughtsman whose way of using words was as painterly as it was literary; a poet whose love for ebullient nonsense veiled his emotional sensitivity. His drawings have a kinship with bestiaries and surrealism, Breughel and Bosch. He was particularly fond of Dickens, admiring the 'farcical aptness' of his characters' names, and 'his dark and deathless rabble of long shadows'.[12] His description of darkness descending over the castle salutes the fog-drenched opening of *Bleak House*:

> Darkness over the four wings of Gormenghast. Darkness lying
> against the glass doors of the Christening Room and pressing
> its impalpable body through the ivy leaves of Lady Groan's
> choked window. Pressing itself against the walls, hiding
> them to all save touch alone; … swallowing everything in its
> insatiable omnipresence. Darkness over the stone sky-field
> where clouds moved through it invisibly.[13]

A 1945 commission to illustrate *Bleak House* reacquainted him with the dreary splendours of Chesney Wold, a moss and ivy-drenched 'labyrinth of grandeur' with grotesquely carved stone monsters and a mausoleum. Labyrinth is a key concept in both *Bleak House* and the Gormenghast novels. Dickens's characters are as lost in the corridors of Chancery and the streets of London as Peake's are in Gormenghast Castle and the mysterious Under-River world of *Titus Alone*, where in an arena he likens to a 'dark circus' Titus sees a 'great conclave of the displaced' who are close kin to the wretched inhabitants of the *Bleak House* slum, Tom-All-Alone. Also woven into Peake's rich mental furnishings are John Donne and Coleridge, Gerard Manley Hopkins and Herman Melville, James Joyce, T.F. Powys and T.S. Eliot, whose *The Waste Land* echoes through *Titus Alone*.

In *A World Away*, her memoir of her husband, Maeve Gilmore emphasizes the constant presence in Peake's imagination of his childhood in China. His parents met there: Ernest Peake practised as a mission doctor and Bessie was a mission assistant. All but two of Mervyn's first eleven years were spent there, mainly in Tientsin. He watched his father perform amputations and visited the mortuary. The freaks and cripples which haunt his poetry and prose derive from the miseries of the shanty towns that hemmed the walls of Chinese cities like the huts of Gormenghast's Outer Dwellers. China's dramatic landscapes, distinctively shaped mountains, dense forests, vast deserts, meandering rivers and scattered islands fed his imagination, as did its exotic art and architecture, highly developed caste system and ancient rituals. Peake saw words 'as if he were listening to an unknown language, in shapes',[14] something natural to an upbringing among pictograms.

The family returned to England for good in 1922. Dr Peake became a GP in Wallington, Surrey, and Mervyn joined his brother Lonnie, who was already boarding at Eltham College, a South-east London school founded for the sons of missionaries. Eric Drake and his brother Burgess were inspiring teachers, full of modern theories. Mervyn left in 1929, and went first to Croydon Art College, and then to the Royal Academy Schools. In 1933 he moved to Sark, where he spent two years working in the studio of the artist's colony

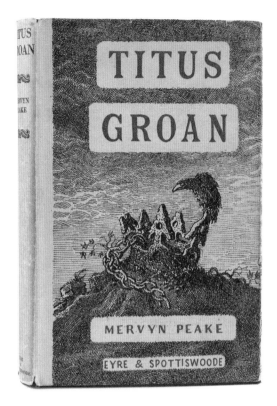

Mervyn Peake's design for the dust jacket for *Titus Groan*, the first of his Gormenghast novels, conveyed the sense that its heir Titus has of being chained to his destiny.

which Eric Drake had set up there. On his return in 1935 he became a teacher at Westminster School of Art, where he met Maeve Gilmore, whom he married in 1937. They lived in a Battersea flat provided by her mother, and both flourished professionally, holding several exhibitions. Peake began illustrating books to great acclaim.

When war threatened in 1939, Mervyn applied to become a war artist, backed by a recommendation by Augustus John, but to no avail. Had he been accepted, the Titus books would probably not have been written. Instead, a racehorse harnessed to a cart, he went into the regular army, moving around England six times in three years as one department after another perceived his unfitness. Long spells spent away from his studio and the comforts of family life in quasi-imprisonment in army camps around Britain left him with plenty of time to write and no material but his own imagination. What he planned to create, he said later in a radio talk, was 'a kind of pantechnicon book, in which I could shove in any mental furniture, however horrible, however beautiful'. During these frustrating years he worked intensively on *Titus Groan*: the absurd and pointless rituals of Gormenghast parodied those of the army. Officials, Muzzlehatch would say in *Titus Alone*, 'are nothing, my dear boy, but the pip-headed, trash-bellied putrid scrannel of earth'.

In 1942 army life became too much for him, and he suffered a nervous breakdown; in 1943 he was invalided out of the army. When he recovered he was given several war artist commissions. He returned to Sark with his family to write the second of the Titus books. In it, the castle is closely identified with Sark. Chapter 3 describes 'the rough margins of the castle life' as 'irregular as the coastline of a squall-rent island'; incessant rain transforms the castle itself into an island, with bays and headlands; and during the hunt for Steerpike distinctive geographical features of Sark are named. Countess Gertrude says to Titus:

> You have been in the North Headstones beyond Gory and the
> Silver Mines. I know where you've been. You've been to the
> Twin Fingers where Little Sark begins and the Bluff narrows.
> Between the Twins would be water now. Am I right?[15]

The war and its aftermath influenced the Titus books profoundly. *Titus Groan* is full of Peake's frustration at forced and pointless inactivity; as atrocities mount, *Gormenghast* reflects the sense of being under attack. Neither, however, bore its scars as deeply as *Titus Alone*, written after Peake's imagination had been violently informed by his fact-finding 1945 tour through war-shattered Germany. He visited Belsen alone, witnessing and recording in drawings the human cost of the atrocities performed by its experimental scientists. On his return to England, he had hopes that he would be able to use his experiences in 'a great and glorious rash of work'.

> Groan I feel could grow giant, imaginative wings, flare out
> majestically, ludicrously, fantastically, earthily, gloriously into
> creation, unlike anything else in English literature.[16]

His mindset shifted from fantasies spun round his childhood experiences and his beloved Sark to science fiction derived from what he had seen in Germany, the London Blitz, his brother's experiences in the Far East, and news of the weapons of mass destruction used at Hiroshima and Nagasaki.

Literary influences on Mervyn Peake (1911–1968) included John Donne and Coleridge, Gerard Manley Hopkins and Herman Melville, James Joyce, T.F. Powys and T.S. Eliot, whose *The Waste Land* echoes through *Titus Alone*.

At the end of *Gormenghast* Titus quits the castle, riding away on the classic steed of the romantic hero, a horse. He is determined to live in his own right, though he still clutches a tiny talisman of Gormenghast's corporeal entity, a 'small knuckle of flint'. The third book in the saga, *Titus Alone* (1959), is science fiction rather than fantasy, jumping from archaisms to a high-tech city 'where the scientists worked, like drones, to the glory of science and in praise of death'. Its skies are dominated by tiny mechanical spies (a prescient imagining of drones) and airships, and its society split between wealthy hedonists and an underworld of refugees preyed upon by a mafia of super-crooks. Titus is implacably pursued by a pair of helmeted soldiers, one of whom has facial scarring reminiscent of Steerpike. He finds a splendid ally in the joyously eccentric Muzzlehatch, is initiated sexually by the statuesque Juno, and pursued though the subterranean world of Under-River by

Veil, the personification of evil, and preyed upon by Cheeta, whose room, with 'the white camel skins of the carpet and the dusky red of the tapestries', is a bizarre echo of Gertrude's.

Titus gradually realizes that Gormenghast, for all his loathing of its demands, provided him with an identity. In 'a long waft of memory', he sees

> the long coruscated outline of Gormenghast and the stones of his home where the lizards lazed, and there, blotting out all else, his mother as he had last seen her at the door of the shanty, the great dripping castle drawn up like a backcloth behind her. 'You will come back,' she had said. 'All roads lead back to Gormenghast.'[17]

And he does, trudging through lonely voids until at last he recognizes a great lichened boulder as the one on which he played 'king of the castle' as a boy, and from which, if he climbed it, he would see the castle itself.

> A gun boomed. It boomed again. It boomed seven times.
>   There it lay behind the boulder; the immemorial ritual of his home. It was the dawn salvo. It boomed for him, for the Seventy-Seventh Earl, Titus Groan, Lord of Gormenghast, wherever he might be.[18]

But Titus does not go home. Reassured that Gormenghast will always be there for him, he can internalize the strength it imparts. He sets off to explore new worlds.

What those would have amounted to will never be known. The fourth book in the series never went beyond two opening pages and lists of the new territories Titus was to explore. Peake's mind was failing, and he struggled to finish *Titus Alone*, which has several agonized references to what he was experiencing. 'I have lost my bearings', mourns Titus during his trial. He cannot convey 'the truth in my head' to his listeners. At the age of 47 Peake was diagnosed variously with Parkinson's disease and premature senility, and underwent the then fashionable treatments first of

ECT (electro-convulsive-therapy) and then frontal lobotomy. 'It feels like everything has been stolen', he told his friend Michael Moorcock after the operation. He spent the last decade of his life in private care homes, and died at the age of 57.[19] His had been a rich life, full of laughter and friendship, and astonishingly productive. In the poem that marks his grave, he wrote 'To live at all is miracle enough ... Come what come may the imagination's heart / Is constellation high and can't be weighed.' Gormenghast Castle lives on to haunt the imagination of every one of its readers.

The hill : hobbiton-across-the Water

DEEP ROOTS
Bag End and J.R.R. Tolkien

I feel that as long as the Shire lies behind, safe and
comfortable, I shall find wandering more bearable: I shall know
that somewhere there is a firm foothold, even if my feet cannot
stand there again.

> Frodo, in J.R.R. Tolkien, *The Fellowship of the Ring*[1]

Bag End gives Bilbo purpose: it is, in fact, the true object of
his quest. For him it is like a sacred place, whose image he
invokes ... in moments of distress, as if he was saying a prayer.

> Wayne Hammond, 1987[2]

Like *Alice in Wonderland*, another famous children's book written
by an Oxford don, *The Hobbit, or There and Back Again* (1937)
begins with a hole in the ground. There the resemblance ends: the
hole in the ground is not a tunnel to a dream world, but one of
the most memorable and desirable residences in fiction: Bag End,
Underhill, home of the hobbit Bilbo Baggins.[3] Its round front door
is smartly painted green and sports 'a shiny yellow brass knob in
the exact middle'. It opens onto

J.R.R. Tolkien's painting of the orderly little world of Hobbiton-on-the-Hill
shows the circular green front door of Bag End, home of Bilbo and Frodo
Baggins, and the essential starting and finishing point of *The Hobbit* and
The Lord of the Rings.

a tube-shaped hall like a tunnel: a very comfortable tunnel without smoke, with panelled walls, and floors tiled and carpeted, provided with polished chairs, and lots and lots of pegs for hats and coats – the hobbit was fond of visitors.[4]

The tunnel leads to a succession of rooms: those on the left-hand side have deep-set round windows looking out onto neat gardens and meadows that slope down to a river; on the right are well-filled larders and capacious cellars. The hobbit lands, referred to in *The Lord of the Rings* as the Shire, are 'a wide respectable country inhabited by decent folk, with good roads, an inn or two, and now and then a dwarf or a farmer ambling by on business'. Hobbiton is an especially peaceful place.

> In this neighbourhood heroes are scarce, or simply not to be found. Swords in these parts are mostly blunt, and axes are used for trees, and shields as cradles or dish-covers.[5]

Burrowing out underground homes emphasizes the importance of roots and is the habit of the most ancient hobbit families; newcomers often build houses above ground, though they still adopt such traditions as round windows.

Into Bilbo's placid world walks a renowned wizard called Gandalf, looking for someone 'to share an adventure I am arranging'. By the end of the next day a throng of dwarves have filled Bag End, and Bilbo has, much to his own surprise, agreed to go with them to recover from a notorious dragon the hoard of treasure that it stole long ago from their forefathers. His mother's wild Tookish blood has triumphed over his Baggins father's timid tendencies. But as the perils and miseries of the expedition increase, his resolve wavers. 'Bother burgling and everything to do with it! I wish I was at home in my nice hole by the fire, with the kettle just beginning to sing', he mutters to himself. After some unpleasant encounters, and narrowly escaping trolls, they finally reach a safe domestic space, 'the Last Homely House', the Rivendell dwelling place of Elrond and his elves.

His house was perfect, whether you liked food, or sleep, or work, or story-telling, or singing, or just sitting and thinking best, or a pleasant mixture of them all.[6]

Although Rivendell is a place of healing and inspiration, and one to which Bilbo will opt to retire when he reaches the grand old age of 111 at the beginning of *The Lord of the Rings*, it is no substitute for the familiar comforts of the Shire. References to Bilbo's far-away home recur through *The Hobbit* like a tolling bell. Here are two of more than a dozen. When an eagle saving him from certain death at the hands of the goblins asks him ecstatically 'What is finer than flying?'

Bilbo would have liked to say: 'A warm bath and late breakfast on the lawn afterwards'; but he thought it better to say nothing at all.[7]

And when he is trapped among the elves

He was thinking once again of his comfortable chair before the fire in his favourite sitting-room in his hobbit-hole, and of the kettle singing. ... 'I wish I was back in my hobbit-hole by my own warm fireside!'[8]

Throughout the book, battles with wargs, goblins, spiders and wood-elves, and Bilbo's theft of a ring with a very significant history and escape from the dragon Smaug, alternate with comforting episodes of companionable pipe-smoking and rounds of drinks in warm hostelries, of scrumptious meals, hot baths and proper beds. Domestic cosiness is an unusual quality to single out for recurring praise in a tale of a quest for dragon-guarded treasure that will climax in a war between five great armies. However, references to 'comfort', 'roots' and especially 'home' permeate *The Hobbit* and recur as a trademark of Tolkien's writings.

The Hobbit was a bedtime story full of in-jokes that Tolkien intended to be enjoyed by his own children and his faerie-friendly colleagues. It was also a taster of the far more ambitious project on which he had been working intermittently for two decades and would continue refining to the end of his life: *The Silmarillion*.

I had a mind to make a body of more or less connected
legend, ranging from the large and cosmogonic to the level
of romantic fairy-story – the larger founded on the lesser in
contact with the earth, the lesser drawing splendour from the
vast backcloths – which I could dedicate simply: to England; to
my country.[9]

'The *Lord of the Rings* is only the end part of a work nearly twice
as long which I worked at between 1936 and 53', he explained in
answer to an admiring letter from W.H. Auden (7 June 1955). His
extensive *legendarium* was the fruit of a lifetime spent studying the
language and literature of Old English, Welsh and Old Norse, and
writing in time off from being Reader and then Professor of English
Language at Leeds, and later Professor of English Language and
Literature at Oxford.

The first hint of halflings appeared in 'The Cottage of Lost
Play', a story written in a school exercise book (now in the Bodleian
Library) while Tolkien was recovering from a bout of trench fever.
A traveller arrives at the foot of a hill and sees

a tiny dwelling whose many small windows were curtained
snugly, yet only so that a most warm and delicious light, as of
hearts content within, looked forth. Then his heart yearned for
kind company, and the desire for wayfaring died in him – and
impelled by a great longing he turned aside at this cottage
door.

Knocking, he asks whose house it is, and is told that it is Mar
Vanwa Tyaliéva, the Cottage of Lost Play, built many years ago
by Lindo and Vairë, and now full of their friends and relations.
Perceiving the traveller's surprise that such an apparently tiny place
held so many people, the doorman says:

Small is the dwelling, but smaller still are they that dwell here
– for all who enter must be very small indeed, or of their own
good wish become as very little folk even as they stand upon
the threshold.[10]

Invited in for a night of 'guest-kindliness', he finds himself in a room called the Hall of Play Regained. A host of laughing children arrive, and after the meal everyone goes to 'the Room of the Log Fire for the telling of tales'. The tales that follow are the first versions of the elvish myths which Tolkien's son Christopher would eventually publish as *The Book of Lost Tales*. By 1936, Tolkien's fondness for small people led him to imagine a new race of beings: hobbits.

Two decades later, in *The Lord of the Rings* trilogy (1954–5), Tolkien's voice changed from the confiding and avuncular tone of *The Hobbit* to that of a bard creating a patriotic myth 'fit for the more adult mind of a land long steeped in poetry'.[11] It was, wrote C.S. Lewis,

> like lightning from a clear sky. … In it heroic romance, gorgeous, eloquent, and unashamed, has suddenly returned at a period almost pathological in its anti-romanticism.[12]

Once again, Tolkien prefaces the perilous adventures to come with loving details of a stable, rooted world. Bag End is both the starting point and the finishing point. The Prologue of *The Fellowship of the Ring* is an encomium on the peaceful world of the Shire, home of hobbits, we are told, for over a thousand years. Hobbit country is affectionately detailed in the next three chapters, before the action shifts to the wider world of Middle-earth, realm of elves, men and dwarves, trolls and giants, sinister ghouls and spectres, the tree-like Ents, talking animals and wizards dealing death and destruction from the tops of inhospitable towers. The hobbit lands play a central part in this invented universe. In Humphrey Carpenter's words,

> The theme of his new story was large, but it was to have its centre in the courage of these small people; and the heart of the book was to be found in the inns and gardens of The Shire, Tolkien's representation of all that he loved best about England.[13]

Bag End is 'a thread of familiarity through the web of the fantastic', a 'bridge between world of the reader and the world of the story'.[14] Just as Bilbo Baggins, disillusioned by his adventures, realizes that the real treasure is back in his own 'quiet Western land, and the Hill, and his hobbit-hole under it', so, in *The Lord of the Rings*, Frodo, Merry, Pippin and Sam are fortified by remembering the Shire. The story opens in Bag End on 22 September 1401 (Shire Reckoning), when Bilbo puts on a splendidly embroidered silk waistcoat and throws a party to celebrate the gross of years that he and his cousin and adopted heir Frodo tot up between them. The celebration ends with Bilbo's disappearance, leaving Bag End and the ring to Frodo. That night, Gandalf explains to Frodo that the Shire, which 'has always seemed so safe and familiar', is under threat. The blanket of the dark is descending.

The ring Frodo now holds is not merely one that enables invisibility. It is the One Ring, a means of world domination sought by Sauron, the Dark Lord of Mordor, It is Frodo's mission to destroy it, in order to save not only the Shire but all of Middle-earth. Frodo is appalled. Nevertheless, he takes on the mission, supported by three valiant friends: his cousins Meriadoc Brandybuck (Merry) and Peregrin Took (Pippin), and his gardener Samwise Gamgee, who will emerge as the greatest hero of the piece. Merry and Pippin echoed the schoolfellows who, like Tolkien, enlisted as officers to fight in World War I. Sam was, Tolkien later wrote, 'a reflection of the English soldier, of the privates and batmen I knew in the 1914 war, and recognised as so far superior to myself'.[15]

All frequently long to be back home. Looking back from the ruined fortress of Weathertop, 'Frodo for the first time fully realized his homelessness and danger. He wished bitterly that his fortune had left him in the quiet and beloved Shire.' It is thoughts of the Shire and all it stands for that make their journey bearable. Its thriving and prosperous state is contrasted with the dead or dying realms through which they pass. When he is in the mines of Moria, Frodo's thoughts wander to

Bag End in the days while Bilbo was still there. He wished with all his heart that he was back there, and in those days, mowing the lawn, or pottering among the flowers, and that he had never heard of Moria, or *mithril* – or the Ring.[16]

But he concentrates on his quest, although he becomes so dominated by the Ring that he finds it increasingly difficult to bring his home to mind. It is Merry and Pippin and above all Sam who can still use Bag End and the Shire as empowering mental touchstones. Reflecting on the strangeness of their situation high in a tower in Minas Tirith, Merry says to Pippin:

'It is best to love first what you are fitted to love, I suppose: you must start somewhere and have some roots, and the soil of the Shire is deep.[17]

'A supper, or a breakfast, by the fire in the old kitchen at Bagshot Row' is what Sam longs for as he and Frodo crawl through Mordor, dogged by Gollum. When Frodo collapses, Sam lifts him onto his back 'with no more difficulty than if he were carrying a hobbit-child pig-a-back in some romp on the lawns or hayfields of the Shire' and carries him onwards. After the Ring and Gollum have plunged into the fiery abyss of the Cracks of Doom, Sam realizes that Frodo has become himself again, 'the dear master of the sweet days in the Shire'. When the celebrations are over, Frodo asks leave to return to the Shire 'that is my home'; Aragorn gives it, saying 'the tree grows best in the land of its sires'.

The last chapters, 'Homeward Bound' and 'The Scouring of the Shire' describe how the desecration of Bag End and the Shire is made good. But Frodo, sick in mind and body, decides to sail with the Elves, who are leaving Middle-earth for the West. It is Sam Gamgee, his wife Rosie and innumerable small Gamgees who will make Bag End a home again. In making Sam the owner of the place that remained a lodestar to them throughout their perils, Tolkien was thanking the young working-class men who fought so selflessly for their country in 1914–18 and 1939–45.

What inspired Tolkien's unmistakably English Shire and the literally down-to-earth Bag End, so strangely at odds with the bleak towers of the wizards, the romantic greenwood dwellings of elves, the palatial mountain caves of dwarves and the mighty cities of men? John Ronald Reuel Tolkien was born on 3 January 1892 in Bloemfontein, capital of the Orange Free State. Diamonds and gold had been discovered in Kimberley and Witwatersrand in the 1870s and 1880s, and his father Arthur Tolkien exhibited all Bilbo's Tookish eagerness for a quest for treasure when in 1889, at the age of 32, he boarded a ship for Cape Town. He had exchanged low pay at the Birmingham branch of Lloyds Bank for a post with the Bank of Africa in the hopes of making enough money to justify his marriage to his young fiancée Mabel Suffield. By the end of 1890 he was manager of the Bloemfontein branch. He invited his beloved Mab out to join him, and they were married in Cape Town Cathedral in 1891. A second son, Hilary, was born in February 1894.

After a freezing summer and a plague of locusts, Mabel took the children back to England in April 1895 to meet their grandparents and build up their strength; they lived with her parents John and Emily Suffield in Kings Heath, on the fringes of Birmingham. In November, news came that Arthur had contracted rheumatic fever; Mabel prepared to go to him, but before she could leave he died. Mabel moved with her two sons to a modest semi-detached villa in Sarehole, a peaceful hamlet 2 miles from Kings Heath and 4 miles from the centre of Birmingham. Tolkien described the four years that he spent in Sarehole as 'the longest-seeming and most formative part of my life'.[18] The countryside around his home between the ages of 4 and 8 was 'a kind of lost paradise'.

> I was brought back to my native heath with a memory of
> something different – hot, dry and barren – and it intensified
> my love of my own countryside. I could draw you a map of
> every inch of it. I loved it with an intensity of love that was
> a kind of nostalgia reversed. It was a kind of double coming
> home, the effect on me of all these meadows... There was an

old mill that really did grind corn with two millers, a great big pond with swans on it, a sandpit, a wonderful dell with flowers, a few old-fashioned village houses and, further away, a stream with another mill.[19]

Tolkien always felt closer to his mother's family, writing to his son Michael that,

> Though a Tolkien by name, I am a Suffield by tastes, talents, and upbringing, and any corner of that county (however fair or squalid) is in an indefinable way 'home' to me, as no other part of the world is.[20]

In a 1955 letter to his publisher bemoaning the identification of the Shire with Oxfordshire, he declared that 'it is in fact more or less a Warwickshire village of about the period of the Diamond Jubilee of Queen Victoria', explaining that he had himself been brought up in just such a place. His famous painting of 'The Hill: Hobbiton-across-the Water', with its mill, round-windowed farmhouses and flower-filled gardens, is an idealized picture of Sarehole and its surrounding countryside.

In 1900 Mabel took her sons closer into Birmingham so that they could attend schools. When she died in 1904, memories of Sarehole and the Worcestershire and Warwickshire countryside became even more hallowed. Tolkien paid them tribute by using local names in both *The Hobbit* and *The Lord of the Rings*. The name Bag End was a nod at the name of his beloved paternal aunt Jane Neave's Worcestershire farmhouse, Dormston Manor Farm, an ancient hotchpotch of a house at the end of a lane. Tolkien first visited it to convalesce in 1923, and enjoyed his anglicization of the French *cul-de-sac* so much that he reversed the process by calling Bilbo's snobbish cousins the Sackville [*sac+ville*]-Bagginses. When Frodo, Sam, Merry and Pippin set off for Took country in Book I of *The Lord of the Rings*, they pass through Green Hill Country and the Woody End, perhaps salutes to Sarehole's Green Hill and Wood End.

Although Tolkien served in the First World War, once he was settled in academe he preferred imagining adventures to having them. For most of his working life he lived in North Oxford, bicycling between the family home in Northmoor Road and the University's colleges, libraries and lecture rooms, and enjoying convivial sessions in local pubs with such kindred spirits as C.S. Lewis and Charles Williams. He was, he wrote to Deborah Webster in 1958,

> a hobbit in all but size. I like gardens, trees, and unmechanized farmlands; I smoke a pipe, and like good plain food (unrefrigerated), but detest French cooking; I like, and even dare to wear in these dull days, ornamental waistcoats. I am fond of mushrooms (out of a field); have a very simple sense of humour (which even my appreciative critics find tiresome); I go to bed late and get up late (when possible). I do not travel much.[21]

But he had a grander side. W.H. Auden wrote to him saying:

> I don't think I have ever told you what an unforgettable experience it was for me as an undergraduate, hearing you recite Beowulf. The voice was the voice of Gandalf.[22]

Tolkien's father died when Tolkien was just 4 years old, and he lost his mother when he was 12. Gandalf and Galadriel were idealized creations that perhaps went some way to substitute for them, and he liked to romanticize his wife as the elf-maid Lúthien and himself as her mortal soulmate Beren. What stabilized his flights of fancy, just as the Shire anchored the hobbits, was his everyday world, 'the simple and ordinary' one of home and children, where deep roots held him. There he was the benign Father Christmas of the annual letters he wrote to John, Michael, Christopher and Priscilla, the blundering motorist Mr Bliss, and the toiling artist Niggle, who is so impeded by everyday obligations that he completes only one perfect Leaf of the infinitely various Tree he embarked on creating. The lines that Gandalf leaves at the Prancing Pony originally

'I am a hobbit in all but size', J.R.R. Tolkien told a journalist in 1958. 'I like gardens, trees, and ... even dare to wear in these dull days, ornamental waistcoats.'

had a rather different purpose, but it seems to me they accord well with Tolkien's belief in the importance of a secure heartland.

All that is gold does not glitter,
Not all those who wander are lost;
The old that is strong does not wither,
Deep roots are not reached by the frost.[23]

CASTLE OF
ANCIENT MAGIC
Hogwarts School and J.K. Rowling

Voldemort and Harry ... share an essential kinship – the
kinship of two boys who grew up alone without the people who
should have loved them and who find the replacement for that
love in a place rather than a person. They find it in Hogwarts.

Beatrice Groves, 2017[1]

Hogwarts is a world in itself and more of a character than a
place.

Claudia Fenske, 2008[2]

Powerful castles begin and end my book. Hogwarts School, 'stronghold of ancient magic',[3] is, like my starting point, *The Castle of
Otranto*, full of mystery and menace: subterranean passages, magical
monsters, ghosts emerging from portraits, ambulant suits of armour.
But it is also an exceptionally benevolent place, a home where the
apprentice wizard Harry Potter feels loved and appreciated for the
first time in his life.

Orphaned as a baby, Harry grows up with his mother's sister's
family, the grotesque and unkind Dursleys in 4 Privet Drive in the
Surrey suburb of Little Whinging. His first eleven years are spent
in Cinderella style, despised and exploited, his bedroom a cupboard
under the stairs. But at the beginning of *Harry Potter and the*

Philosopher's Stone (1997), the first volume of Rowling's seven-book saga, a shaggy giant of a man called Rubeus Hagrid explodes into his life, and tells him that his parents were a witch and a wizard. He must leave the world of 'Muggles' (as unmagical people are known) and be educated at Hogwarts School of Witchcraft and Wizardry, travelling from King's Cross's Platform 9¾ on the Hogwarts Express, a magnificent steam train which thunders the length of Britain to a remote and mountainous destination.

At the first sight of the castle, there is a 'loud 'Oooooh!' from the new pupils.

> The narrow path had opened suddenly on to the edge of a
> great black lake. Perched atop a high mountain on the other
> side, its windows sparkling in the starry sky, was a vast castle
> with many turrets and towers.[4]

Led by Hagrid, soon revealed as the school's keeper of magical creatures, Harry and his fellow new pupils glide across the lake in a fleet of little boats, which take them through a curtain of ivy into an underground harbour. They disembark, and climb a rock passageway until they emerge on the lawn in front of the castle, and go through its huge oak front door.

> The stone walls were lit with flaming torches ... the ceiling
> was too high to make out, and a magnificent marble staircase
> facing them led to the upper floors.[5]

After being startled by a throng of ghosts who stream past them, chattering busily, they are led into the Great Hall, which is lit by floating candles. Here they are sorted into houses named after the school's four founders according to their character: Gryffindor is the home of the brave of heart, Ravenclaw of the clever, Hufflepuff of the faithful and fair, Slytherin of the cunning and ambitious. The choice is made by a magical Sorting Hat, which muses in verse as to where each will go. To Harry's relief, the Hat, after considering Slytherin, accepts his own wish to be in Gryffindor. After a dinner featuring every child's favourite foods, he goes up to his dormitory, and falls asleep in a four-poster bed hung with red curtains and made cosy with a warming pan. The house common room has comfortable armchairs set around the fire, on which they toast crumpets and marshmallows. 'Your house will be something like your family', explains the stern but kindly Professor McGonagall.

So it proves. Harry finds he is already famous as the baby that the evil wizard Voldemort failed to kill. Ugly duckling turned swan, he is at last in his element. Very soon, 'the castle felt more like home than Privet Drive had ever done'. He builds up a substitute family: a paternal mentor in its headmaster Albus Dumbledore, and an unexpectedly maternal one in Hagrid, who tenderly delivered the swaddled baby Harry to the Dursleys in *Stone*.[6] In the last book (*Harry Potter and the Deathly Hallows*), Hagrid carries Harry's apparently lifeless body back to Hogwarts with similar tenderness, 'arms trembling with the force of his heaving sobs, great tears splashed down upon him', an image evocative of a pietà.[7]

In Gryffindor, Harry finds faithful friends in Ron Weasley and Hermione Granger. The castle constantly surprises its pupils.

> There were a hundred and forty-two staircases at Hogwarts: wide, sweeping ones; narrow, rickety ones; some that led somewhere different on a Friday... Then there were doors that wouldn't open unless you asked politely, or tickled them in exactly the right place, and doors that weren't really doors at all, but solid walls just pretending. It was also very hard to remember where anything was, because it all seemed to move around a lot.[8]

It presents challenges as well as comforts and wonders. As in *Mansfield Park*, the security of this new-found home is under threat. The snide and snobbish Draco Malfoy pursues the family's feud against Muggle-born wizards. The mysterious Potions master Severus Snape is equally antagonistic. Terrifying creatures lurk in the castle's pipes, secret passages and maze-like under-regions. Worst of all, Voldemort, once a Hogwarts boy called Tom Riddle, is

In the first of Harry Potter's seven adventures he is whirled away by steam train to Hogwarts Castle, the all but animate magical stronghold which becomes both home and saviour as he learns how to defeat the arch-villain Voldemort.

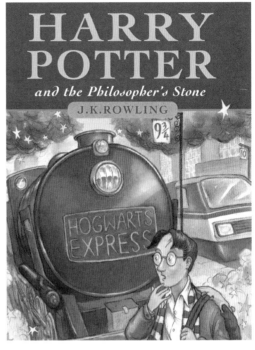

seeking to become immortal and to dominate the world. Eleven years earlier, he was defeated, but not before he had murdered Harry's parents and tried to murder their baby. But Harry survived, to become legendary as 'the Boy who Lived'. As the series progresses, it emerges that Dumbledore is carefully educating Harry in the defence of the school and himself against the 'Dark Lord'.

Each book takes place over the course of a school year, beginning in September and ending with the summer holidays. Hogwarts is always central. In the course of the books, Harry and his friends rise through the school; they are 11 years old in *Harry Potter and the Philosopher's Stone* and 17 in *Deathly Hallows*. In *Philosopher's Stone* (1997), a magical talisman offering immortality and wealth has been hidden in Hogwarts, defended by a gigantic and fearsome three-headed dog.[9] In *Chamber of Secrets* (1998), Harry and his friends have to discover the lair of the murderous basilisk hidden deep in the school's dungeons by Salazar, the founder of Slytherin. In *Prisoner of Azkaban* (1999), Hogwarts appears to be under threat from the notorious Sirius Black, but the real villain of the piece turns out to be Ron's rat Scabbers, the disguise adopted by Peter Pettigrew, the betrayer of both Harry's parents and Sirius. In *Goblet of Fire* (2000), the champions of European wizarding schools arrive for the Triwizard Tournament, rigged by Voldemort to entrap Harry.

Menace increases in *Order of the Phoenix* (2003), in which Hogwarts is taken under the control of the Ministry of Magic's enforcer Dolores Umbridge. The castle fights back by opening the Room of Requirement as a sanctuary for the rebels against her rule. There they can practise the vital Defences against the Dark Arts needed to foil Voldemort's next assault on the school. In *Half-Blood Prince* (2005), Hogwarts is invaded by the soul-stealing Dementors (close kin to the Dark Riders who threaten the Shire), and climaxes with the death of Dumbledore. Finally, *Deathly Hallows* (2007) describes a devastating attack on the school, and the Dark Lord's final defeat thanks to Harry's inspired sacrifice of himself for the good of others. His acceptance of death is crucial: Harry overcomes his fear of dying, while Lord Voldemort is desperate to escape death.

Hogwarts Castle is a fantastical and romantic creation well calculated to appeal to imaginative children, including those educated, as Rowling herself was, in a comprehensive day school. Confessing in an interview with Stephen Fry that she had never been inside a boarding school, she went on to say:

> It was essential for the plot that the children could be enclosed somewhere together overnight. This could not be a day school, because the adventure would fall down every second day if they went home and spoke to their parents, and then had to break back into school every week to wander around at night, so it *had* to be a boarding school.[10]

She explained in another interview that

> in fiction, boarding school comes over as a surrogate family. The pupils are with their contemporaries and free of their parents and the guilt attached to upsetting them.[11]

The boarding school setting is a uniquely English and very popular literary contrivance that began with *Tom Brown's School Days* (1857), and continued through countless books by Angela

J.K. Rowling, sketched here by Stuart Pearson Wright in 2006, confessed to Stephen Fry in 2005 that she had never been inside a boarding school. She invented Hogwarts because it left her characters free to adventure without their parents, but also acted as a surrogate family.

Brazil, Frank Richards, Anthony Buckeridge and Enid Blyton. But the buildings themselves are never as much to the fore and beloved as Hogwarts. It is all-important in the Potter stories, the focus of loyalty, the ultimate prize.

Families, both happy and unhappy, are drivers of the plots. The series revolves around the connection between Harry Potter, Tom Riddle and Severus Snape, the three abandoned boys who each, at different times, find a home from home in Hogwarts. Dumbledore tells Harry that

> 'Voldemort was, I believe, more attached to this school than he has ever been to a person. Hogwarts was where he had been happiest; the first and only place he had felt at home.' Harry felt slightly uncomfortable at these words, for this was exactly how he felt about Hogwarts, too.[12]

The difference between the three is that both Voldemort and Snape came from unhappy families, unlike Harry, who, though orphaned as a baby, knows from magical visions that he had loving parents. The family home reflects the inner state of the family. The Dursleys' Privet Drive is constipated with conventionality. The Blacks' Grimmauld Place is as grim and ancient as its name suggests, and in *Order of the Phoenix* it becomes as animate as Hogwarts: 'In Harry's opinion they were really waging war on the house, which was putting up a very good fight.' The homes of Voldemort's parents the Gaunts and the Riddles are desolate and forlorn. The only really satisfactory home is the Weasleys' 'The Burrow', a place as cosy as Bag End. Harry joins the family circle, finding a brother-like friend in Ron, a substitute mother in Mrs Weasley, and eventually a bride in Ron's sister Ginny.

Making a school the most memorable character in the books reflects J.K. Rowling's belief, implicit in the impressively wide range of literary and mythic reference in her books, that knowledge is power. Albus Dumbledore is determined to teach the young wizards in his charge to use magic in the right way. He believes in their learning by example, experiment, research and intuition (with comically little thought of health and safety). The trio realize in the final book how important their education has been. Hermione's knowledge of Herbology, Ron's skill in playing chess and Harry's adroitness as the Quidditch Seeker all prove essential skills. Learning how to use the magical and sometimes violently active Hogwarts Library is also crucial. It is a memory palace with 'tens of thousands of books, thousands of shelves, hundreds of narrow rows' in which the books protect themselves fiercely. Rowling uses it to show that knowledge can be used for both good and evil. Tom Riddle consults *Secrets of the Darkest Art*, Hagrid learns about the rearing of dragons, Hermione finds out how to make Polyjuice in *Moste Potente Potions*, Ron keeps *Quidditch Through the Ages* until it is long overdue.

Harry's adventures, like those of Tolkien's hobbits, observe many of the conventions of the epic identified by Joseph Campbell in his classic of comparative mythology, *The Hero with a Thousand Faces*. The hero and his faithful sidekicks go on quests, undergoing challenges of all kinds. John Granger has pointed out that

> Every Harry Potter adventure is a circle, and like Odysseus's, Aeneas's, and Dante's adventures before him, each conforms to the three steps of separation from the mundane world to the mystical, initiation there, and divine return, usually with a trip to the underworld thrown in.[13]

But there are few epics in which the setting has been as heroic as the hero. In the course of the final Battle of Hogwarts, elements of the castle take on active roles. Its portrait people leave their frames, a cavalcade of the ghosts known as the Headless Hunt gallop into battle, statues and suits of armour stride into action; even the classroom desks rise up and fight. Its obstreperous poltergeist Peeves drops Snarglepods on the Death-Eaters' heads, and the fantastic beasts and magical plants in its grounds join in the fray. The house-elves swarm into the Entrance Hall with knives and cleavers; pupils, elves, wizards, and even, it appears, Harry Potter himself die for it. But Harry is resurrected, and returns to the fray in his Invisibility Cloak.

> The castle was empty. He felt ghostly striding through it alone, as if he had already died. The portrait people were still missing from their frames; the whole place was eerily still, as if all its remaining lifeblood were concentrated in the Great Hall, where the dead and the mourners were crammed.[14]

Once again, he confronts Voldemort, who is at last defeated by his own rebounding curse. Dumbledore's triumphant army will magically restore the school to even greater glory. Nineteen years later, Harry's son, named Albus Severus after the mentors to whom he owed most, sets off on the Hogwarts Express.

Does Rowling's own life illuminate the invention of Hogwarts? Born in 1960, Joanne Rowling grew up with a younger sister near the Forest of Dean, and went to Wyedean School, Sedbury. She read widely from earliest childhood; E. Nesbit, Dorothy L. Sayers, Nancy Mitford, C.S. Lewis, Charles Dickens and J.R.R. Tolkien were among her favourite authors. She has cited Jane Austen's *Emma* as a guiding light, and in an interview for *The Scotsman* said that the profoundly Christian Elizabeth Goudge's *The Little White Horse* (1946) had 'more than any other book … a direct influence on the Harry Potter books'.[15] Moonacre Manor is certainly as important to the novel as Hogwarts is to Harry Potter's adventures. Rowling pays it direct homage by imagining Harry Potter sleeping in a four-poster made cosy with a warming pan in a tower with a starry ceiling, exploring subterranean passages and being guided by a unicorn, all experiences enjoyed sixty years earlier by Maria Merryweather.

Scholars such as Beatrice Groves and John Granger have revealed the remarkable length and breadth of Rowling's literary knowledge, and have ingeniously traced her literary allusions, from the playfully obvious (calling the caretaker's cat Mrs Norris after the obnoxious aunt in *Mansfield Park*) to the obscure (an epigram from Aeschylus opens *Deathly Hallows*, and its second chapter is titled 'In Memoriam', a reference to a doubt-filled poem by Tennyson).[16] The series is also profoundly influenced by alchemical ideas – Rowling said in 1998 that she read 'a boatload of books on alchemy' before she started writing.[17] The philosopher's stone is a form of Voldemort's holy grail: the Elixir of Life.[18] Alchemical allusions are woven into all seven books. The four school houses are matched to the four elements of earth, air, fire and water; the names of Albus Dumbledore, Rubeus Hagrid and Sirius Black evoke the white (Albedo), red (Rubedo) and black (Nigredo) stages of alchemical transfiguration. Alchemists thought of themselves as seekers, and Harry plays Seeker in his house Quidditch team; his guardian spirit (Patronus) is a stag, which has the alchemical meaning of a longing for God. New souls are born in 'God's hollow place', and we are told that Harry was born in a little West Country village called Godric's Hollow. A website devoted to the spiritual aspects of the Hogwarts series describes it as 'the most popular alchemical work ever written'.[19]

Rowling's seven-part epic, which has over a million words, is 30 per cent longer than the authorized version of the King James Bible. It is unusually moral for a modern fiction. Fundamentalist Christians who deplore magic in any form and critics who dismissed the series as an unaccountably successful but essentially trivial throwback to boarding school literature were alike confounded by the seventh and final book, in which the opus reaches its climax. Harry, the Chosen One, emerges as a Christ-like figure, prepared to die to save the world from evil. 'My belief and my struggling with religious belief and so on I think is quite apparent in this book', Rowling said after its publication.[20]

Rowling's central concern is with what makes a nurturing and supportive home, a universally popular message. The larger theme of the books is to show that upbringing in such a home is a potent weapon in the ceaseless battle between good and evil.

AFTERWORD

My twenty portraits of fictional dwellings are a mix of the humble and the awesome, the cosy and the terrifying, the forlorn and the highly prized. Some suffered destruction; others were saved from it. Some were thankfully returned to; others wisely rejected. Running as a subtext behind the essays has been an exploration of the nature of a home. Is it a trophy to crown a successful career or marriage, or an inherited burden? A place to fight for or one so tangled with our childhood that it arrests our development? Should we stay there, or make it a launchpad to high endeavours? At different times of our lives we use our homes to different ends. What the varieties of fictional experiences of home in these chapters endorse is how essential a home is to humankind.

Times are changing. For a few decades after World War II, domesticity was highly prized, but its deskilling by modern technology led to its rejection in the 1960s. The rise of the 1970s' 'Me Generation' brought the worship of individualism, and a fascination with being nomadic, investing in self rather than family. In 1983 Leonard Lutwack could opine that 'A moving place – automobile, van, spacecraft – may be the nest for people of the twentieth and twenty-first centuries.'[1] However, the romance of the road declined in the face of the soaring pecuniary value of bricks and mortar in the last thirty years, and leapfrogging from one improved home to another became a normal way of life. Today, making money by moving house is becoming less possible, and, for many young people, buying a house is financially impossible. Renting is the new normal.

It seems to me that we are now re-evaluating the homes we have lost, seeking out old roots and putting down new ones, making new connections and rediscovering old ones, something that Internet search engines and social media make easier than it has ever been. Exploring family history and establishing gardens to embellish homes is hugely popular, and we are rising to the challenge of creating homes, rented and owned alike, that our children can look back on nostalgically. Writers are once again interesting themselves in offering fictional messages emphasizing the psychological, rather than monetary, value of the homes we live in. Novels in which a house is the hero are reappearing.

GAZETTEER

THE CASTLE OF OTRANTO

Otranto Castle, Puglia Horace Walpole never visited the Aragonese castle that dominates the little Italian seaport of Otranto, in south-east Puglia. It is suitably gothic and imposing.

Strawberry Hill, Twickenham Walpole's own mock-Gothic creation is the place to discover more about the workings of his mind. The gardens are open, free, seven days a week. The house is open on Sundays 11 am–4 pm and Mondays 12 am–4 pm.

MANSFIELD PARK

Godmersham Park, Chilham While writing *Mansfield Park*, Jane Austen often visited the house in Kent that her brother Edward inherited in 1808; it is pictured behind the image of Jane Austen on the new £10 note. A footpath running through the estate has good views of the house and its eighteenth-century folly, and it is open for National Gardens Scheme open days in June each year. The Godmersham Park Heritage Centre is open on Mondays 9–12 am and 1–5 pm in the summer (godmershamheritage.webs. com).

Stoneleigh Abbey, Warwickshire was the home of Jane's maternal relatives, the Leighs, for 400 years. In 1806, Jane, with her mother and her sister Cassandra, visited Stoneleigh Abbey with their cousin, the Reverend Thomas Leigh. Its chapel and grounds, designed by Humphrey Repton, appear in *Mansfield Park* as those of Sotherton. The grounds are open Sundays– Thursdays 11 am–5 pm. Guided tours give access to the house.

Chawton, Hampshire Jane Austen's home for ten years is now a museum dedicated to her memory. It is open seven days a week except over Christmas and in January (ww.jane-austens-house-museum.org.uk).

WAVERLEY

Abbotsford, Melrose, Roxburghshire The house, gardens and estate of Walter Scott's dream castle is open to visitors; the house also offers accommodation (www.scottsabbotsford.com).

Traquair House, Innerleithen, Peebleshire is frequently open to the public; its main gates, topped with stone bears that must have inspired those of Tully-Veolan, have never been opened since the Stuart cause was lost (www.traquair.co.uk).

WUTHERING HEIGHTS

Haworth Parsonage, Yorkshire is now a museum to the Brontë family (www.bronte.org.uk)

Top Withens, a ruined farmhouse high on the moors above Haworth, often assumed to be Wuthering Heights, is in fact a much humbler house.

THE HOUSE OF SEVEN GABLES

Salem, Massachusetts is the location of the house on which Hawthorne is thought to have based his novel; it is now a museum to his memory and that of the book (www.7gables.org).

BLEAK HOUSE

Bleak House, Broadstairs An attractively higgledy-piggledy house, once Charles Dickens's summer retreat, it was renamed Bleak House many years later, and run as a museum. It is now once again a private house.

Rockingham Castle, Leicestershire Dickens often visited the Castle, which was the home of his friends the Watsons, and said that it had elements of Chesney Wold. Still owned by the Watson family, it is regularly open to the public (www.rockinghamcastle.com).

UNCLE TOM'S CABIN

Uncle Tom's Cabin Museum, Dresden, Ontario celebrates the escaping slave route known as the Underground Railway, but has no actual connection with Harriet Beecher Stowe's novel.

221B BAKER STREET

The Sherlock Holmes Museum has been created in honour of Sherlock Holmes in the present 221B Baker Street (a number which did not exist when Conan Doyle created Holmes) (www.sherlock-holmes.co.uk).

THE SPOILS OF POYNTON

Lamb House, Rye, Sussex became Henry James's home shortly after he finished *The Spoils of Poynton*. Now owned by the National Trust and regularly open to visitors, it epitomizes James's domestic ideal, resembling Mrs Geraint's final tasteful but unassuming home Ricks, rather than Poynton itself (www.nationaltrust.org.uk/lamb-house).

THE FORSYTE SAGA

Robin Hill Galsworthy's own drawings of Robin Hill are preserved in the British Museum. Its site is that of his childhood home Combe House, on Kingston Hill.

HOWARDS END

Rooks Nest, Stevenage E.M. Forster's childhood home in Hertfordshire is a private house. The countryside around it offers fine walks.

THE GREAT GATSBY

Sands Point, Long Island Although Beacon Towers has been demolished, many of the magnificent mansions on Sands Point survive; a tour allows visitors to see them (sandspointpreserveconservancy.org).

ORLANDO & THE EDWARDIANS

Knole House, Sevenoaks Now owned by the National Trust, Knole is regularly open to visitors (www.nationaltrust.org.uk/knole).

REBECCA

Menabilly House, near Fowey The inspiration for Mandalay is a private house, all but invisible in a shroud of woods. However, the estate rents out two holiday cottages, one close to the famous boathouse (www.menabilly. com).

BRIDESHEAD REVISITED

Castle Howard, Yorkshire matches Waugh's description of Brideshead's exterior, and was used in the recent film. It is regularly open to visitors (www.castlehoward.co.uk).

Madresfield Court, Malvern The home of Waugh's friends the Lygons, Madresfield Court has elements of Brideshead about it, especially the Arts & Crafts chapel. It is occasionally open to visitors (www.madresfieldestate. co.uk).

I CAPTURE THE CASTLE

Wingfield Castle, Suffolk A private house, visible from the adjoining common.

GORMENGHAST

Sark, Channel Islands Although Gormenghast is an imaginary creation, Peake's second book mentions many specific locations on the island, his home for many years.

THE LORD OF THE RINGS

Sarehole Mill, Birmingham Much more hemmed around with houses than it was in Tolkien's day, Sarehole held an almost sacred place in his imagination, inspiring the rural haven that was the Shire. It has been preserved as a museum (www.birminghammuseums.org.uk/sarehole).

NOTES

INTRODUCTION

1. Gaston Bachelard, *The Poetics of Space* (1958), trans. Maria Jolas, Penguin, 2014.
2. Virginia Woolf, *Orlando*, Hogarth Press, 1928, ch. 4.
3. Reprinted in Ursula le Guin, *The Wave in the Mind: Talks and Essays on the Writer, the Reader, and the Imagination*, Shambala, 2004, pp. 42–3.

A TRIUMPHANT ILLUSION

1. Frederick S. Frank, Introduction to Horace Walpole, *The Castle of Otranto and The Mysterious Mother*, Broadview Press, 2003, p. 19.
2. Horace Walpole, *The Castle of Otranto, a Gothic Story*, London, 1764, ch. 1.
3. Cited in Jessica Esa, 'A Brief Insight into the Relationship between Gothic Literature and Architecture', http://exeter.academia.edu/JessicaEsa.
4. Now in the keeping of the Sarah Campbell Blaffer Foundation, Houston, Texas.
5. Horace Walpole, letter to Henry Seymour Conway, June 1747, Yale University online edition of *Horace Walpole's Correspondence*, vol. 37, p. 269.
6. R.W. Ketton-Cremer, *Horace Walpole*, Methuen, 1964, p. 140.
7. Joseph Addison, *The Spectator* 415, 26 June 1712
8. Horace Walpole, letter, 21 August 1762, quoted in R.R. Mehatra, *Horace Walpole and the English Novel,* Blackwell, 1934, p. 9. Walpole was referring to Alma's decidedly anthropomorphic castle in Spenser's *The Faerie Queene.*
9. Marion Harney, Preface, *Place-making for the Imagination: Horace Walpole and Strawberry Hill*, Ashgate, 2013, p. 7.
10. Or Gothic script.
11. *The Castle of Otranto,* Preface.
12. *The Letters of Horace Walpole, Earl of Orford*, vol. 3.
13. William Blackstone, *Commentaries on the Laws of England*, Clarendon Press, 1766–1770, vol. 2, p. 208.
14. *The Castle of Otranto*, Preface to 2nd edn, 1765.
15. Her preface describes it as 'the literary offspring of the Castle of Otranto' (Warren Hunting Smith, *Architecture in English Fiction*, Yale University Press, 1970, p. 83).
16. Now owned by the National Trust, The Vyne also had a part to play in Jane Austen's life; see Chapter 2.
17. Thomas Gray to Horace Walpole, 15 July 1736, quoted in Harney, Preface, *Place-making for the Imagination*, p. 8.
18. Ketton-Cremer, *Horace Walpole*, p. 41.

THE BEWILDERED HOUSE

1. Jane Austen, letter to Cassandra, 13 June 1814, in Deirdre Le Faye, *Jane Austen's Letters*, 4th edn, Oxford University Press, 2011.

2. George Meredith, *The Empty Purse, with Odes to the Comic Spirit, to Youth in Memory and Verses*, Macmillan, London, 1892.
3. It was completed by 1799, though not published until December 1817, five months after her death.
4. Jane Austen, *Mansfield Park*, Thomas Egerton, 1814, ch. 5.
5. Calling the house Mansfield Park may be a salute to a milestone ruling against slavery in England made by the judge Lord Mansfield in 1772.
6. A letter to Cassandra, 29 January 1813, refers to her interest in ordination; in *Jane Austen's Letters*, p. 210.
7. Austen, *Mansfield Park*, ch. 25.
8. Fanny's mother had hoped that Sir Thomas would further the prospects of her son William. Adopting Fanny was a cheaper option, though the baronet worried both about 'cousins in love' and the need to provide adequately for her; her Aunt Norris reassures him that it might not be necessary.
9. Austen, *Mansfield Park*, ch. 2.
10. Austen, *Mansfield Park*, ch. 1.
11. Whether this was intended is much disputed, but Austen continues 'Now, do not be suspecting me of a pun, I entreat', a tongue-in-cheek denial that shows she knew her remark's implications.
12. Cowper was Austen's favourite poet; she also quotes from him in *Emma* and *Sense and Sensibility*, and mentions him in her letters.
13. Austen, *Mansfield Park*, ch. 9.
14. Austen, *Mansfield Park*, ch. 16.
15. Austen, *Mansfield Park*, ch. 38.
16. Austen, *Mansfield Park*, ch. 41.
17. Austen, *Mansfield Park*, ch. 48.
18. Caroline Austen, *My Aunt Jane Austen: A Memoir*, Jane Austen Society, 1867.
19. Chawton had no chapel. The modern one that Jane gave to Sotherton that so disappointed Fanny's romantic mind was borrowed from that of Stoneleigh, in Warwickshire; Jane visited the house with her mother on 6 August 1806, and stayed about ten days.
20. The oldest, Edward, then 19, was 'ever the foremost and always up with the hounds'. Quoted in Linda Slothouber, *Jane Austen, Edward Knight, & Chawton: Commerce and Community*, Woodpigeon Publishing, 2015, p. 88.
21. Quoted in David Nokes, *Jane Austen: A Life*, University of California Press, 1998, p. 424; from *The Austen Papers, 1704–1856*, ed. R.A. Austen-Leigh, Spottiswoode, 1942, no. 252.
22. Jane Austen, letter to Frank Austen, 26 July 1809, *Jane Austen's Letters*, p. 184.

BRIDGING TWO WORLDS
1. Walter Scott, *Tales of a Grandfather*, vol. 2, Robert Cadell, 1831, p. 73.
2. Mavis Batey, 'The High Phase of English Landscape Gardening', *Eighteenth Century Life*, NS, 2, 1983, p. 47.
3. Walter Scott, *Count Robert of Paris*, Robert Cadell, 1832, ch. 25.
4. C.R. Leslie, *Autobiographical Recollections*, ed. Tom Taylor, Ticknor & Fields, 1855, p. 219.
5. *The Ballantyne Press and Its Founders 1796–1908*, Ballantyne, 1909, p. 39.
6. Walter Scott, *Waverley*, Preface to 1828 edition.
7. *Quarterly Review*, 14 March 1826, quoted in William Reistzel, 'Sir Walter Scott's Review of Jane Austen's Emma', *PMLA*, vol. 43, no. 2, 1928, p. 48.
8. Kathryn J. Kirkpatrick, Introduction to Maria Edgeworth, *Castle Rackrent*, Oxford University Press, 1995.
9. Walter Scott, 'General Preface to the Waverley Novels', Magnum Opus edn, 48 vols, Robert Cadell, 1829–33.

10. Walter Scott, *Waverley*, ch. 8.
11. Scott, *Waverley*, ch. 63.
12. Scott, *Waverley*, ch. 71.
13. Scott, *Waverley*, ch. 3.
14. Scott, *Waverley*, ch. 3. Description of Oldbuck's study runs for several pages.
15. W.S. Crockett, *The Scott Country*, A & C Black, 1902.
16. Charles Sharpe, 'Recollections of Sir Walter Scott', *Fraser's Magazine*, January 1836, p. 113.
17. Sir Walter Scott, Journal, 23 November 1831, www.online-literature.com/walter_scott/journal-of-scott/53.

A PLAGUE ON BOTH YOUR HOUSES

1. *Letters of Dante Gabriel Rossetti to William Allington 1854–1870*, Unwin, 1897, p. 58.
2. Emily Brontë, *Wuthering Heights*, Thomas Cautley Newby, 1847, ch. 1.
3. For clarity's sake I use Cathy for Cathy/Catherine Earnshaw and Catherine for Cathy/Catherine Linton, except in quotations from the text. It was then common to name a child after a parent, but Emily is twinning them for deliberate effect, and varies their naming.
4. The effect of entail in the male line and the consequent dispossession of women from a beloved home is a recurring plot issue in nineteenth-century fiction; it also lay behind Vita Sackville-West's and Virginia Woolf's fictions built around Knole (see Chapter 13).
5. Brontë, *Wuthering Heights*, ch. 3.
6. Brontë, *Wuthering Heights*, ch. 34.
7. These were first detailed by C.P. Sanger in a perceptive 1926 monograph for the Woolfs' Hogarth Press, *The Structure of Wuthering Heights*.
8. Brontë, *Wuthering Heights*, ch. 7.
9. Brontë, *Wuthering Heights*, ch. 13.
10. Brontë, *Wuthering Heights*, ch. 33.
11. Brontë, *Wuthering Heights*, ch. 32.
12. Emily Brontë, 'Remembrance'.
13. Walter Scott, *Rob Roy*, Archibald Constable, 1817, ch. 14.
14. Lyndall Gordon, *Charlotte Brontë: A Passionate Life*, Virago, 2008, ch. 5.
15. Matthew Arnold, 'Hawarth Churchyard'.
16. In *The Genesis of Wuthering Heights* (Hong Kong University Press, 1958), Mary Visick comments on the 'Casaubon-like burrowing' of scholars into the text; sixty years later this has grown to a daunting Everest of comment and criticism.

DARK ROMANCE

1. Nathaniel Hawthorne, *The House of the Seven Gables*, Ticknor & Fields, 1851, ch. 12.
2. Herman Melville, 'Hawthorne and His Mosses', *The Literary World*, New York, 17 and 24 August 1850.
3. Hawthorne, *The House of the Seven Gables*, ch. 1.
4. Hawthorne, *The House of the Seven Gables*, ch. 1.
5. Arthur Ransome, *A History of Story-telling: Studies in the Development of Narrative*, new edn, intro. Philip Pullman, Arthur Ransome Trust, 2019 (1904), ch. 14, 'Hawthorne and Moral Romance'.
6. Hawthorne, *The House of the Seven Gables*, ch. 1.
7. Hawthorne, *The House of the Seven Gables*, ch. 13.
8. Hawthorne, *The House of the Seven Gables*, ch. 15.
9. Hawthorne, *The House of the Seven Gables*, ch. 2.
10. Hawthorne, *The House of the Seven Gables*, ch. 5.
11. Hawthorne, *The House of the Seven Gables*, ch. 7.
12. Hawthorne, *The House of the Seven Gables*, ch. 9.

13. Hawthorne, *The House of the Seven Gables*, ch. 18.
14. Hawthorne, 'Fire Worship', in *Mosses from an Old Manse*, Putnam, 1846.
15. Hawthorne, *The House of the Seven Gables*, ch. 17.
16. Letter to Henry Conolly, Boston, May 1840, in Joel Myerson, *Selected Letters of Nathaniel Hawthorne*, Ohio State University Press, 2001, p. 77.
17. 'Hawthorne's Castle in the Air: Form and Theme in *The House of the Seven Gables*', *English Literary History*, vol. 38, no. 2, June 1971, pp. 294–317.

TOMB FOR THE LIVING

1. Charles Dickens, *Bleak House*, Bradbury & Evans, 1853, ch. 28.
2. Peter W. Graham, 'From Mansfield Park to Gosforth Park: The English Country House from Austen to Altmann', *Persuasions, the Journal of the Jane Austen Society of North America*, 2002.
3. Dickens, *Bleak House*, ch. 1.
4. Dickens, *Bleak House*, ch. 1.
5. Dickens, *Bleak House*, ch. 7.
6. Dickens, *Bleak House*, ch. 12.
7. Dickens, *Bleak House*, ch. 12.
8. Dickens, *Bleak House*, ch. 6.
9. Dickens, *Bleak House*, ch. 45. When he was writing, Dickens was engaged in the replacement of such slums by model artisan dwellings; he visited the Great Exhibition of 1851 and admired Prince Albert's Model Dwellings. Tom-all-Alone's was later replaced by Peabody Buildings, the work of the great American philanthropist George Peabody (1795–1869).
10. Dickens, *Bleak House*, ch. 64.
11. Dickens, *Bleak House*, ch. 66.

KITCHEN TABLE SOCIETY

1. Harriet Beecher Stowe, *Uncle Tom's Cabin*, John P. Jewett, 1852, ch. 4.
2. George Sand, 'La case de l'oncle Tom', *La Presse*, 17 December 1852; my translation.
3. Charles Edward Stowe, *Harriet Beecher Stowe: The Story of her Life*, Houghton Mifflin, 1911, p. 203.
4. Annie Fields, *Life and Letters of Harriet Beecher Stowe*, Houghton Mifflin, 1898, pp. 132–3.
5. Stowe, *Uncle Tom's Cabin*, ch. 9.
6. Stowe, *Uncle Tom's Cabin*, ch. 13.
7. Stowe, *Uncle Tom's Cabin*, ch. 13.
8. It might be argued that a cardinal weakness of Stowe's book is its disinclination to accept black and white people mingling; on the other hand, she knew the prejudices of her readership in the north all too well.
9. Stowe, *Uncle Tom's Cabin*, ch. 14.
10. Stowe, *Uncle Tom's Cabin*, ch. 18.
11. Stowe, *Uncle Tom's Cabin*, ch. 15.
12. Lori Askeland warns, however, that just as 'a vestige of the rough logs' of Uncle Tom's cabin can always be seen beneath its beflowered exterior, so a vestige of slavery and male-dominated culture can be seen beneath even the most idyllic utopias in the book. Lori Askeland, 'Remodelling the Model Home in *Uncle Tom's Cabin* and *Beloved*', *American Literature*, vol. 64, no. 4, December 1992, p. 788.
13. Stowe, *Uncle Tom's Cabin*, ch. 32.
14. Stowe, *Uncle Tom's Cabin*, ch. 41.
15. 'Getting in the Kitchen with Dinah: Domestic Politics in *Uncle Tom's Cabin*', *American Quarterly*, vol. 36, no. 4, Autumn 1984, pp. 503–23. See also Jane Tompkins, *Sensational Designs: The Cultural Work of American Fiction 1790–1860*, Oxford University Press, 1986.

BACHELOR LAIR

1. Robert Harbison, *Eccentric Spaces*, André Deutsch, 1977, pp. 25–6.
2. 'It is most certainly to you that I owe Sherlock Holmes', he wrote to Bell on 4 May 1892; www.arthur-conan-doyle.com/index. php?title=Letter_to_Mr_Bell_about_Sherlock_Holmes_(4_may_1892).
3. In the final set of stories, *The Case-Book of Sherlock Holmes*, published in *Strand Magazine* between 1921 and 1927, he announced that Holmes once had rooms in Montagu Street.
4. Arthur Conan Doyle, *A Study in Scarlet*, Ward Lock, 1887, ch. 2.
5. Doyle, *A Study in Scarlet*, ch. 2.
6. Arthur Conan Doyle, 'The Adventure of the Empty House'.
7. 'Mrs Hudson is without a doubt *the* woman in the Canon' writes Catherine Cooke admiringly in 'Mrs. Hudson: A Legend in Her Own Lodging-House', *Baker Street Journal* 55, 2007, p. 1. Robert Harbison agrees: 'Mrs Hudson warms and protects without demanding anything in return, so if she falls sick, Watson prescribes, and if Holmes does she nurses'; *Eccentric Spaces*, p. 25.
8. Joseph Kestner calls it 'a club in microcosm'; *Sherlock's Men: Masculinity, Conan Doyle and Cultural History*, Ashgate, 1997, p. 34.
9. Jon Lellenberg, *Arthur Conan Doyle: A Life in Letters*, Harper, 2005, p. 512.

HOUSEHOLD GODS

1. Henry James, *The Spoils of Poynton*, Heinemann, 1896, ch. 3.
2. R.S. Thomas, 'Henry James', from *Frequencies*, 1978.
3. Henry James, Preface, *The Portrait of a Lady*, Macmillan, 1881.
4. Frances Matthiessin, ed., *The Notebooks of Henry James*, Oxford University Press, 1947, pp. 40–41.
5. He was probably inspired by the poem of that title written by his friend Robert Louis Stevenson. James was a great friend of the Stevensons when they lived at Skerryvore in Bournemouth; they kept Louis's father's chair empty for him.
6. James, *The Spoils of Poynton*, ch. 6.
7. James, *The Spoils of Poynton*, ch. 7.
8. James, *The Spoils of Poynton*, ch. 7.
9. James, *The Spoils of Poynton*, ch. 21.
10. James, *The Spoils of Poynton*, ch. 21.
11. James, *The Spoils of Poynton*, ch. 21.
12. James, *The Spoils of Poynton*, ch. 18.
13. James, Preface, *The Spoils of Poynton*.
14. Henry James, *English Hours*, Heinemann, 1905.
15. James, Preface, *The Spoils of Poynton*.
16. James, *The Spoils of Poynton*, ch. 10. James makes the point that it is the first issue of the magazine, and he may well have been taking a sidelong swipe at the magazine *House Beautiful*, which was launched while he was working on the book and forced him to change its title.
17. Candace Wheeler (1827–1923), an innovative interior and textile designer, was co-founder of Tiffany's.
18. Quoted in Bill Brown, 'A Thing about Things', *Henry James Review* 23, 2002, pp. 222–32.
19. Letter to W.E. Norris, 23 December 1907, in *Letters of Henry James*, ed. Percy Lubbock, Macmillan, 1920, p. 496.
20. Henry James, *The Awkward Age*, Book Seventh, Heinemann, 1899.

PROPERTY

1. John Galsworthy, *The Man of Property*, Heinemann, 1907, ch. 8.
2. Svetlana Nikitina, 'Forsyte's *Bildungsroman*: A Saga of a Place', *Interdisciplinary*

Literary Studies, vol. 13, no. 1/2, Fall 2011 (Penn State University Press).
3. John Galsworthy, handwritten note, British Library Add MS. 41752.
4. Galsworthy, *The Man of Property*, ch. 10.
5. Galsworthy, *The Man of Property*, ch. 8.
6. Galsworthy, *The Man of Property*, ch. 3.
7. John Galsworthy, Preface, *The Forsyte Saga*, Heinemann, 1922.
8. Galsworthy, *The Man of Property*, ch. 3.
9. Geoffrey Harvey, 'Reading The Forsyte Saga', *The Yearbook of English Studies* 26, 1996, p. 131.
10. Galsworthy, *The Man of Property*, ch. 5.
11. Galsworthy, *The Man of Property*, ch. 4.
12. This and earlier quotations in this paragraph are from Hermann Muthesius, *The English House*, trans. and ed. Dennis Sharp, BSP Professional Books, 1987 (originally published in 1904 as *Das Englishe Haus*).
13. Galsworthy, *The Man of Property*, ch. 8.
14. Galsworthy, *The Man of Property*, ch. 13.
15. Galsworthy, *The Man of Property*, ch. 9.
16. Ford Madox Ford, 'Literary Portraits VI – Mr Galsworthy and *the Dark Flower*', *Outlook* (London), 18 October 1913, quoted in James Gindin, *John Galsworthy's Life and Art: An Alien's Fortress*, University of Michigan Press, 1987, p. 31.
17. Nikitina, 'Forsyte's *Bildungsroman*', pp. 61–76.
18. Frank Lloyd Wright, *A Testament*, Horizon Press, 1957, p. 219.
19. Frank Lloyd Wright, Preface, *Studies and Executed Buildings*, Verlag Ernst Wasmuth, 1910.
20. John Galsworthy, *To Let*, Heinemann, 1921, ch. 9.

ANCHORAGE

1. R.A. Scott-James, Daily News, November 1910; quoted in Philip Gardner, ed., *E.M. Forster: The Critical Heritage*, Routledge, 1973, p. 138.
2. E.M. Forster, *Commonplace Book*, Scolar Press, 1978.
3. Anniversary postscript to *A Room with a View*, Penguin, 1958.
4. E.M. Forster, *Howards End*, Edward Arnold, 1910, ch. 1.
5. Forster, *Howards End*, ch.22.
6. Forster, *Howards End*, ch. 19.
7. Forster, *Howards End*, ch. 18.
8. Forster, *Howards End*, ch. 17.
9. Forster, *Howards End*, ch. 44.
10. Forster, *Howards End*, ch. 33.
11. John Stape, *E.M. Forster: Interviews and Recollections*, Macmillan, 1993, p. 81.
12. Nicola Beauman, *Morgan: A Biography of E.M. Forster*, Hodder, 1993, p. 16.
13. E.M. Forster, *Marianne Thornton*, Edward Arnold, 1956.
14. P.N. Furbank, *E.M. Forster: A Life*, vol. 1, Cardinal, 1988, p. 16.
15. I was then an undergraduate at Newnham (1964–67). John Cooke, a friend at King's College, took me to meet Forster, who enjoyed talking to students. He talked about the importance of recording dreams, thoughts and favourite quotations. Fifteen years after his death in 1970, his *Commonplace Book* was published by Stanford University Press.

COLOSSAL ILLUSION

1. F. Scott Fitzgerald, *The Great Gatsby*, Charles Scribner's Sons, 1925, ch. 3.
2. Kathleen Parkinson, *Critical Studies: The Great Gatsby*, Penguin, 1988, p. 142.
3. 'Echoes of the Jazz Age', *Scribner's Magazine*, November 1931.
4. Fitzgerald, *The Great Gatsby*, ch. 3.
5. Fitzgerald, *The Great Gatsby*, ch. 4.

6. Fitzgerald, *The Great Gatsby*, ch. 4.
7. Fitzgerald, *The Great Gatsby*, ch. 5.
8. Andrew Turnbull, *Scott Fitzgerald*, Charles Scribner's Sons, 1962.
9. A reference to Sinclair Lewis's recent novel about an estate agent, *Babbitt*, 1922.
10. 'When Harper & Brothers asked Zelda to contribute to *Favorite Recipes of Famous Women*, she wrote: "See if there is any bacon, and if there is, ask the cook which pan to fry it in. Then ask if there are any eggs, and if so try and persuade the cook to poach two of them. It is better not to attempt toast, as it burns very easily. Also, in the case of bacon, do not turn the fire too high, or you will have to get out of the house for a week. Serve preferably on china plates, though gold or wood will do if handy."' Dorothy Lanahan, Introduction to *Dear Scott, Dear Zelda: The Love Letters of F. Scott and Zelda Fitzgerald*, ed. J. Bryer and C. Barks, St Martin's Press, 2002, p. xxvii.
11. It was demolished in 1945; the 2013 film of *Gatsby* modelled his house on it.
12. Fitzgerald, *The Great Gatsby*, ch. 7.
13. Fitzgerald, *The Great Gatsby*, ch. 8.
14. It was very similar to Marlow's vision of Roman London in Conrad's *Heart of Darkness*; Fitzgerald admitted that he had borrowed his use of a semi-objective narrator from Conrad.
15. F. Scott Fitzgerald, 'Author's House', *Esquire*, 1 July 1936.
16. H.L. Mencken, review of *The Great Gatsby*, *Chicago Sunday Tribune*, 3 May 1925.

THE QUEEREST SENSE OF ECHO

1. Quoted in Clare Hanson, *Virginia Woolf*, Palgrave Macmillan, 1994, p. 95.
2. Nigel Nicolson, *Sunday Times*, 4 September 1966.
3. Vita Sackville-West, *Knole and the Sackvilles*, Heinemann, 1922, p. 2.
4. Vita Sackville-West, *Pepita*, Hogarth Press, 1937, p. 192.
5. Vita Sackville-West, *The Heir*, Heinemann, 1922, ch. 5.
6. Virginia Woolf, *The Diary of Virginia Woolf*, vol. II, ed. Anne Oliver Bell, Hogarth Press, 1977, p. 61.
7. Ibid., p. 236.
8. Vita's diary, 17 August, 1926, quoted in Matthew Dennison, *Behind the Mask: The Life of Vita Sackville-West*, Collins, 2014, p. 163.
9. Letter to Vita, 31 January–2 February 1927, in Nigel Nicolson, *The Letters of Virginia Woolf*, 5 vols, Hogarth Press, 1975–1980, vol. III, p. 319.
10. Lyndall Gordon, *Virginia Woolf: A Writer's Life*, Virago, 1984. The 2018 film considerably distorts the facts.
11. 'I can't have it said "Vita's great friends Dottie, Hilda & Virginia". I detest the 2nd rate schoolgirl atmosphere' (*Diary*, vol. III, p. 267). Hilda Mathieson, a BBC producer, and Dorothy Wellesley were both Vita's lovers.
12. Virginia Woolf, 5 October 1927, in *A Writer's Diary*, Hogarth Press, 1953.
13. Quoted in Harry Blamires, *A Guide to Twentieth Century Literature in English*, Methuen, 1983, p. 307.
14. *The Diary of Virginia Woolf*, vol. II, 5 July 1924.
15. The name Shelmerdine is borrowed from Michael Arlen's *The London Venture* (1920), a stream-of-consciousness novel in which 'a delightful adventuress' called Shelmerdine has a throng of lovers.
16. Virginia Woolf, *Orlando: A Biography*, Hogarth Press, 1928, ch. 2.
17. Woolf, *Orlando*, ch. 6.
18. Vita Sackville-West, *The Edwardians*, Hogarth Press, 1930, ch. 1.
19. Sackville-West, *The Edwardians*, ch. 2.
20. Sackville-West, *The Edwardians*, ch. 2.
21. Sackville-West, *The Edwardians*, ch. 7.
22. Sackville-West, *The Edwardians*, ch. 7.

SHEER FLAPDOODLE

1. Stella Gibbons, *Cold Comfort Farm*, Longman, 1932, ch. 3, ch. 2.
2. 'The trouble about Mr Mybug was that ordinary objects, which are not usually associated with sex even by our best minds, did suggest sex to Mr Mybug.' When he and Flora go for a walk, young trees 'make him think of phallic symbols and the buds of nipples and virgins'. He points out to Flora 'that he and she were walking on seeds which were germinating in the womb of the earth. He said it made him feel as if he were trampling on the body of a great brown woman. He felt as if he were a partner in some mighty rite of gestation.' Gibbons, *Cold Comfort Farm*, ch. 11.
3. Gibbons, *Cold Comfort Farm*, ch. 1.
4. Gibbons, *Cold Comfort Farm*, ch. 8.
5. Gibbons, *Cold Comfort Farm*, ch. 3.
6. Gibbons, *Cold Comfort Farm*, ch. 22.
7. Gibbons, *Cold Comfort Farm*, ch. 23.
8. I suspected that this too was a parody, but no; H.L. Manhood (1904–1991) was serious; he lived in a converted railway carriage in deepest Sussex and wrote many short stories in the Powys/A.E. Coppard mode. He turned away from literature in disgust at editorial interference and poor pay in 1953, bought more land, and took to growing his own food and brewing cider.
9. 'The large agonised faces in Mary Webb's book annoyed me', she wrote in a 1966 *Punch* article about writing *Cold Comfort Farm*. 'I did not believe people were any more despairing in Herefordshire than in Camden Town.' It seems likely that Gibbons was referring to the stylized wooden expressions of Rowland Hilder's and Norman Hepple's illustrations for the 1930s' Cape editions of Webb's novels.
10. Mary Webb, *Gone to Earth*, Constable, 1917, ch. 3.
11. Stella Gibbons, *Westwood*, Longman, 1946, ch. 4.
12. Stella Gibbons, *Conference at Cold Comfort Farm*, Longman, 1949.
13. Faye Hammill, 'Cold Comfort Farm, D.H. Lawrence, and English Literary Culture Between the Wars', *Modern Fiction Studies*, vol. 47, no. 4, Winter 2001, pp. 831–54; Faye Hammill, 'Literature or "just sheer flapdoodle"?' Stella Gibbons's *Cold Comfort Farm*', *Women, Celebrity and Literary Culture between the Wars*, University of Texas Press, 2007; Mara Reisman, 'Civilizing Projects, Feminism and Comedy in Stella Gibbons's *Cold Comfort Farm*', *Modern Language Studies*, vol. 43, no. 1, 2013, pp. 30–49.

HOUSE OF SECRETS

1. Daphne du Maurier, 'House of Secrets', *The Rebecca Notebook and Other Memories*, Gollancz, 1981, p. 135.
2. Sally Beauman, 'Afterword', p. 431.
3. Du Maurier, 'House of Secrets', p. 134.
4. Margaret Forster, *Daphne du Maurier*, Chatto, 1993, p. 58; Judith Cook, *Daphne: A Portrait of Daphne du Maurier*, Bantam, 1991, p. 80.
5. Beauman, 'Afterword'.
6. Daphne du Maurier, *Rebecca*, Gollancz, 1938, ch. 7.
7. Du Maurier, *Rebecca*, ch. 14.
8. Du Maurier, *Rebecca*, ch. 1.
9. Du Maurier, *Rebecca*, ch. 16.
10. Du Maurier, *Rebecca*, ch. 17.
11. Du Maurier, *Rebecca*, ch. 21.
12. Du Maurier, *Rebecca*, ch. 23.
13. Du Maurier, *Rebecca*, ch. 19.
14. Du Maurier, *Rebecca*, ch. 27.
15. Du Maurier, *Rebecca*, ch. 1.

A HOUSEHOLD OF THE FAITH

1. Rodney Delasanta and Mario L. D'Avanzo, 'Truth and Beauty in *Brideshead Revisited*', *Modern Fiction Studies*, vol. 11, no. 2, Summer 1965, p. 145.
2. Evelyn Waugh, Preface, *Brideshead Revisited: The Sacred and Profane Memories of Captain Charles Ryder*, Penguin, 1959.
3. 7 January 1945, in *The Letters of Nancy Mitford and Evelyn Waugh*, ed. Charlotte Mosley, Houghton Mifflin, 1996.
4. Evelyn Waugh, *Brideshead Revisited*, 1945, Penguin edn, book I, ch. 1.
5. Waugh, *Brideshead Revisited*, book I, ch. 1.
6. Waugh, *Brideshead Revisited*, book I, ch. 2.
7. Waugh, *Brideshead Revisited*, book I, ch. 4.
8. Evelyn Waugh, *A Little Order: Selected Journalism*, ed. Donat Gallagher, Penguin, 2000, ch. 4.
9. Waugh, *Brideshead Revisited*, book I, ch. 4.
10. Waugh, *Brideshead Revisited*, book I, ch. 5.
11. Waugh, *Brideshead Revisited*, book II, ch. 1.
12. Waugh, *Brideshead Revisited*, book II, ch. 3.
13. Waugh, *Brideshead Revisited*, book III, ch. 1. The explicit connection with property was an addition in the revised 1960 edition.
14. Waugh, *Brideshead Revisited*, book II, ch. 3.
15. Quoted in Paula Byrne, *Mad World: Evelyn Waugh and the Secrets of Brideshead*, HarperCollins, 2010.
16. Waugh, *Brideshead Revisited*, book I, ch. 4.
17. Waugh, *Brideshead Revisited*, book III, ch. 5
18. Waugh, *Brideshead Revisited*, Epilogue.
19. Waugh, *Brideshead Revisited*, Epilogue.

THE SORCERER'S TOWER

1. Dodie Smith, *Look Back in Gratitude*, Appendix, Muller, 1985, p. 271.
2. Dodie Smith, *I Capture the Castle*, Heinemann, 1948, ch. 15.
3. Smith, *I Capture the Castle*, ch. 10.
4. Smith, *I Capture the Castle*, ch. 3.
5. Smith, *I Capture the Castle*, ch. 1.
6. It was rescued in 1943 by Graham, Baron Ash of Packwood, who took it (like James Mortmain) on a forty-year lease (from the Adair family), and remained there until his death in 1980. In private hands today, it is still exceptionally romantic in its moat-bound isolation, and very well cared for.
7. Dodie Smith, *Look Back in Astonishment*, W.H. Allen, 1979.
8. W.H. Ainsworth, *The Lancashire Witches*, H. Colburn, 1849, p. 234.
9. Smith, *I Capture the Castle*, ch. 12.
10. Smith, *I Capture the Castle*, ch. 5.

VAST SHAMBLES

1. Mervyn Peake, *Gormenghast*, Eyre & Spottiswoode, 1950, ch. 52.
2. Lesley Glyn Marx, 'Dark Circus: An Examination of the Work of Mervyn Peake with Selected Reference to Prose and Verse', M.A. thesis, University of Cape Town, 1983.
3. Peake, *Gormenghast*, ch. 9.
4. Mervyn Peake, *Titus Groan*, Eyre & Spottiswoode, 1946, ch. 78.
5. Peake, *Titus Groan*, ch. 1.
6. Peake, *Gormenghast*, ch. 15.
7. Peake, Peake, *Titus Groan*, ch. 69.
8. Peake, BBC radio play of *Titus Groan* and *Gormenghast*, February 1956.

I am indebted to Peter Winnington for scanning this for me; it was published in *Mervyn Peake Review*, 1987.

9. Peake, *Gormenghast*, ch. 39.
10. Peake, *Gormenghast*, ch. 76.
11. Peake, *Gormenghast*, ch. 78.
12. Working notebook for chapters 60 and 61 of *Titus Groan*, quoted in Hadas Elber-Aviram, 'Dark and Deathless Rabble of Long Shadows: Peake, Dickens, Tolkien, and 'this dark hive called London', *Peake Studies*, vol. 14, no. 2, 2015, p. 9.
13. Peake, *Titus Groan*, ch. 20.
14. Maeve Gilmore, Introduction to Mervyn Peake, *A Book of Nonsense*, Peter Owen, 1972, p. 10,
15. Peake, *Gormenghast*, ch. 76.
16. Peter Winnington, 'Mervyn Peake's Letters to Maeve Gilmore', *Peake Studies*, vol. 13, no. 3, October 2013, p. 17.
17. Mervyn Peake, *Titus Alone*, Eyre & Spottiswoode, 1959, ch. 34.
18. Peake, *Titus Alone*, ch. 122.
19. Peake's notes towards the fourth book were published in 1992 as an addendum to the Overlook edition of *Titus Alone* (ed. Peter Winnington). They also appeared as the opening chapter to *Search Without End*, Maeve Gilmore's very personal sequel, which identified Titus and Peake very closely, ending by providing a sanctuary for Titus in an island that is recognizably Sark. An edited version of this was published by Vintage as *Titus Awakes: The Lost Book of Gormenghast* in 2011, the centenary of Peake's birth.

DEEP ROOTS

1. J.R.R. Tolkien, *The Fellowship of the Ring*, George Allen & Unwin, 1954, book I, ch. 2.
2. Wayne Hammond, 'All the Comforts: The Image of Home in *The Hobbit* and *The Lord of the Rings*, *Mythlore* 51, Autumn 1987
3. Tolkien gave Bag End a hyphen in *The Hobbit*, perhaps to emphasize its affinity with *cul-de-sac* (see below), but not in *Lord of the Rings*. I have decided to use Bag End throughout.
4. J.R.R. Tolkien, *The Hobbit, or There and Back Again*, George Allen & Unwin, 1937, ch. 1.
5. Tolkien, *The Hobbit*, ch. 1.
6. Tolkien, *The Hobbit*, ch. 3.
7. Tolkien, *The Hobbit*, ch. 7.
8. Tolkien, *The Hobbit*, ch. 9.
9. Letter to Milton Waldman of Collins (no. 131), c.1951, in *Letters of J.R.R. Tolkien*, ed. Humphrey Carpenter, Allen & Unwin, 1981.
10. Tolkien, 'The Cottage of Lost Play' (1915), in *The Book of Lost Tales*, vol. 1, ed. Christopher Tolkien, HarperCollins, 2015.
11. Letter to Milton Waldman of Collins (no. 131).
12. C.S. Lewis, *Time and Tide*, 14 August 1954.
13. Humphrey Carpenter, *J.R.R. Tolkien: A Biography*, Allen & Unwin, 1977, part V, ch. 2.
14. Wayne Hammond, 'All the Comforts: The Image of Home in *The Hobbit* and *The Lord of the Rings*', *Mythlore* 51, Autumn 1987 (Mythopoeic Society, California), pp. 29–33.
15. Letter to H. Cotton Minchin, 16 April 1956 (no. 187), in *Letters*.
16. Tolkien, *The Fellowship of the Ring*, book II, ch 4.
17. J.R.R. Tolkien, *The Return of the King*, George Allen & Unwin, 1955, book 5, ch. 8.
18. Carpenter, *J.R.R. Tolkien: A Biography*, part 2, ch. 2.

19. J.R.R. Tolkien, interview with John Ezard, *Guardian*, 28 December 1966.
20. Letter to Michael Tolkien, 18 March 1941 (no. 44) in *Letters*. Carpenter inserts 'Worcestershire' in square brackets; however, though Sarehole was originally part of Worcestershire, in 1911, overtaken by Birmingham's urban sprawl, it was annexed to Warwickshire, which explains Tolkien's reference to that county, rather than Worcestershire, in the 1955 letter to his publisher, below.
21. Letter to Deborah Webster, 25 October 1958 (no. 213), in *Letters*.
22. Carpenter, *J.R.R. Tolkien: A Biography*, part IV, ch. 3.
23. Gandalf, in Tolkien, *The Fellowship of the Ring*, book I, ch. 10.

CASTLE OF ANCIENT MAGIC

1. Beatrice Groves, *Literary Allusion in Harry Potter*, Routledge, 2017, p. 16.
2. Claudia Fenske, *Muggles, Monsters and Magicians: A Literary Analysis of the Harry Potter Series*, Peter Lang, 2008, p. 115.
3. Dumbledore, in J.K. Rowling, *Harry Potter and the Half-Blood Prince*, Bloomsbury, 2005, ch. 20.
4. J.K. Rowling, *Harry Potter and the Philosopher's Stone*, Bloomsbury, 1997, ch. 6.
5. Rowling, *Harry Potter and the Philosopher's Stone*, ch. 7.
6. Hagrid is also distinctly motherly towards his fabulous beasts. His cosy cabin has a patchwork quilt on its bed, and he bakes perfect rock cakes; he even thoughtfully packs a teddy in the crate in which he has to send away his pet dragon, 'in case he gets lonely'.
7. I am indebted to Beatrice Groves for discovering that Rowling intended this analogy. *Literary Allusion in Harry Potter*, Routledge, 2017, p. 64.
8. Rowling, *Harry Potter and the Philosopher's Stone*, ch. 8.
9. One of Rowling's many references to classical myth. 'Fluffy', as Hagrid cheerfully calls him, is clearly Cerberus, the Hound of Hades who prevents the dead from escaping the underworld.
10. www.accio-quote.org/articles/2005/1205–bbc-fry.html.
11. Jennie Renton, 'Wild about Harry', *Candis*, November 2001.
12. Rowling, *Harry Potter and the Half-Blood Prince*, ch. 20.
13. John Granger, *Harry Potter's Bookshelf: The Great Books behind the Hogwarts Adventures*, Berkley Books, 2009, p. 213.
14. Rowling, *Harry Potter and the Deathly Hallows*, Bloomsbury, 2007, ch. 34.
15. www.accio-quote.org/articles/2002/1102–fraser-scotsman.html.
16. Groves, *Literary Allusion in Harry Potter*, pp. xiii and 129; John Granger, 'The Aesychlus Epigraph', www.hogwartsprofessor.com/the-aeschylus-epigraph-in-deathly-hallows.
17. *Scottish Herald*, 26 September 2012.
18. Rowling is far from the first, but undoubtedly the most successful, in building a fiction around this theme, which occurs in Honoré de Balzac's *L'Elixir de longue vie* (1830), W.H. Ainsworth's *Auriol* (1844), Edward Bulwer-Lytton's *A Strange Story* (1845), Nathaniel Hawthorne's *Septimus Felton* (1872), H. Rider Haggard's *She* (1886) and Arthur Ransome's *The Elixir of Life* (1915).
19. www.harrypotterforseekers.com/alchemy/alchemy.php. It compares it to the Rosicrucian classic of death and resurrection *The Chymical Wedding of Christian Rosycross* (1616).
20. Interview with Meredith Vieira, NBC *Today* show, 31 July 2007; www.nbcnews.com/id/20001720/print/1/displaymode/1098.

AFTERWORD

1. Leonard Lutwack, *The Role of Place in Literature*, Syracuse University Press, 1984.

FURTHER READING

GENERAL

Bachelard, Gaston, *The Poetics of Space*, trans. Marie Jolas, Penguin, 2014.
Briganti, Chiara, *The Domestic Space Reader*, Toronto University Press, 2012.
Frank, Ellen Eve, *Literary Architecture: Essays toward a Tradition: Walter Pater, Gerard Manley Hopkins, Marcel Proust, Henry James*, California University Press, 1979.
Gill, Richard, *Happy Rural Seat: The English Country House and the Literary Imagination*, Yale University Press, 1972.
Harbison, Robert, *Eccentric Spaces*, André Deutsch, 1977.
Humble, Nicola, *The Feminine Middlebrow Novel*, Oxford University Press, 2001.
Kelsall, Malcolm Miles, *The Great Good Place*, Harvester, 1993.
Kelsall, Malcolm Miles, *Literary Representations of the Irish Country House*, Palgrave Macmillan, 2002.
Lutwack, Leonard, *The Role of Place in Literature*, Syracuse University Press, 1984.
McEntyre, Marion Chandler, *Dwelling in the Text Houses in American Fiction*, California University Press, 1991.
Page, Judith W., *Women, Literature, and the Domesticated Landscape*, Cambridge University Press, 2014.
Richardson, Phyllis. *The House of Fiction: From Pemberley to Brideshead, Great British Houses in Literature and Life*, Kindle edn, 2017.
Romines, Ann, *The Home Plot: Women, Writing and Domestic Ritual*, Massachusetts University Press, 1992.
Saggini, Francesca, *The Houses of Fiction as the House of Life: Representations of the House from Richardson to Woolf*, Cambridge Scholars, 2012.
Smith, Warren Hunting, *Architecture in English Fiction*, Yale University Press, 1970.
Tindall, Gillian, *Countries of the Mind: The Meaning of Place to Writers*, Hogarth Press, 1991.
Tristram, Philippa, *Living Space in Fact and Fiction*, Routledge, 1989.
Whitehead, Christiania, *Castles of the Mind: A Study of Medieval Architectural Allegory*, University of Wales Press, 2003.

THE CASTLE OF OTRANTO

Davison, Carol Margaret, *Gothic Literature, 1764–1824*, University of Wales Press, 2009.
Harney, Marion, *Place-making for the Imagination: Horace Walpole and Strawberry Hill*, Ashgate, 2013.
Ketton-Cremer, Robert Wyndham, *Horace Walpole*, Methuen, 1964.
Lewis, Wilmarth Sheldon, *The Genesis of Strawberry Hill*, Metropolitan Museum of Art, New York, 1934.

Walpole, Horace, *The Castle of Otranto and The Mysterious Mother*, ed. Frederick S. Frank, Broadview Press, 2002.

MANSFIELD PARK

Austen, Caroline, *My Aunt Jane Austen: A Memoir*, Jane Austen Society, 1867.
Baker, William, *Critical Companion to Jane Austen: A Literary Reference to Her Life and Work*, Facts on File, 1944.
Barcas, Janine, *Matters of Fact in Jane Austen*, Johns Hopkins University Press, 2012.
Faye, Deirdre, *Jane Austen's Letters*, 4th edn, Oxford University Press, 2011.
Grey, David, et al., *The Jane Austen Companion*, Macmillan, 1986.
Nokes, David, *Jane Austen: A Life*, University of California Press, 1998.
Slothouber, Linda, *Jane Austen, Edward Knight, & Chawton: Commerce & Community*, Woodpigeon Publishing, 2015.
Tomalin, Claire, *Jane Austen: A Life*, Viking, 1997.

WAVERLEY

Brown, Iain Gordon, *Abbotsford and Sir Walter Scott: The Image and the Influence*, Society of Antiquaries, 2003.
Buchan, John, *Sir Walter Scott*, Cassell, 1932.
Crockett, William Shillinglaw, *The Scott Country*, A & C Black, 1902.
Daiches, David, *Sir Walter Scott and his World*, Thames & Hudson, 1971.
Kelly, Stuart, *Scott-Land: The Man Who Invented a Nation*, Polygon, 2010.
Leslie, Charles Robert, *Autobiographical Recollections*, ed. Tom Taylor, Ticknor & Fields, 1855.
Lockhart, John Gibson, *Memoirs of the Life of Sir Walter Scott*, Robert Cadell, 1848.
Reed, James, *Sir Walter Scott: Landscape and Reality*, Athlone, 1990.
Scott, Walter, *Waverley*, ed. Peter Garside, Edinburgh University Press, 2007.

WUTHERING HEIGHTS

Barker, Juliet, *The Brontës*, Abacus, 1994.
Barnard, Robert, *Emily Brontë*, British Library, 2000.
Brontë, Charlotte, et al., *Tales of Glass Town, Angria and Gondal: Selected Writings*, Oxford University Press, 2010.
Brontë, Emily, *Wuthering Heights*, ed. Richard Dunn, 4th edn, Norton, 2003.
Dry, Florence Swinton, *The Sources of 'Wuthering Heights'*, Heffer and Sons, 1937.
Gordon, Lyndall, *Charlotte Brontë: A Passionate Life*, Virago, 2008.
Sanger, Charles Percy, *The Structure of Wuthering Heights*, Hogarth Press, 1926.
Turner, Joseph Horsfall, *Brontëana: The Rev. Patrick Brontë, A.B., His Collected Works and Life. The Works; and the Brontës of Ireland*, T. Harrison, 1895.
Visick, Mary, *The Genesis of Wuthering Heights*, Hong Kong University Press, 1965.

THE HOUSE OF THE SEVEN GABLES

Hawthorne, Nathaniel, *Mosses from an Old Manse*, Putnam, 1846.
Hawthorne, Nathaniel, *Selected Letters of Nathaniel Hawthorne*, ed. Joel Myerson, Ohio State University Press, 2001.
Mellow, James Robert, *Nathaniel Hawthorne in His Times*, Houghton Mifflin, 1980.
Stokes, Edward, *Hawthorne's Influence on Dickens and George Eliot*, University of Queensland Press, 1985.

BLEAK HOUSE

Ackroyd, Peter, *Dickens*, HarperCollins, 1990.
Armstrong, Frances, *Dickens and the Concept of Home*, University of Michigan Press, 1990.

Dickens, Charles, *The Letters of Charles Dickens*, ed. Graham Storey and Kathleen Tillotsen, Clarendon Press, 1995.
Jordan, John O., *Supposing Bleak House*, University of Virginia Press, 2011.
Tomalin, *Charles Dickens: A Life*, Penguin, 2012.

UNCLE TOM'S CABIN

Fields, Annie, *Life and Letters of Harriet Beecher Stowe*, Houghton Mifflin, 1898.
Gates, Henry Louis, Jr, *The Annotated Uncle Tom's Cabin*, W.W. Norton, 2007.
Stowe, Charles Edward, *Harriet Beecher Stowe: The Story of Her Life*, Houghton Mifflin, 1911.
Tompkins, Jane, *Sensational Designs: The Cultural Work of American Fiction 1790–1860*, Oxford University Press, 1986.

SHERLOCK HOLMES

Baring-Gould, William S., *Sherlock Holmes of Baker Street: A Life of the World's First Consulting Detective*, Random House, 1995.
Bell, Harold Winnering, *Baker Street Studies*, Constable, 1934.
Doyle, Adrian Conan, and John Dickson Carr, *The Exploits of Sherlock Holmes*, Sphere, 1978.
Doyle, Arthur Conan, *Through the Magic Door*, Thomas Nelson & Sons, 1918.
Kestner, Joseph, *Sherlock's Men: Masculinity, Conan Doyle and Cultural History*, Ashgate, 1997.
Lellenburg, Jon L., *Arthur Conan Doyle: A Life in Letters*, Harper, 2007.
Starrett, Vincent, *The Private Life of Sherlock Holmes*, George Allen & Unwin, 1961.
Starrett, Vincent, ed., *221B: Studies in Sherlock Holmes*, Kessinger Publishing, 2007.

THE SPOILS OF POYNTON

Cohen, Deborah, *Household Gods: The British and their Possessions*, Yale University Press, 2006.
Gordon, Lyndall, *Henry James: His Women and His Art*, Virago, 2012.
Hyde, Harford Montgomery, *Henry James at Home*, Methuen, 1969.
James, Henry, *English Hours*, ed. and intro. Alma Louise Lowe, Heinemann, 1960.
Stallman, Robert Wooster, *The Houses that James Built and Other Literary Studies*, Michigan State University Press, 1961.

THE FORSYTE SAGA

Dupré, Catherine, *John Galsworthy, A Biography*, Collins, 1976.
Gindin, James Jack, *John Galsworthy's Life and Art: An Alien's Fortress*, Macmillan, 1987.
Marrot, Harold Vincent, *The Life and Letters of John Galsworthy*, Heinemann, 1935.
Nikitina, Svetlana, 'Forsytes' Bildungsroman: A Saga of a Place', *Interdisciplinary Literary Studies* (Penn State University Press), vol. 13, no. 1/2, Fall 2011.
Sternlicht, Sanford, *John Galsworthy*, Twayne, 1987.

HOWARDS END

Beauman, Nicola, *Maurice: A Biography of the Novelist E.M. Forster*, Hodder, 1993.
Forster, E.M., *Commonplace Book*, Scolar Press, London, 1978.
Forster, E.M., *Howards End*, ed. Alistair M. Duckworth, Bedford/St. Martin's, 1997.
Forster, E.M., *Selected Letters of E.M. Forster*, ed. Mary Dago, 2 vols, Collins, 1983–85.
Furbank, Philip Nicholas, *E.M. Forster: A Life*, Cardinal, 1988.
Gardner, Philip, *E.M. Forster: The Critical Heritage*, Routledge, 1973.
Stape, John, ed., *E.M. Forster: Interviews and Recollections*, Macmillan, 1993.

THE GREAT GATSBY

Fitzgerald, Francis Scott, *The Letters of F. Scott Fitzgerald*, ed. Andrew Turnbull, Bodley Head, 1964.

Fitzgerald, Francis Scott, *Dear Scott, Dear Zelda: The Love Letters of F. Scott and Zelda Fitzgerald*, ed. J. Bryer and C. Barks, St Martin's Press, 2002.

Fitzgerald, Francis Scott, *My Lost City: Personal Essays, 1920–1940*, ed. James W. West, Cambridge University Press, 2005.

Mizener, Arthur, *Scott Fitzgerald and His World*, Thames & Hudson, 1972.

Parkinson, Kathleen, *Critical Studies: The Great Gatsby*, Penguin, 1988.

Turnbull, Andrew, *Scott Fitzgerald*, Bodley Head, 1962.

ORLANDO & THE EDWARDIANS

Bell, Anne Oliver, ed., *The Diary of Virginia Woolf*, 5 vols, Hogarth Press, 1977–84.

Dennison, Matthew, *Behind the Mask: The Life of Vita Sackville-West*, Collins, London, 2014.

Gordon, Lyndall, *Virginia Woolf: A Writer's Life*, Oxford University Press, 1984.

Harris, Alexandra, *Virginia Woolf*, Thames & Hudson, 2011.

Lee, Hermione, *Virginia Woolf*, Chatto, 1996.

Nicolson, Nigel, *Portrait of a Marriage*, Weidenfeld & Nicolson, 1990.

Sackville-West, Vita, *Knole and the Sackvilles*, Heinemann, London, 1922.

Sackville-West, Vita, *The Letters of Vita Sackville-West to Virginia Woolf*, ed. Louise DeSalvo and Mitchell A. Leaska, Hutchinson, 1984.

Woolf, Virginia, *The Letters of Virginia Woolf*, 5 vols, ed. Nigel Nicolson, Hogarth Press, 1975–80.

COLD COMFORT FARM

Hammill, Faye, 'Literature or "just sheer flapdoodle"? Stella Gibbons's *Cold Comfort Farm*', in *Women, Celebrity, and Literary Culture between the Wars*, University of Texas Press, 2007.

Oliver, Reggie, *Out of the Woodshed: A Portrait of Stella Gibbons*, Bloomsbury, 1998.

Reisman, Mara, 'Civilizing Projects, Feminism, and Comedy in Stella Gibbons's *Cold Comfort Farm*', *Modern Language Studies*, vol. 43, no. 1, 2013.

REBECCA

Cook, Judith, *Daphne: A Portrait of Daphne du Maurier*, Bantam, 1991.

Du Maurier, Daphne, *Letters from Menabilly: Portrait of a Friendship*, ed. Oriel Malet, Weidenfeld & Nicolson, 1993.

Du Maurier, Daphne, *Rebecca*, afterword Sally Beauman, Virago, 2002.

Du Maurier, Daphne, *The Rebecca Notebook and Other Memories*, Gollancz, 1981.

Forster, Margaret, *Daphne du Maurier*, Chatto, 1993.

BRIDESHEAD REVISITED

Byrne, Paula, *Mad World: Evelyn Waugh and the Secrets of Brideshead*, Harper, 2009.

Davie, Michael, *The Diaries of Evelyn Waugh*, Penguin, 1997.

Garnett, Robert Reginald, *From Grimes to Brideshead: The Early Novels of Evelyn Waugh*, Bucknell, 1990.

Hastings, Selina, *Evelyn Waugh*, Capuchin, 2013.

Heath, Jeffrey, *Picturesque Prison: Evelyn Waugh and His Writing*, McGill–Queen's University Press, 1982.

Waugh, Evelyn, *Brideshead Revisited*, rev. edn, intro. Frank Kermode, Campbell, 1993.

Waugh, Evelyn, *A Little Order: Selected Journalism*, ed. Donat Gallagher, Penguin, 2000.

I CAPTURE THE CASTLE

Grove, Valerie, *Dear Dodie: The Life of Dodie Smith*, Chatto, 1996.
Smith, Dodie, *Look Back in Astonishment*, W.H. Allen, 1979.
Smith, Dodie, *Look Back with Gratitude*, Muller, 1985.

GORMENGHAST

Batchelor, John, *Mervyn Peake: A Biographical and Critical Exploration*, Duckworth, 1974.
Gilmore, Maeve, *A World Away: A Memoir of Mervyn Peake*, Gollancz, 1970.
Gilmore, Maeve, *Peake's Progress: Selected Writings and Drawings of Mervyn Peake*, Penguin, 2000.
Moorcock, Michael, 'Architect of the Extraordinary: The Work of Mervyn Peake', *Vector* 9, June 1960.
Peake, Claire, *Under a Canvas Sky: Living Outside Gormenghast*, Constable, 2011.
Smith, Gordon, *Mervyn Peake*, Gollancz, 1984.
Watney, John, *Mervyn Peake*, Michael Joseph, 1976.
Winnington, G. Peter, *Mervyn Peake's Vast Alchemies: The Illustrated Biography*, Peter P. Owen, 2009.
Winnington, G. Peter, ed., *Miracle Enough: Papers on the Works of Mervyn Peake*, Cambridge Scholars, 2013.
Yorke, Malcolm, *Mervyn Peake: My Eyes Mint Gold*, John Murray, 2000.

THE HOBBIT & THE LORD OF THE RINGS

Blackman, Robert S., *The Roots of Tolkien's Middle Earth*, Tempus, 2006.
Carpenter, Humphrey, *J.R.R. Tolkien: A Biography*, George Allen & Unwin, 1977.
Eaglestone, Robert, ed., *Reading The Lord of the Rings: New Writings on Tolkien's Classic*, Continuum, 2005.
Hammond, Wayne G., and Christina Scull, 'All the Comforts: The Image of Home in *The Hobbit* and *The Lord of the Rings*', *Mythlore* 51 (Mythopoeic Society, California), Autumn 1987.
Hammond, Wayne G., and Christina Scull, *The Lord of the Rings: A Reader's Companion*, Harper, 2005.
Tolkien, J.R.R., *Letters of J.R.R. Tolkien*, ed. Humphrey Carpenter, George Allen & Unwin, 1981.
Tolkien, J.R.R., *The Annotated Hobbit*, intro. and notes Douglas A. Anderson, Harper, 2002.

HARRY POTTER & HOGWARTS SCHOOL

Berndt, Katrin, *Heroism in the Harry Potter Series*, Ashgate, 2011.
Colbert, David, *The Magical World of Harry Potters: A Treasury of Myths, Legends and Fascinating Facts*, Puffin, 2007.
Fenske, Claudia, *Muggles, Monsters and Magicians: A Literary Analysis of the Harry Potter Series,* Peter Lang, 2008.
Granger, John, *Harry Potter's Bookshelf: The Great Books behind the Hogwarts Adventures*, Berkley, 2009.
Groves, Beatrice, *Literary Allusion in Harry Potter*, Routledge, 2017.
Reagan, Nancy Ruth, *Harry Potter and History*, Wiley, 2011.
Weiss, Shira Wolosky, *The Riddles of Harry Potter: Secret Passages and Interpretive Quests*, Palgrave Macmillan, 2010.

ACKNOWLEDGEMENTS

The idea of writing a book offering in-depth portraits of twenty famous fictional dwellings arose in discussions with Samuel Fanous and Janet Phillips of Bodleian Library Publishing. I am indebted to the generosity of such experts in their fields as Wayne Hammond (for Tolkien), Peter Winnington (for Mervyn Peake) and Beatrice Groves (for J.K. Rowling) in reading and commenting upon relevant draft chapters, and to the 'common readers' who supportively persevered in giving me feedback on the rambling first versions of all twenty chapters: Hugh Griffith, Martin Meredith, Graeme Stones, Peter Snow and especially architect Phil Tabor – the rooftop apartment in Venice that he shares with Gillian Crampton Smith is my favourite home from home. Above all, I thank Lyndall Gordon, who gave me courage to rush in where wise angels circumspectly tiptoe.

CREDITS

TEXT

INDEX